Study Guide

for use with

Financial Accounting
Fundamentals

2009 Edition

John J. Wild
University of Wisconsin at Madison

Prepared by
April Mohr
Jefferson Community and Technical College, NW

 McGraw-Hill
Irwin

Boston   Burr Ridge, IL   Dubuque, IA   New York   San Francisco   St. Louis
Bangkok   Bogotá   Caracas   Kuala Lumpur   Lisbon   London   Madrid   Mexico City
Milan   Montreal   New Delhi   Santiago   Seoul   Singapore   Sydney   Taipei   Toronto

McGraw-Hill
Irwin

Study Guide for use with
FINANCIAL ACCOUNTING FUNDAMENTALS
John J. Wild

Published by McGraw-Hill/Irwin, an imprint of The McGraw-Hill Companies, Inc., 1221 Avenue of the Americas, New York, NY 10020. Copyright © 2009, 2007 by The McGraw-Hill Companies, Inc. All rights reserved.

1 2 3 4 5 6 7 8 9 0 BKM/BKM 0 9 8

ISBN: 978-0-07-336041-6
MHID: 0-07-336041-4

www.mhhe.com

TO THE STUDENT

This study guide was prepared as a learning tool for your study of *Financial Accounting Fundamentals* by John J. Wild. The materials provided in this study guide are not a substitute for your textbook. Rather, the objectives of this study guide are to:

▶ Summarize important information that is explained in the textbook. For example, the **chapter outline** of each chapter identifies important topics in the chapter. While you are reading each chapter's outline, you should ask yourself whether or not you clearly understand the listed topics that are set forth in the outline. If not, you should return to the appropriate chapter in your *Financial Accounting Fundamentals* textbook and carefully reread the sections that explain the topics about which you are unclear.

▶ Provide you with copies of **visuals** that your instructor may use in class to introduce selected topics.

▶ Provide you with copies of **alternative demonstration problems** that your instructor may use in class to review selected topics.

▶ Provide you with a quick means of testing your knowledge of the chapter. The **problems** included for each chapter include true-false and multiple-choice questions, matching of key terms and definitions, fill-in-the-blank questions, and a variety of exercises requiring application and analysis of many of the concepts covered in the chapter. If you are unable to correctly answer the problems, you should again return to the appropriate chapter in your *Financial Accounting Fundamentals* textbook and review the sections about which you are unclear.

How can you get the most out of this study guide? The best approach may be summarized as follows:

▶ **First**, read the learning objectives and the related summary paragraphs. Then, ask whether your understanding of the chapter seems adequate for you to accomplish the objectives. If not, return to and reread the relevant sections of the related chapter in your *Financial Accounting Fundamentals* textbook.

▶ **Second**, review the chapter outline, taking time to think through (describing to yourself) any explanations that would be required to expand the outline. Use the notes column to make note of questions that arise or concepts that seem particularly difficult. Return to your *Financial Accounting Fundamentals* textbook to locate the answers to your questions and review the difficult concepts.

▶ **Third**, review the visuals. The visuals reinforce major concepts of the chapter.

▶ **Fourth**, read and then complete the requirements of each of the problems. Check your answers against the solutions that are provided after the problems. Return to your *Financial Accounting Fundamentals* textbook for additional review of any material that you haven't fully mastered.

▶ **Fifth**, raise any unanswered questions that you may have in class and/or see your Instructor for help.

You may also find it helpful to **bring the chapter outlines, visuals and alternative demonstration problems to class** as explained below.

▶ You can highlight the sections of the chapter outline and/or visuals that your instructor emphasizes.

▶ You may use the notes column of the chapter outline to record additional information that is provided by your instructor. In this regard, don't forget to note whether or not your Instructor will hold you responsible for the information covered in the appendices, if any, that conclude each chapter. (The outlines of the appendices always appear at the end of the chapter outline.)

▶ Instructors often use the alternative demonstration problem(s) in class to illustrate key concepts in the chapter. You can use your copy of the alternative demonstration problem as a starting point for solving the problem in class. (If a given alternative demonstration problem in not covered in class, you may wish to solve it anyway; see your instructor for the solution.)

▶ Often, in addition to assigning various quick study questions, exercises and problems from the end-of-chapter textbook materials as homework, instructors select additional questions, exercises and/or problems for use in class. You can make note of those questions, exercises and/or problems in the notes column of the chapter outline. Later, as you study the chapter outline, you will have a list of quick study questions, exercises and/or problems that were covered by your instructor during class in addition to those that were assigned as homework (which are typically listed on your class syllabus).

The next two pages are provided to recommend an **overall approach to succeeding** in your accounting course.

I would truly appreciate your feedback as to the usefulness of this study guide and any ideas you would like to share.

April Mohr
april.mohr@kctcs.edu

Financial Accounting Fundamentals

HOW TO SUCCEED IN YOUR ACCOUNTING COURSE

A. **Stay Up-To-Date**

Accounting is a unique discipline in that learning takes place in "building blocks." The best analogy is that it is almost impossible to learn to read without learning the sounds of the letters in the alphabet. In is almost impossible for you to learn topics in accounting without having a level of understanding of the previously addressed topic. Accounting is the language of business, and like any language, it is learned through a developmental process.

Staying up-to-date includes completing all assignments on a timely basis. This allows you to take full advantage of classroom assignment check. The best insurance for staying up-to-date is to use good time management skills. This means that you need to commit to a regular weekly study schedule—and stick to it! Staying up-to-date will give you the foundations to learn and *succeed!*

B. **Make Effective Use of Your Textbook**

1. Overview the chapter.

   a. Preview the learning objectives and mark those that the instructor has listed in the course outline or mentioned in class.

   b. Read the opening page of each chapter, which provides a very brief look at contents, as well as a look back and ahead. This allows you to see the links or building blocks you will put in place.

   c. Read the Summary of Learning Objectives found at the end of the chapter. This first pass on summaries is just to get a broad perspective of the contents. Do not expect to understand all that you read at this point.

2. Read the chapter.

   a. Use a highlighter or take notes as you read to keep you mentally alert and focused.

   b. Writing is a proven vehicle for learning. Use the wide text margins to note key concepts as well as questions that arise. This will clarify your thoughts as you read.

   c. Use the Quick Check feature. The Quick Check sections are interspersed throughout each chapter. The brief Quick Check questions are designed to help you assess whether you are grasping the essential concepts. Guidance Answers to Quick Checks are found at the end of each chapter.

   d. Reread the Summary of Learning Objectives. Make sure you thoroughly understand those specified by the instructor.

3. Solve the demonstration problem(s) at the end of each chapter. *Don't overlook these!* Students find these most helpful in learning how to solve accounting problems. They address all major topics of the chapter. If you need help getting started, refer to the approach to planning the solution that is provided. Compare your answers to the complete solution that follows each demonstration problem.

C.   Get Involved and Stay Involved

1. The more actively involved you are in the learning process, the more you will understand and retain the course materials. Don't hesitate to ask questions that arise while you were reading the chapter, completing homework assignments, or otherwise studying.

2. Participate fully in each and every classroom activity.

3. Form a study group or a learning team. Meet regularly outside of class. Support each other's learning. Teaching others is proven to be the most effective way of reinforcing learning and increasing your retention. Every student will benefit.

TABLE OF CONTENTS

CHAPTER 1
INTRODUCING FINANCIAL ACCOUNTING

Learning Objective C1:

Explain the purpose and importance of accounting in the information age.

Accounting is an information and measurement system that identifies, records, and communicates relevant, reliable, and comparable information about an organization's business activities. It helps assess opportunities, products, investments, and social and community responsibilities.

Learning Objective C2:

Identify users and uses of accounting.

Users of accounting are both internal and external. Some users and uses of accounting include (a) managers in controlling, monitoring, and planning; (b) lenders for measuring the risk and return of loans; (c) shareholders for assessing the return and risk of stock; (d) directors for overseeing management; and (e) employees for judging employment opportunities.

Learning Objective C3:

Identify opportunities in accounting and related fields.

Opportunities in accounting include financial, managerial, and tax accounting. They also include accounting-related fields such as lending, consulting, managing, and planning.

Learning Objective C4:

Explain why ethics are crucial to accounting.

The goal of accounting is to provide useful information for decision making. For information to be useful, it must be trusted. This demands ethical behavior in accounting.

Learning Objective C5:

Explain generally accepted accounting principles, and define and apply several key accounting principles.

Generally accepted accounting principles are a common set of standards applied by accountants. Accounting principles aid in producing relevant, reliable, and comparable information. Four principles underlying financial statements were introduced: cost, revenue recognition, matching, and full disclosure. Financial statements also reflect four assumptions: going-concern, monetary unit, time period, and business entity.

Learning Objective C6 (Appendix 1B):

Identify and describe the three major activities of organizations.

Organizations carry out three major activities: financing, investing, and operating. Financing is the means used to pay for resources such as land, buildings, and machines. Investing refers to the buying and selling of resources used in acquiring and selling products and services. Operating activities are those necessary for carrying out the organization's plans.

Learning Objective A1:

Define and interpret the accounting equation and each of its components.

The accounting equation is: Assets = Liabilities + Equity. Assets are resources owned by a company. Liabilities are creditors' claims on assets. Equity is the owner's claim on assets (the residual). The expanded accounting equation is: Assets = Liabilities + [Common Stock – Dividends + Revenues – Expenses].

Learning Objective A2:

Analyze business transactions using the accounting equation.

A transaction is an exchange of economic consideration between two parties. Examples include exchanges of products, services, money, and rights to collect money. Transactions always have at least two effects on one or more components of the accounting equation. This equation is always in balance.

Learning Objective A3:

Compute and interpret return on assets.

Return on assets is computed as net income divided by average assets. For example, if we have an average balance of $100 in a savings account and it earns $5 interest for the year, the return on assets is $5/$100, or 5%.

Learning Objective A4 (Appendix 1A):

Explain the relation between return and risk.

Return refers to income, and risk is the uncertainty about the return we hope to make. All investments involve risk. The lower the risk of an investment, the lower its expected return. Higher risk implies higher, but riskier, expected return.

Learning Objective P1:

Identify and prepare basic financial statements and explain how they interrelate.

Four financial statements report on an organization's activities: balance sheet, income statement, statement of retained earnings, and statement of cash flows.

Chapter Outline

Notes

I. Importance of Accounting

Accounting is an information and measurement system that identifies, records and communicates relevant, reliable, and comparable information about an organization's business activities. **Recordkeeping**, or **bookkeeping**, which includes just one function of accounting, is the recording of transactions and events, either manually or electronically. Technology is a key part of modern business and has changed the way we store, process, and summarize large masses of data. Technology has allowed accounting to expand to include consulting, planning and other financial services.

A. Users of Accounting Information

Accounting is the *language of business* because all organizations set up an accounting information system to communicate data to help people make better decisions.

1. **External information users** are not directly involved in running the organization; they include shareholders, lenders, directors, customers, suppliers, regulators, lawyers, brokers, and the press. External users have limited access to an organization's information but they must receive information that is relevant, reliable and comparable. **Financial accounting** is the area of accounting aimed at serving external users by providing them with *general-purpose financial statements*.

2. **Internal information users** are those directly involved in managing and operating an organization. They use the information to help improve the efficiency and effectiveness of an organization. **Managerial accounting** is the area of accounting that serves the decision-making needs of internal users. Internal users and the information they require include:

   a. Research and development managers need data on current and projected costs and revenues to decide whether to pursue or continue research and development projects.

   b. Purchasing managers need data on quality and quantity of merchandise and materials purchases.

   c. Human resource managers need data on current payroll costs, employee benefits, performance and compensation.

   d. Production managers need data on costs and quality of production processes.

   e. Distribution managers need data on quantity and delivery schedules.

   f. Marketing managers need data on sales and costs to effectively target consumers and set prices.

   g. Servicing managers need data on warranties and maintenance information to provide a valuable product to its customers.

3. Both internal and external users rely on internal controls to monitor and control company activities. **Internal controls** are procedures designed to protect company property, ensure reliable reports, promote efficiency, and encourage adherence to company policies.

B. **Opportunities in Accounting**

1. The four broad areas of opportunities in accounting include financial accounting, managerial accounting, taxation, and accounting-related careers.

2. The majority of accounting opportunities are in *private accounting. Public accounting* offers the next largest number of opportunities while still other opportunities exist in government (and not-for-profit) agencies, including business regulation and investigation of law violations.

3. The professional standing of accounting specialists are denoted by a certificate such as certified public accountant (CPA), certified management accountant (CMA), certified internal auditor (CIA), certified bookkeeper (CB), certified payroll professional (CPP), personal financial specialist (PFS), certified fraud examiner (CFE) and certified forensic accountant (CrFA).

II.   **Fundamentals of Accounting**

A. **Ethics – A Key Concept**
   Ethics are beliefs that distinguish right from wrong; they are accepted standards of good and bad behavior.

1. Ethical behavior is important in all successful organizations. Users must be able to trust accounting information. Good ethics are good business.

2. The AICPA and IMA have set up ethical codes of conduct to be followed.

B. **Generally Accepted Accounting Principles**
   Financial accounting is governed by rules known as **generally accepted accounting principles, GAAP.** GAAP aims to make accounting information relevant, reliable and comparable. Two main groups establish GAAP.

1. **Setting Accounting Principles**

   a. The Financial Accounting Standards Board (FASB) is the private group that sets both broad and specific principles.

   b. The **Securities and Exchange Commission** (SEC) is the government group that establishes reporting requirements for companies that issue stock to the public.

   c. The **International Accounting Standards Board** (IASB) issues *International Financial Reporting Standards* (IFRS) that identify preferred accounting practices. The IASC hopes to create more harmony among accounting practices of different countries; however, it does not have authority to impose its standards on companies.

2. **Principles and Assumptions of Accounting**
    Accounting principles (and assumptions) are both general (basic assumptions, concepts and guidelines for preparing financial statements) and specific (detailed rules used in reporting transactions). The principles discussed in this chapter are:

    a. **Cost principle**—accounting information is based on actual costs incurred in business transactions. Cost is measured on a cash or equal-to-cash basis.

    b. **Revenue recognition principle**—provides guidance on when a company must recognize revenue; to *recognize* means to record it.

    c. **Matching principle**—a business must record its expenses incurred to generate the revenue reported.

    d. **Full disclosure principle**—requires a company to report the details behind financial statements that would impact users' decisions.

    e. **Going-concern assumption**—accounting information reflects a presumption that the business will continue operating instead of being closed or sold

    f. **Monetary unit assumption**—transactions and events are expressed in monetary, or money, units (generally the currency of the country in which the business operates).

    g. **Time period assumption**—presumes that the life of a company can be divided into time periods and that useful reports can be prepared for those periods.

    h. **Business entity assumption**—a business is accounted for separately and distinctly from its owner(s). A business entity can take one of three legal forms:

        i. *Sole proprietorship* is a business owned by one person that has unlimited liability. Requires no special legal requirements. The business is not subject to an income tax but the owner is responsible for personal income tax on the net income of the entity.

        ii. *Partnership* is a business owned by two or more people, called partners, who are subject to unlimited liability. No special legal requirements must be met. The only requirement is an oral or written agreement between the partners which usually outlines how profits and losses are to be shared. The business is not subject to an income tax, but the owners are responsible for personal income tax on their individual share of the net income of the entity.

        iii. *Corporation* is a business that is a separate legal entity whose owners are called shareholders or stockholders. These owners have limited liability because the business is legally responsible for its own actions and debts. The entity is responsible for a business income tax and the owners are responsible for personal income tax on profits that are distributed to them in the form of dividends. **Sarbanes-Oxley (SOX)** is an act which requires documentation and verification of internal controls. The goal of this act is to provide more transparency, accountability and truthfulness in reporting transactions.

III. Transaction Analysis and the Accounting Equation

  A. Accounting Equation

The accounting system reflects two basic aspects of a company: what it owns and what it owes. Together, liabilities and equity are the source of funds to acquire assets. The relation of assets, liabilities and equity is reflected in the **accounting equation**:

Assets = Liabilities + Owner's Equity (A = L + OE)

1. **Assets** are resources owned or controlled by a company; these resources are expected to yield future benefits.

2. **Liabilities** are creditors' claims on assets.

3. **Owner's Equity** is the owner's claim on assets; equity is also called *net assets* or *residual equity (interest)*.

    A corporation's equity—often called stockholders' or shareholders' equity—has two parts: contributed capital and retained earnings:

    a. **Contributed capital**, refers to the amount that stockholders invest in the company—included under the title **common stock**.

    b. **Retained earnings** refer to income (revenues less expenses) that is not distributed to stockholders. The distribution of assets to stockholders is called **dividends**, which reduce retained earnings. **Revenues** increase retained earnings and are the assets earned from a company's earnings activities. **Expenses** decrease retained earnings and are the cost of assets or services used to earn revenues.

4. The above breakdown of equity yields the expanded accounting equation:

    A= L + Contributed Capital + Retained Earnings

    A = L + Common Stock – Dividends + Revenues – Expenses

5. **Net income** occurs when revenues exceed expenses. A **net loss** occurs when expenses exceed revenues, which decreases equity.

B. **Transaction Analysis**

Business activities can be described in terms of transactions and events. **External transactions** are exchanges of value between two entities, which yield changes in the accounting equation. **Internal transactions** are exchanges within an entity; they can also affect the accounting equation. **Events** refer to those happenings that affect an entity's accounting equation and can be reliably measured. The following section uses the accounting equation to analyze eleven selected transactions and events. Remember that each transaction leaves the accounting equation in balance and assets always equal the sum of liabilities and equity.

Transaction 1: Investment by Owner
+ Assets (Cash) = + Equity (Common Stock)
After this transaction, the cash (an asset) and the stockholders' equity each equal the amount invested. The source of the increase in equity is the owner's investment (stock issuance), which is included in the column titled Common Stock.

Transaction 2: Purchase supplies for cash
+Assets (Supplies) = – Assets (Cash)
This transaction merely changes the form of assets from cash to supplies; the decrease in cash is exactly equal to the increase in supplies.

Transaction 3: Purchase Equipment for Cash
+ Assets (Equipment) = – Assets (Cash)
Like Transaction 2, this transaction is an exchange of one asset, cash, for another asset, equipment; the equipment is an asset because of its expected future benefits.

Transaction 4: Purchase Supplies on Credit
+Assets (Supplies) = + Liability (Account Payable)
The supplies are acquired in exchange for a promise to pay for them later; the liability created is referred to as *accounts payable*.

Transaction 5: Provide Services for Cash
+ Assets (Cash) = + Equity (Revenues)
The company earns revenues by providing services to its clients; the increase in equity is included in revenues because the cash received from clients is earned by providing services.

Transactions 6 and 7: Payment of Expenses in Cash
– Assets (Cash) = – Equity (Expenses)
These two transactions involve the payment of cash for this month's rent and employee salary; the costs of both rent and salary are expenses, as opposed to assets, because their benefits are used in the current month (they have no further benefits after the current month). Both transactions decrease equity which is included in the column titled Expenses.

Transaction 8: Provide Services and Facilities for Credit

+ Assets (Accts Receivable) = + Equity (Revenues)

The company earns revenues by providing services to its clients; the clients are billed for the services. This transaction results in an asset, called *accounts receivable*, which is the amount owed by this client, and also yields an increase in equity reflected in the column titled Revenues.

Transaction 9: Receipt of Cash from Accounts Receivable

+ Assets (Cash) = – Assets (Accounts Receivable)

The client pays the company the amount that it was billed for the services provided in Transaction 8. This transaction does not change the total amount of assets and does not affect liabilities or equity; it converts the receivable (an asset) to cash (an asset). It does not create new revenue. The revenue was recognized in Transaction 8.

Transaction 10: Payment of accounts payable

– Assets (Cash) = – Liability (Accounts Payable)

The company made a partial payment to the vendor for the supplies acquired in Transaction 4. This transaction decreases cash and decreases its liability to the vendor. Equity does not change; this event does not create an expense. The expense will be recorded in the future when the company derives the benefits from these supplies by using them.

Transaction 11: Payment of cash dividend

– Assets (Cash) = – Equity (Dividends)

The company declared and paid a dividend to its owner. Dividends (decreases in equity) are not reported as expenses because they are not part of the company's earnings process, and they are not used in computing net income.

IV. **Financial Statements**

A *Income Statement*

Reports on operating revenue and expense activities *over a period of time*. Net income (or loss) is computed as sales less all costs and expenses. Revenues are reported first followed by expenses. Expenses reflect the costs to generate the revenue reported.

B. *Statement of Retained Earnings*

Reports changes in retained earnings of the business over a period of time. Changes result from net income, which increases retained earnings. A net loss and dividends decrease retained earnings. Ending retained earnings is reported on the balance sheet.

C. *Balance Sheet*

Reports a listing of amounts for assets, liabilities, and equity *at a point in time*.

D. *Statement of Cash Flows*

Reports on cash flows for operating, investing, and financing activities over a period of time.

Chapter Outline

Notes

V.   Decision Analysis—Return on Assets (ROA)

A. Return on assets, also called return on investment (ROI), is a profitability measure; useful in evaluating management, analyzing and forecasting profits, and planning activities.

B. It is calculated by dividing net income by average total assets.

VI.   Return and Risk Analysis (Appendix 1A)

A. Net income is often linked to return. Return on assts (ROA) is stated in ratio form as income divided by assets invested.

B. **Risk** is the uncertainty about the return we will earn. All business investments involve risk, but some involve more risk than others.

C. The lower the risk of an investment, the lower is our expected return. Higher risk implies higher, but riskier, expected returns.

D. The trade-off between risk and return is a normal part of business. We use accounting information to assess both return and risk.

VII. Business Activities and the Accounting Equation (Appendix 1B)

There are three major types of business activities:

A. Financing Activities—provide the means organizations use to pay for resources such as land, buildings, and equipment to carry out plans.

B. Investing Activities—the acquiring and disposing of resources (assets) that an organization uses to acquire and sell its products or services.

C. Operating Activities—involve using resources to research, develop, purchase, produce, distribute, and market products and services.

WARNING: <u>NO MATTER WHAT HAPPENS</u> ALWAYS KEEP THIS SCALE IN BALANCE

Basic Accounting Equation

ASSETS = LIABILITIES + EQUITY

<u>TRANSACTION ANALYSIS RULES</u>

1) Every transaction affects at least two items.
2) Every transaction must result in a balanced equation.

TRANSACTION ANALYSIS POSSIBILITIES:					
A		=	L	+	E
(1)	+	and		+	
or (2)	−	and		−	
or (3)	+ and −	and		No change	
or (4)	No change	and		+ and −	

One spring, Jane Smith decided to earn money as a lawn service professional. After discussions with neighbors, she obtained enough commitments for lawn servicing jobs that she thought she could be successful at it. On June 1, 20X9, on the basis of these commitments, Jane started her business under the name of Ultimate Lawn Care, Inc.

On August 31, 20X9, Jane noted the following events which occurred during the first three months of business:

- On June 1, Jane personally invested $2,000 in the business by depositing the $2,000 in the business's bank account.

- Deposits during the first three months, all from customer collections, totaled $11,400.

- Checks written during the 3-month period included the following:

  - Truck and equipment rental, $1,800

  - Gas, oil, and lubrication, $880

  - Miscellaneous supplies used, $90

  - Helpers, $4,700; including payroll taxes, $500;

  - Insurance, $175;

  - Telephone, $100

  - Dividend (transferred to personal bank account), $2,000.

At the end of August:

- Customers still owed $600 for services that were performed.

- The business owed another $100 to a vendor for gas and oil.

Required:

1. Show the effect of each transaction on the accounting equation.

2. Prepare an income statement for Ultimate Lawn Care, Inc. for the three months ended August 31, 20X9.

3. Prepare a balance sheet for Ultimate Lawn Care, Inc. at August 31, 20X9.

4. Explain why`the company's cash balance at the end of the summer does not agree with the amount of net income earned during the summer.

(If this alternative demonstration problem is not covered in class, see your instructor for the solution.)

Problem I

The following statements are either true or false. Place a (T) in the parentheses before each true statement and an (F) before each false statement.

1. ( ) Two businesses with the same owner must have separate accounting records.

2. ( ) Land appraised at $40,000 and worth that much to its purchaser should be recorded at its worth ($40,000), even though it was purchased through hard bargaining for $35,000.

Problem II

You are given several words, phrases, or numbers to choose from in completing each of the following statements or in answering the following questions. In each case select the one that best completes the statement, or answers the question, and place its letter in the answer space provided.

_____ 1. The board that currently has the primary authority to identify generally accepted accounting principles is the:

    a. APB.

    b. FASB.

    c. FEI.

    d. ASB.

    e. AICPA.

_____ 2. If Kay Bee Company rendered services for a customer in exchange for $175 cash, what would be the effects on the accounting equation?

    a. Assets, $175 increase; Liabilities, no effect; Owner's Equity, $175 increase.

    b. Assets, no effect; Liabilities, $175 decrease; Owner's Equity, $175 increase.

    c. Assets, $175 increase; Liabilities, $175 increase; Owner's Equity, no effect.

    d. Assets, $175 increase; Liabilities, $175 decrease; Owner's Equity, $350 increase.

    e. There is no effect on the accounting equation.

Problem III

Many of the important ideas and concepts discussed in Chapter 1 are reflected in the following list of key terms. Test your understanding of these terms by matching the appropriate definitions with the terms. Record the number identifying the most appropriate definition in the blank space next to each term.

_____ Accounting	_____ Internal users
_____ Accounting equation	_____ International Accounting Standards
_____ Assets	Board (IASB)
_____ Audit	_____ Liabilities
_____ Balance sheet	_____ Managerial accounting
_____ Bookkeeping	_____ Matching principle
_____ Business entity assumption	_____ Monetary unit assumption
_____ Common stock	_____ Net assets
_____ Contributed capital	_____ Net income
_____ Corporation	_____ Net loss
_____ Cost principle	_____ Partnership
_____ Dividends	_____ Proprietorship
_____ Equity	_____ Recordkeeping
_____ Ethics	_____ Retained earnings
_____ Events	_____ Return*
_____ Expanded accounting equation	_____ Return on assets
_____ Expenses	_____ Revenues
_____ External transactions	_____ Revenue recognition principle
_____ External users	_____ Risk*
_____ Financial accounting	_____ Securities and Exchange Commission
_____ Financial Accounting Standards	(SEC)
Board (FASB)	_____ Shareholders
_____ Full disclosure principle	_____ Shares
_____ Generally Accepted Accounting	_____ Sole proprietorship
Principles (GAAP)	_____ Statement of cash flows
_____ Going-concern assumption	_____ Statement of retained earnings
_____ Income	_____ Stock
_____ Income statement	_____ Stockholders
_____ Internal transactions	_____ Time period assumption

Key term discussed in Appendix 1A

1. An information and measurement system that identifies, records, and communicates relevant information about a company's business activities.

2. Rules that specify acceptable accounting practice.

3. Persons using accounting information who are not directly involved in running the organization.

4. A business owned by two or more people that is not organized as a corporation.

5. The federal agency charged by Congress to set reporting rules for organizations that sell ownership shares to the public.

6. Part of accounting that involves recording transactions and events, either manually or electronically (also called bookkeeping).

7. An analysis and report of an organization's accounting system and its records using various tests.

8. Assets = Liabilities + [Common Stock – Dividends + Revenues – Expenses].

9. Activities within an organization that can affect the accounting equation.

10. Business owned by one person that is not organized as a corporation; also called a *sole proprietorship.*

11. Area of accounting mainly aimed at serving external users.

12. Codes of conduct by which actions are judged as right or wrong, fair or unfair, honest or dishonest.

13. Owners of a corporation (also called shareholders).

14. A business owned by one person that is not organized as a corporation (also called a proprietorship).

15. A business that is a separate legal entity under state or federal laws with owners called shareholders or stockholders.

16. Refers to the amount that stockholders invest in the company; included under the title common stock.

17. Prescribes that a company must record its expenses incurred to generate the revenue reported.

18. A report of changes in retained earnings over a period of time; adjusted for increases (owner investment and net income) and for decreases (dividends and net loss).

19. Resources expected to produce current and future benefits.

20. Creditor's claims on an organization's assets.

21. Group that identifies preferred accounting practices and encourages global acceptance; issues International Financial Reporting Standards.

22. The income from an investment.

23. Owner's (shareholders') claims on an organization's assets.

24. The equality where Assets = Liabilities + Owner's Equity.

25. The amount of uncertainty about an expected return.

26. Equity of a corporation divided into units (also called shares).

27. A corporation's basic ownership share (also called capital stock).

28. The principle that requires a business be accounted for separately from its owner(s).

29. Persons using accounting information who are directly involved in managing the organization.

30. Financial statement that lists the types and amounts of assets, liabilities, and equity at a specific date; also called the statement of financial position.

31. Amount earned after subtracting all expenses necessary for its sales (also called earnings, income or profit).

32. Exchanges of economic consideration between one entity and another entity.

33. A ratio reflecting operating efficiency; defined as net income divided by average total assets (also called return on investment).

34. The accounting principle that requires financial statement information to be based on actual costs incurred in business transactions.

35. Area of accounting aimed at serving the decision-making needs of internal users.

36. Equity of a corporation divided into units (also called stock).

37. The costs incurred to earn sales.

38. A corporation's distributions of assets to its owners.

39. A part of accounting that involves recording transactions and events, either manually or electronically (also called recordkeeping).

40. Happenings that both affect an organization's financial position and can be reliably measured.

41. Amounts earned from selling products or services (also called sales).

42. A principle that requires financial statements to reflect the assumption that the business will continue operating.

43. An independent group of seven full-time members who are responsible for setting accounting rules.

44. Owners of a corporation (also called stockholders).

45. Amount earned after subtracting all expenses necessary for sales (also called earnings, net income or profit).

46. Financial statement that subtracts expenses from revenues to yield a net income or loss over a specified period of time.

47. A principle that assumes transactions and events can be expressed in money units.

48. Another name for equity.

49. The excess of expenses over revenues for a period.

50. A corporation's accumulated net income and losses that have not been distributed (in dividends) to shareholders.

51. The principle that requires that revenue is recognized when earned.

52. A financial statement that lists cash inflows (receipts) and cash outflows (payments) during a period; arranged by operating, investing, and financing activities.

53. Presumes that the life of a company can be divided into time periods and that useful reports can be prepared for those periods.

54. Requires a company to report the details behind financial statements that would impact users' decisions.

Problem IV

Complete the following by filling in the blanks.

1. The cost principle requires financial statement information to be based on _____ incurred in business transactions. The _____ assumption requires financial statements to reflect the assumption that the business will continue operating instead of being closed or sold. The _____ principle requires a company to report the details behind financial statements that would impact users' decisions.

2. The balance sheet equation is _____ equals _____ plus _____. It is also called the _____ equation.

3. The statement of cash flows shows the events that caused _____ to change. It classifies the cash flow into three major categories: _____, _____, and _____ activities.

Problem V

The following are eight transactions completed by Cornell, Inc., a law firm.

1. Paid the rent for three months in advance on the law office, $3,000.

2. Paid cash to purchase a new computer for the office, $900.

3. Completed legal work for Ray Holland and immediately collected the full payment of $2,500 in cash.

4. Purchased law books on credit, $700.

5. Completed $1,500 of legal work for Julie Landon on credit, and immediately entered in the accounting records both the right to collect and the revenue earned.

6. Paid for the law books purchased in Transaction 4.

7. Received $1,500 from Julie Landon for the legal work in Transaction 5.

8. Paid the weekly salary of the office secretary, $575.

The assets, liabilities, and owner's equity of Linda Cornell's law practice prior to the above eight transactions are shown below. In the spaces provided below, show (by additions and subtractions) the effects of each transaction on the company's assets, liabilities, and equity. Include new totals after each transaction as in Exhibit 1.9 in the text.

		Assets				=	Liabilities +		Equity		
Cash	+ Accounts Receivable +	Prepaid Rent	+ Law Library	+ Office Equipment =			Accounts Payable	+ Common Stock	+ Revenues	− Expenses
$4,000			$12,000	$3,250				$19,250		
1.										
2.										
3.										
4.										
5.										
6.										
7.										
8.										

Refer to the above and complete the following by filling in the blanks.

a. Did each transaction affect two items of the equation? _____

b. Did the equation remain in balance after the effects of each transaction were entered?

_____

c. If the equation had not remained in balance after the effects of each transaction were entered, this would have indicated that _____.

d. Cornell, Inc. earned $2,500 of revenue upon the completion of Transaction 3, and the asset that flowed into the business as a result of this transaction was in the form of _____.

e. Cornell, Inc. earned $1,500 of revenue upon the completion of Transaction 5, and the asset that flowed into the business upon the completion of this transaction was

_____.

f. The right to collect $1,500 from Julie Landon was converted into _____ in Transaction 7. Nevertheless, the revenue was earned upon the completion of the _____ in Transaction 5.

g. The $1,500 collected in Transaction 7 was recognized as revenue in Transaction 5 because of the _____ principle, which states that (1) revenue should be recognized at the time it is _____, (2) the inflow of assets associated with revenue may be in a form other than _____, and (3) the amount of revenue should be measured as the cash plus the cash equivalent value of any _____received from customers in exchange for goods or services.

Solutions for Chapter 1

Problem I

1. T
2. F

Problem II

1. B
2. A

Problem III

1	Accounting	29	Internal users
24	Accounting equation	21	International Accounting Standards Board (IASB)
19	Assets		
7	Audit	20	Liabilities
30	Balance sheet	35	Managerial accounting
39	Bookkeeping	17	Matching principle
28	Business entity assumption	47	Monetary unit assumption
27	Common stock	48	Net assets
16	Contributed capital	31	Net income
15	Corporation	49	Net loss
34	Cost principle	4	Partnership
38	Dividends	10	Proprietorship
23	Equity	6	Recordkeeping
12	Ethics	50	Retained earnings
40	Events	22	Return*
8	Expanded accounting equation	33	Return on assets
37	Expenses	41	Revenues
32	External transactions	51	Revenue recognition principle
3	External users	25	Risk*
11	Financial accounting	5	Securities and Exchange Commission (SEC)
43	Financial Accounting Standards Board (FASB)		
54	Full disclosure principle	44	Shareholders
2	Generally Accepted Accounting Principles (GAAP)	36	Shares
		14	Sole proprietorship
		52	Statement of cash flows
42	Going-concern assumption	18	Statement of retained earnings
45	Income	26	Stock
46	Income statement	13	Stockholders
9	Internal transactions	53	Time period assumption

Key term discussed in Appendix 1A.

©The McGraw-Hill Companies, Inc., 2009

Problem IV

1. costs; going-concern; full disclosure
2. assets; liabilities; equity; accounting
3. cash; operating; investing; financing

Problem V

	Cash	+	Accounts Receivable	+	Prepaid Rent	+	Law Library	+	Office Equipment	=	Accounts Payable	+	Common Stock	+	Revenues	–	Expenses
	$4,000						$12,000		$3,250				$19,250				
1. –	3,000			+	$3,000												
	1,000				3,000		12,000		3,250				19,250				
2. –	900							+	900								
	100				3,000		12,000		4,150				19,250				
3. +	2,500														+	$2,500		
	2,600				3,000		12,000		4,150				19,250		2,500		
4.							+	700			+	$700						
	2,600				3,000		12,700		4,150		700		19,250		2,500		
5.		+	$1,500												+	1,500		
	2,600		1,500		3,000		12,700		4,150		700		19,250		4,000		
6. –	700									–	700						
	1,900		1,500		3,000		12,700		4,150		0		19,250		4,000		
7. +	1,500	–	1,500														
	3,400		0		3,000		12,700		4,150		0		19,250		4,000		
8. –	575																–	$575
	$2,825	+	$0	+	$3,000	+	$12,700	+	$4,150	=	$0	+	$19,250	+	$4,000	–	$575

a. Yes
b. Yes
c. an error had been made
d. cash
e. an account receivable
f. cash; legal work
g. revenue recognition; earned; cash; noncash assets

CHAPTER 2
ACCOUNTING FOR TRANSACTIONS

Learning Objective C1:

Explain the steps in processing transactions.

The accounting process identifies business transactions and events, analyzes and records their effects, and summarizes and presents information useful in making decisions. Transactions and events are the starting points in the accounting process. Source documents help in their analysis. The effects of transactions and events are recorded in journals. Posting along with a trial balance helps summarize and classify these effects.

Learning Objective C2:

Describe source documents and their purpose.

Source documents identify and describe transactions and events. Examples are sales tickets, checks, purchase orders, bills, and bank statements. Source documents provide objective and reliable evidence, making information more useful.

Learning Objective C3:

Describe an account and its use in recording transactions.

An account is a detailed record of increases and decreases in a specific asset, liability, equity, revenue, or expense item. Information from accounts is analyzed, summarized, and presented in reports and financial statements for decision makers.

Learning Objective C4:

Describe a ledger and a chart of accounts.

A ledger (or general ledger) is a record containing all accounts used by a company and their balances. It is referred to as the *books*. The chart of accounts is a list of all accounts and usually includes an identification number assigned to each account.

Learning Objective C5:

Define *debits* and *credits* and explain double-entry accounting.

Debit refers to left, and *credit* refers to right. Debits increase assets, expenses, and dividends, while credits decrease them. Credits increase liabilities, common stock, and revenues; debits decrease them. Double-entry accounting means each transaction affects at least two accounts and has at least one debit and one credit. The system for recording debits and credits follows from the accounting equation. The left side of an account is the normal balance for assets, dividends, and expenses, and the right side is the normal balance for liabilities, common stock, and revenues.

Learning Objective A1:

Analyze the impact of transactions on accounts and financial statements.

We analyze transactions using the concepts of double-entry accounting. This analysis is performed by determining a transaction's effects on accounts. These effects are recorded in journals and posted to ledgers. We also identify the financial statements affected by each transaction.

Learning Objective A2:

Compute the debt ratio and describe its use in analyzing company performance.

A company's debt ratio is computed as total liabilities divided by total assets. It reveals how much of the assets are financed by creditor (nonowner) financing. The higher this ratio, the more risk a company faces because liabilities must be repaid at specific dates.

Learning Objective P1:

Record transactions in a journal and post entries to a ledger.

Transactions are recorded in a journal. Each entry in a journal is posted to the accounts in the ledger. This provides information that is used to produce financial statements. Balance column accounts are widely used and include columns for debits, credits, and the account balance.

Learning Objective P2:

Prepare and explain the use of a trial balance.

A trial balance is a list of accounts from the ledger showing their debit or credit balances in separate columns. The trial balance is a summary of the ledger's contents and is useful in preparing financial statements and in revealing recordkeeping errors.

Learning Objective P3:

Prepare financial statements from business transactions.

The balance sheet, the statement of retained earnings, the income statement, and the statement of cash flows use data from the trial balance (and other financial statements) for their preparation.

I. Analyzing and Recording Process

A. The accounting process identifies business transactions and events, analyzes and records their effects, and summarizes and presents information in reports and financial statements. The steps in the accounting process that focus on *analyzing and recording* transactions and events are: (1) record relevant transactions and events in a journal, (2) post journal information to ledger accounts, and (3) prepare and analyze the trial balance. Accounting records are informally referred as the *accounting books*, or simply the *books*.

B. **Source documents** identify and describe transactions and events. Source documents are sources of accounting information and can be in either hard copy or electronic form. Examples are sales tickets, checks, purchase orders, bills from suppliers, employee earnings records, and bank statements. Source documents provide objective and reliable evidence about transactions and events.

C. An **account** is a record of increases and decreases in a specific asset, liability, equity, revenue, or expense item. The **general ledger**, or **ledger**, is a record containing all accounts used by a company.

D. Accounts are arranged in three basic categories based on the accounting equation. A separate account is kept for each of the following:

1. **Asset Accounts**—resources owned or controlled by a company that have expected future benefits; examples include Cash, Accounts Receivable, Note Receivable, Prepaid Accounts, Supplies, Equipment, Buildings, and Land.

2. **Liability Accounts**—claims by creditors against assets; obligations to transfer assets or provide products or services to other entities; examples include Accounts Payable, Note Payable, Unearned Revenue, and Accrued Liabilities.

3. **Equity Accounts**—owner's residual interest in the assets of the business after deducting liabilities; examples include Common Stock, Dividends, Revenues, and Expenses.

II. Analyzing and Processing Transactions

A. Ledger and Chart of Accounts

1. A ledger (or general ledger) is the sum of all the accounts a company uses.

2. The **chart of accounts** is a list of all the accounts in the ledger with their identification numbers.

B. Debits and Credits
1. A **T-account** represents a ledger account and is used to understand the effects of one or more transactions.
2. The *left* side of an account is called the **debit** side. A debit is an entry on the left side of an account.
3. The *right* side of an account is called the **credit** side. A credit is an entry on the right side of an account.
4. Whether a debit or a credit is an increase or decrease depends on the account.
5. In an account where a debit is an increase, the credit is a decrease. In an account where a credit is an increase, the debit is a decrease.
6. The **account balance** is the difference between the total debits and the total credits recorded in an account.

C. Double-Entry Accounting
1. The total amount that is debited to accounts must equal the total amount credited to accounts for each transaction. The sum of debit account balances in the ledger must equal the sum of credit account balances.
2. Assets are on the left side of the equation; therefore, the left, or debit, side is the *normal balance* side for assets.
3. Liabilities and equities are on the right side; therefore, the right, or credit, side is the *normal balance* side for liabilities and equity.
4. Equity increases from revenues and stock issuances and it decreases from expenses and dividends. Increases (credits) to common stock and revenues *increase* equity; increases (debits) to dividends and expenses *decrease* equity.
5. The normal balance of each account (assets, liability, common stock, dividends, revenue, or expense) refers to the left or right (debit or credit) side where *increases* are recorded.

D. Journalizing and Posting Transactions
1. A **journal** gives a complete record of each transaction in one place; it shows the debits and credits for each transaction. The process of recording each transaction in a journal is called **journalizing**. The process of transferring journal entry information to the ledger is called **posting**.

2. The **general journal** can be used to record any type of transaction. Steps for recording entries in a general journal include:

   a. Date the transaction; enter the year at the top of the first column and the month and day on the first line of each journal entry.

   b. Enter titles of accounts debited (account titles are taken from the chart of accounts and aligned with the left margin of the column), and then enter amounts in the Debit column on the same line.

   c. Enter titles of accounts credited (account titles are taken from the chart of accounts and indented from the left margin of the column to distinguish them from debited accounts), and then enter amounts in the Credit column on the same line.

   d. Enter a brief explanation of the transaction on the line below the entry.

3. A blank line is left between each journal entry for clarity.

4. When a transaction is first recorded, the **posting reference (PR) column** is left blank (in a manual system); later, when posting entries to the ledger, the identification numbers of the individual ledger accounts are entered in the PR column.

5. T-accounts are simple and direct means to show how the accounting process works; however, actual accounting systems need more structure and therefore use **balance column accounts.** The balance column account format is similar to a T-account in having columns for debits and credits; it is different in including date and explanation columns.

6. The heading of the Balance column does not show whether it is a debit or credit balance; instead, an account is assumed to have a *normal balance* (that is, the side where increases are recorded). Unusual events can temporarily give an account an *abnormal balance* (that is, the side where decreases are recorded).

7. To ensure the ledger is up-to-date, entries are posted as soon as possible using the following steps:

   a. First, identify the ledger account that is debited in the entry; then, in the ledger, enter the date, the journal and page in its PR column, the debit amount, and the new balance of the ledger accounts.

   b. Second, enter the ledger account number in the PR column of the journal.

   c. Repeat the first two steps for credit entries and amounts.

E. **Analyzing Transactions – An Illustration**

The illustrations below follow the four steps in processing transactions. Each transaction is analyzed in terms of its effect on the accounting equation. Double-entry accounting is used to record the transaction in journal entry form, and the financial statements affected by each transaction are identified. (The following abbreviations are used for the financial statements: IS for income statement, BLS for balance sheet, SCF for statement of cash flows, and SRE for statement of retained earning.) The first eleven transactions are from Chapter 1; five additional transactions are included.

Transaction 1: Investment by owner
Analysis:
+ Assets (Cash) = + Equity (Common Stock)
Double entry:
Debit Cash and credit Common Stock
Statements affected:
BLS and SCF

Transaction 2: Purchase supplies for cash
Analysis:
+Assets (Supplies) = – Assets (Cash)
Double entry:
Debit Supplies and credit Cash
Statements affected:
BLS and SCF

Transaction 3: Purchase equipment for cash
Analysis:
+ Assets (Equipment) = – Assets (Cash)
Double entry:
Debit Equipment and credit Cash
Statements affected:
BLS and SCF

Transaction 4: Purchase supplies on credit
Analysis:
+Assets (Supplies) = + Liability (Account Payable)
Double entry:
Debit Supplies and credit Accounts Payable
Statements affected:
BLS

Transaction 5: Provide services for cash
Analysis:
+ Assets (Cash) = + Equity (Revenues)
Double entry:
Debit Cash and credit Revenue (type of revenue would be identified in account name)
Statements affected:
BLS, IS, SCF, and SRE

Transactions 6 and 7: Payment of expenses in cash
Analysis:
– Assets (Cash) = – Equity (Expenses)
Double entry:
Debit Expenses (type of expense would be identified in account name) and credit Cash
Statements affected:
BLS, IS, SCF, and SRE

Transaction 8: Provide consulting and rental services on credit
Analysis:
+ Assets (Accts Receivable) = + Equity (Revenues)
Double entry:
Debit Accounts Receivable and credit Revenue (type of revenue would be identified in account name)
Statements affected:
BLS, IS, SCF, and SRE

Transaction 9: Receipt of cash on account
Analysis:
+ Assets (Cash) = – Assets (Accounts Receivable)
Double entry:
Debit Cash and credit Accounts Receivable
Statements affected:
BLS and SCF

Transaction 10: Partial payment of accounts payable
Analysis:
– Assets (Cash) = – Liability (Accounts Payable)
Double entry:
Debit Accounts Payable and credit Cash
Statements affected:
BLS and SCF

Transaction 11: Payment of cash dividend
Analysis:
– Assets (Cash) = – Equity (Dividends)
Double entry:
Debit Dividends and credit Cash
Statements affected:
BLS, SCF, and SRE

Transaction 12: Receipt of cash for future services
Analysis:
+ Assets (Cash) = + Liabilities (Unearned Revenue)
Double entry:
Debit Cash and credit Unearned Revenue (type of unearned revenue is often identified in account name)
Statements affected:
BLS and SCF

Transaction 13: Pay cash for future insurance coverage
Analysis:
– Assets (Cash) = + Assets (Prepaid Insurance)
Double entry:
Debit Prepaid Insurance and credit Cash
Statements affected:
BLS and SCF

Transaction 14: Purchase supplies for cash
Analysis:
+ Assets (Supplies) = – Assets (Cash)
Double entry:
Debit Supplies and credit Cash
Statements affected:
BLS and SCF

Transactions 15 and 16: Payment of expenses in cash
Analysis:
– Assets (Cash) = – Equity (Expenses)
Double entry:
Debit Expense (type of expense would be identified in account name) and credit Cash
Statements affected:
BLS, IS, SCR, and SRE

III.   **Trial Balance**

A. Preparing a Trial Balance

1. A **trial balance** is a list of accounts and their balances at a point in time.

2. The three steps to preparing a trial balance are as follows:

a. List each account and its amount (from the ledger),

b. Compute the total debit balances and the total credit balances, and

c. Verify (prove) total debit balances equal total credit balances.

B. Searching for and Correcting Errors

1. If a trial balance does not balance (the columns are not equal), the error(s) must be found and corrected. Find the errors by checking the following:

a. Verify that the trial balance columns are correctly added.

b. Verify that the account balances are accurately entered from the ledger.

c. See whether a debit (or credit) balance is mistakenly listed in the trial balance as a credit (or debit).

d. Recompute each account balance in the ledger.

e. Verify that each journal entry is properly posted.

f. Verify that the original journal entry has equal debits and credits.

2. If an error in a journal entry is discovered before the entry is posted, it can be corrected in a manual system by drawing a line through the incorrect information and writing in the correct information.

3. If an error in a journal entry is not discovered until after it is posted, a *correcting entry* that removes the amount from the wrong account and records it to the correct account should be journalized and posted.

C. Using a Trial Balance to Prepare Financial Statements

The statements prepared in this chapter are called *unadjusted statements* because further account adjustments need to be made (as described in chapter 3).

1. A balance sheet reports on an organization's financial position at a *point in time*. The income statement, statement of retained earnings, and statement of cash flows report on financial performance over a *period of time*.

2. A one-year, or annual, reporting period is known as the *accounting*, or *fiscal*, *year*. A business whose accounting year begins on January 1 and ends on December 31 is known as a *calendar-year* company. A company that chooses a fiscal year ending on a date other than December 31 is known as a *noncalendar-year* company.

3. Income Statement—reports the revenues earned less the expenses incurred by a business over a period of time.

4. Statement of Retained Earnings—reports information about how retained earnings changes over the accounting period.

5. Balance Sheet—reports the financial position of a company at a point in time, usually at the end of a month, quarter, or year. The *account form* of the balance sheet reports assets on the left and liabilities and equity on the right. The *report form* of the balance sheet reports assets on the top and liabilities and equity on the bottom.

6. Presentation Issues:

   a. Dollar signs are not used in journals and ledgers; they do appear in financial statements and other reports such as the trial balance. The usual practice is to put dollar signs beside only the first and last numbers in a column.

   b. Companies commonly round amounts in reports to the nearest dollar, or even to a higher level.

IV.   **Decision Analysis—Debt Ratio**

     A. A company that finances a relatively large portion of its assets with liabilities has a high degree of *financial leverage*. Higher financial leverage involves greater risk because liabilities must be repaid and often require regular interest payments (equity financing does not). The risk that a company might not be able to meet such required payments is higher if it has more liabilities (is more highly leveraged).

     B. One way to assess the risk associated with a company's use of liabilities is to compute the **debt ratio**.

         1. It is calculated as total liabilities divided by total assets.

         2. It tells us how much (what percentage) of the assets are financed by creditors (non-owners) or liability financing; the higher the debt ratio, the more risk a company faces from its financial leverage.

THREE PARTS OF AN ACCOUNT

(1) ACCOUNT TITLE	
Left Side called (2) DEBIT	Right Side called (3) CREDIT

RULES FOR USING ACCOUNTS

Accounts are <u>assigned</u> <u>balance</u> sides (debit or credit).

To <u>increase</u> any account, use the balance side.

To <u>decrease</u> any account, use the <u>side opposite</u> the balance side.

FINDING ACCOUNT BALANCES

If total debits equals total credits, the account balance is zero.

If total <u>debits are greater</u> than total credits, the account has a <u>debit balance</u> equal to the difference of the two totals.

If total <u>credits are greater</u> than total debits, the account has a <u>credit balance</u> equal to the difference of the two totals.

BALANCE SIDES

ALL ACCOUNTS ARE ASSIGNED BALANCE SIDES.

ASSETS	=	LIABILITIES + EQUITY

are on the <u>left</u> side of the
accounting equation
therefore
they increase using the
debit or left side.

are on the <u>right</u> side of the
accounting equation
therefore
they increase using the
credit or right side.

DEBIT BALANCE	CREDIT BALANCE

Asset Accounts		Liability Accounts		Equity Accounts	
Debit	*Credit*	*Debit*	*Credit*	*Debit*	*Credit*
+ side	– side	– side	+ side	– side	+ side
Normal			Normal		Normal
Balance			Balance		Balance

EQUITY ACCOUNTS

Common Stock
(increases equity, which is on the right side of the accounting equation, equity increases with credits)

Debit	Credit
– side	+ side
	Normal
	Balance

Dividends
(decreases equity, equity decreases with debits)

Debit	Credit
+ side	– side
Normal	
Balance	

> Each time assets are distributed to stockholders, the dividends account balance increases. As such, its normal balance is a debit.

All Revenue Accounts
(increases equity, equity increases with credits)

Debit	Credit
– side	+ side
	Normal
	Balance

All Expense Accounts
(decreases equity, equity decreases with debits)

Debit	Credit
+ side	– side
Normal	
Balance	

> Each time an expense is incurred, the expense account balance increases. As such, its normal balance is a debit.

USING ACCOUNTS – SUMMARY

$$\boxed{\text{Assets} = \text{Liabilities} + \text{Equity}}$$

Asset Accounts	Liability Accounts	Equity Accounts
Debit +	Credit +	Credit +
Balance	Balance	Balance

$$\boxed{\text{Equity Accounts}}$$

Common Stock	Dividends
Credit +	Debit +
Balance	Balance

Revenue Accounts	Expense Accounts
Credit +	Debit +
Balance	Balance

RULE REVIEW

Transaction analysis rules:
- Each transaction affects at least two accounts.
- Each transaction must have equal debits and credits.

General account use rules:
- To <u>increase</u> any account, use <u>balance</u> side.
- To <u>decrease</u> any account, use <u>side opposite</u> the balance.

Wigor Inc. completed the following transactions during the year ended December 31, 20×9, its first year of operations:

  a. Bill Wiggins personally invests $30,000 in the new business in exchange for common stock and deposits the cash in a bank account opened under the name of Wigor Inc.

  b. Equipment for use in the business was purchased for $9,000. Two-thirds of the price was paid in cash; the rest was due in a year.

  c. Service fees earned were $60,000; $6,000 of this was on credit.

  d. Operating expenses incurred were $35,000; $4,000 was on credit.

  e. Wigor Inc. collected half the money owed to it.

  f. Wigor Inc. paid off $2,000 it owed.

  g. Wiggins bought a car for $12,000 for his personal use, half paid for now from his personal savings and half to be paid in a year.

Required:

1. Prepare journal entries for each of the events.

2. Prepare a trial balance at the end of the year for Wigor Inc.

(If this alternative demonstration problem is not covered in class, see your instructor for the solution.)

Problem I

The following statements are either true or false. Place a (T) in the parentheses before each true statement and an (F) before each false statement.

1. ( )   Debits are used to record increases in assets, withdrawals, and expenses.

2. ( )   The process of recording transactions in a journal is called posting.

3. ( )   The debt ratio is used to assess a company's risk of failing to pay its debts when they are due.

Problem II

You are given several words, phrases, or numbers to choose from in completing each of the following statements or in answering the following questions. In each case select the one that best completes the statement, or answers the question, and place its letter in the answer space provided.

_____ 1.   Properties or economic resources owned by a business, or probable future economic benefits obtained or controlled by a particular entity as a result of past transactions or events, are called:

    a. Dividends.

    b. Assets.

    c. Retained earnings.

    d. Revenues.

    e. Owner's equity.

_____ 2.   The journal entry to record the completion of legal work for a client on credit and billing the client $1,700 for the services rendered would be:

    a. Accounts Receivable... 1,700

        Unearned Legal Fees..   1,700

    b. Legal Fees Earned... 1,700

        Accounts Receivable...   1,700

    c. Accounts Payable... 1,700

        Legal Fees Earned...   1,700

    d. Legal Fees Earned... 1,700

        Sales   1,700

    e. Accounts Receivable... 1,700

        Legal Fees Earned...   1,700

_____ 3. A ledger is:
- a. A book of original entry in which the effects of transactions are first recorded.
- b. The collection of all accounts used by a business.
- c. A book of original entry in which any type of transaction can be recorded.
- d. A book of special journals.
- e. An account with debit and credit columns and a third column for showing the balance of the account.

Problem III

Many of the important ideas and concepts discussed in Chapter 2 are reflected in the following list of key terms. Test your understanding of these terms by matching the appropriate definitions with the terms. Record the number identifying the most appropriate definition in the blank space next to each term.

_____ Account	_____ Double-entry accounting
_____ Account balance	_____ General journal
_____ Balance column account	_____ Journal
_____ Chart of accounts	_____ Journalizing
_____ Common stock	_____ Ledger
_____ Compound journal entry	_____ Posting
_____ Credit	_____ Posting reference (PR) column
_____ Creditors	_____ Source documents
_____ Debit	_____ T-account
_____ Debt ratio	_____ Trial balance
_____ Dividends	_____ Unearned revenue

1. A liability created when customers pay in advance for products or services; earned when the products or services are delivered in the future.

2. A corporation's distributions of assets to its owners.

3. List of accounts and their balances at a point in time; total debt balances equal total credit balances.

4. An account with debit and credit columns for recording entries and another column for showing the balance of the account after each entry.

5. The source of information for accounting entries and can be in either paper or electronic form; also called _business papers_.

6. Individuals or organizations entitled to receive payments.

7. A record where transactions are recorded before they are posted to ledger accounts.

8. Process of transferring journal entry information to the ledger.

9. Record within an accounting system where increases and decreases in a specific asset, liability, equity, revenue, or expense are entered and stored.

10. Tool used to show the effects of transactions and events on individual accounts.

11. Process of recording transactions in a journal.

12. Recorded on the left side; an entry that increases asset and expense accounts, and decreases liability, equity, and revenue accounts; abbreviated Dr.

13. The difference between the total debits and total credits (including the beginning balance) for an account.

14. A list of accounts used by a company includes an identification number for each account.

15. A journal entry that affects at least three accounts.

16. An all-purpose journal for recording transactions and events.

17. A ratio of total liabilities to total assets; used to describe risk associated with a company's debts.

18. Recorded on the right side; an entry that decreases asset and expense accounts, or increases liability, equity, and revenue accounts; abbreviated Cr.

19. Record containing all accounts (with amounts) for a business.

20. An accounting system in which each transaction affects at least two accounts and has at least one debit and one credit.

21. A column in journals where account numbers are entered when entries are posted to ledger accounts.

22. Corporation's basic ownership share; also generically called *capital stock*.

Problem IV

Complete the following by filling in the blanks.

1. Assets created by selling goods and services on credit are called _____.
   Liabilities created by buying goods and services on credit are called

   _____.

2. Probable future sacrifices of economic benefits arising from present obligations of a particular entity to transfer assets or provide services to other entities in the future as a result of past transactions or events are called _____.

3. An excess of revenues over expenses for a period results in a _____.
   An excess of expenses over revenues results in a _____. The financial statement that lists revenues and expenses is the _____.

4. The process of recording transactions in a journal is called _____. The process of transferring journal entry information to the ledger is called _____.

5. The _____ creates a link between a journal entry and the ledger accounts by providing a cross-reference for tracing the entry from one record to the other.

6. A trial balance that fails to balance is proof that _____ either in journalizing, in posting, or in preparing the trial balance.

7. A trial balance that balances is not absolute proof that no errors were made because

   _____.

8. The steps in preparing a trial balance are:

   _____.

   _____.

_____ .

_____ .

_____ .

9. a. The normal balance of an asset account is a _____ .

    b. The normal balance of a liability account is a _____ .

    c. The normal balance of the common stock account is a _____ .

    d. The normal balance of the retained earnings account is a _____ .

    e. The normal balance of a revenue account is a _____ .

    f. The normal balance of an expense account is a _____ .

Problem V

Following are the first 10 transactions completed by P. L. Wheeler's new business called Wheeler's Repair Shop, Inc.:

    a. Started the business by issuing common stock to P. L. Wheeler in exchange for $1,800 cash, which was deposited in a bank account in the name of the business.

    b. Paid three months' rent in advance on the shop space, $675.

    c. Purchased repair equipment for cash, $700.

    d. Completed repair work for customers and collected cash, $1,005.50.

    e. Purchased additional repair equipment on credit from Comet Company, $415.50.

    f. Completed repair work on credit for Fred Baca, $175.

    g. Paid Comet Company $290.50 of the amount owed from transaction (e).

    h. Paid the local radio station $75 for an announcement of the shop opening.

    i. Fred Baca paid for the work completed in transaction (f).

    j. Paid $350 cash dividend to P. L. Wheeler.

Required:

1. Record the transactions directly in the T-accounts that follow. Use the transaction letters to identify the amounts in the accounts.

2. Prepare a trial balance as of the current date using the form that follows.

Cash

Accounts Payable

Common Stock

Accounts Receivable

Retained Earnings

Prepaid Rent

Repair Services Revenue

Repair Equipment

Advertising Expense

WHEELER'S REPAIR SHOP, INC.
Trial Balance
_____, 20____

Financial Accounting Fundamentals

Problem VI

Journalize the following transactions and post to the accounts that follow.

 a. On November 5 of the current year, started business by issuing common stock to Sherry Dale for $2,450 cash, which was deposited in a bank account in the name of a new business named Dale Real Estate Inc.

 b. On November 6, the business purchased office equipment for $425 cash.

GENERAL JOURNAL

DATE	ACCOUNT TITLES AND EXPLANATION	P.R.	DEBIT	CREDIT

GENERAL LEDGER

Cash   Account No. 101

DATE	EXPLANATION	P.R.	DEBIT	CREDIT	BALANCE

Office Equipment   Account No. 163

DATE	EXPLANATION	P.R.	DEBIT	CREDIT	BALANCE

Sherry Dale, Capital   Account No. 301

DATE	EXPLANATION	P.R.	DEBIT	CREDIT	BALANCE

Solutions for Chapter 2

Problem I

1. T
2. F
3. T

Problem II

1. B
2. E
3. B

Problem III

9	Account	20	Double-entry accounting
13	Account balance	16	General journal
4	Balance column account	7	Journal
14	Chart of accounts	11	Journalizing
22	Common stock	19	Ledger
15	Compound journal entry	8	Posting
18	Credit	21	Posting reference (PR) column
6	Creditors	5	Source documents
12	Debit	10	T-account
17	Debt ratio	3	Trial balance
2	Dividends	1	Unearned revenue

Problem IV

1. accounts receivable; accounts payable
2. liabilities
3. net income (profit); net loss; income statement
4. journalizing; posting
5. Posting reference (PR) column
6. at least one error has been made
7. some types of errors do not create unequal debits and credits
8. (1) Determine the balance of each account;
   (2) List in their ledger order the accounts having balances, with the debit balances in one column and the credit balances in another;
   (3) Add the debit balances;
   (4) Add the credit balances;
   (5) Compare the two totals for equality.
9. (a) debit; (b) credit; (c) credit; (d) credit; (e) credit; (f) debit

Problem V

Cash			
(a)	1,800.00	(b)	675.00
(d)	1,005.50	(c)	700.00
(i)	175.00	(g)	290.50
		(h)	75.00
		(j)	350.00

Repair Equipment		
(c)	700.00	
(e)	415.50	

Retained Earnings		
(j)	350.00	

Accounts Receivable			
(f)	175.00	(i)	175.00

Accounts Payable			
(g)	290.50	(e)	415.50

Repair Services Revenue		
	(d)	1,005.50
	(f)	175.00

Prepaid Rent		
(b)	675.00	

Common Stock		
	(a)	1,800.00

Advertising Expense		
(h)	75.00	

WHEELER'S REPAIR SHOP, INC.
Trial Balance
(Current Date)

Cash..	$ 890.00	
Prepaid rent...	675.00	
Repair equipment..	1,115.50	
Accounts payable		$ 125.00
Common stock..		1,800.00
Retained earnings	350.00	
Repair services revenue...		1,180.50
Advertising expense	75.00	
Totals..	$3,105.50	$3,105.50

Problem VI

GENERAL JOURNAL

DATE	ACCOUNT TITLES AND EXPLANATION	P.R.	DEBIT					CREDIT				
20— Nov. 5	Cash	101	2	4	5	0	00					
	Common Stock	301						2	4	5	0	00
	Owner's initial investment.											
6	Office Equipment	163		4	2	5	00					
	Cash	101							4	2	5	00
	Purchased office equipment											

GENERAL LEDGER

Cash   Account No. 101

DATE	EXPLANATION	P.R.	DEBIT				CREDIT				BALANCE			
20— Nov. 5		G-1	2	4	5	0	00					2	4	5	0	00
6		G-1						4	2	5	00	2	0	2	5	00

Office Equipment   Account No. 163

DATE	EXPLANATION	P.R.	DEBIT				CREDIT				BALANCE			
20— Nov. 6		G-1		4	2	5	00						4	2	5	00

Common Stock   Account No. 301

DATE	EXPLANATION	P.R.	DEBIT				CREDIT				BALANCE			
20— Nov. 5		G-1						2	4	5	0	00	2	4	5	0	00

CHAPTER 3
PREPARING FINANCIAL STATEMENTS

Learning Objective C1:

Explain the importance of periodic reporting and the time period principle.

The value of information is often linked to its timeliness. To provide timely information, accounting systems prepare periodic reports at regular intervals. The time period principle assumes that an organization's activities can be divided into specific time periods for periodic reporting.

Learning Objective C2:

Explain accrual accounting and how it improves financial statements.

Accrual accounting recognizes revenue when earned and expenses when incurred—not necessarily when cash inflows and outflows occur. This information is valuable in assessing a company's financial position and performance.

Learning Objective C3:

Identify steps in the accounting cycle.

The accounting cycle consists of 10 steps: (1) analyze transactions, (2) journalize, (3) post, (4) prepare an unadjusted trial balance, (5) adjust accounts, (6) prepare an adjusted trial balance, (7) prepare statements, (8) close, (9) prepare a post-closing trial balance, and (10) prepare (optional) reversing entries.

Learning Objective C4:

Explain and prepare a classified balance sheet.

Classified balance sheets report assets and liabilities in two categories: current and noncurrent. Noncurrent assets often include long-term investments, plant assets, and intangible assets. A corporation separates equity into common stock and retained earnings.

Learning Objective A1:

Explain how accounting adjustments link to financial statements.

Accounting adjustments bring an asset or liability account balance to its correct amount. They also update related expense or revenue accounts. Every adjusting entry affects one or more income statement accounts *and* one or more balance sheet accounts. An adjusting entry never affects cash.

Learning Objective A2:

Compute profit margin and describe its use in analyzing company performance.

Profit margin is defined as the reporting period's net income divided by its net sales. Profit margin reflects on a company's earnings activities by showing how much income is in each dollar of sales.

Learning Objective A3:

Compute the current ratio and describe what it reveals about a company's financial condition.

A company's current ratio is defined as current assets divided by current liabilities. We use it to evaluate a company's ability to pay its current liabilities out of current assets.

Learning Objective P1:

Prepare and explain adjusting entries.

Prepaid expenses refer to items paid for in advance of receiving their benefits. Prepaid expenses are assets. Adjusting entries for prepaids involve increasing (debiting) expenses and decreasing (crediting) assets. *Unearned* (or *prepaid*) *revenues* refer to cash received in advance of providing products and services. Unearned revenues are liabilities. Adjusting entries for unearned revenues involves increasing (crediting) revenues and decreasing (debiting) unearned revenues. *Accrued expenses* refer to costs incurred in a period that are both unpaid and unrecorded. Adjusting entries for recording accrued expenses involve increasing (debiting) expenses and increasing (crediting) liabilities. *Accrued revenues* refer to revenues earned in a period that are both unrecorded and not yet received in cash. Adjusting entries for recording accrued revenues involve increasing (debiting) assets and increasing (crediting) revenues.

Learning Objective P2:

Explain and prepare an adjusted trial balance.

An adjusted trial balance is a list of accounts and balances prepared after recording and posting adjusting entries. Financial statements are often prepared from the adjusted trial balance.

Learning Objective P3:

Prepare financial statements from an adjusted trial balance.

Revenue and expense balances are reported on the income statement. Asset, liability, and equity balances are reported on the balance sheet. We usually prepare statements in the following order: income statement, statement of retained earnings, balance sheet, and statement of cash flows.

Learning Objective P4:

Describe and prepare closing entries.

Closing entries involve four steps: (1) close credit balances in revenue (and gain) accounts to Income Summary, (2) close debit balances in expense (and loss) accounts to Income Summary, (3) close Income Summary to Retained Earnings, and (4) close Dividends account to Retained Earnings.

Learning Objective P5:

Explain and prepare a post-closing trial balance.

A post-closing trial balance is a list of permanent accounts and their balances after all closing entries have been journalized and posted. Its purpose is to verify that (1) total debits equal total credits for permanent accounts and (2) all temporary accounts have zero balances.

Learning Objective P6 (Appendix 3A):

Explain the alternatives in accounting for prepaids.

Charging all prepaid expenses to expense accounts when they are purchased is acceptable. When this is done, adjusting entries must transfer any unexpired amounts from expense accounts to asset accounts. Crediting all unearned revenues to revenue accounts when cash is received is also acceptable. In this case, the adjusting entries must transfer any unearned amounts from revenue accounts to unearned revenue accounts.

Learning Objective P7 (Appendix 3B):

Prepare a work sheet and explain its usefulness.

A work sheet can be a useful tool in preparing and analyzing financial statements. It is helpful at the end of a period in preparing adjusting entries, an adjusted trial balance, and financial statements. A work sheet usually contains five pairs of columns: Unadjusted Trial Balance, Adjustments, Adjusted Trial Balance, Income Statement, and Balance Sheet.

Chapter Outline

Notes

I.   Timing and Reporting

   A. The Accounting Period
      To provide timely information, accounting systems prepare periodic reports at regular intervals.

      1. The **time-period principle** assumes that an organization's activities can be divided into specific time periods such as a month, a three-month quarter, a six-month interval, or a year. Reports covering a one-year period are known as **annual financial statements. Interim financial statements** cover one, three, or six months of activity.

      2. Annual reporting period:

        a. Calendar year—January 1 to December 31.

        b. **Fiscal year**—any twelve consecutive months used to base annual financial reports on.

        c. **Natural business year**—a fiscal year that ends when a company's sales activities are at their lowest level for the year.

   B. Accrual Basis versus Cash Basis

      1. Accounts are adjusted at the end of a period to record internal transactions and events that are not yet recorded.

      2. **Accrual basis accounting**—uses the adjusting process to recognize revenue when earned and to match expenses with revenues. This means the economic effects of revenues and expenses are recorded when earned or incurred, not when cash is received or paid. Accrual basis is consistent with GAAP.

      2. **Cash basis accounting**—revenues are recognized when cash is received and expenses are recognized when cash is paid. The cash basis is not consistent with GAAP.

      3. Accrual accounting also increases the **comparability** of financial statements from one period to another.

   C. Recognizing Revenues and Expenses

      1. The **revenue recognition principle** requires revenue be recorded when earned, not before and not after.

      2. The **matching principle** requires expenses be recorded in the same period as the revenues earned as a result of these expenses.

II.   Adjusting Accounts

The process of adjusting accounts involves analyzing each account balance and the transactions and events that affect it to determine any needed adjustments. An **adjusting entry** is recorded to bring an asset or liability account balance to its proper amount. This entry also updates a related expense or revenue account.

A. Framework for Adjustments

Adjustments are necessary for transactions and events that extend over more than one period. Adjusting entries are necessary so that revenues, expenses, assets and liabilities are correctly reported. Each adjusting entry affects one or more income statement accounts and one or more balance sheet accounts (but not the cash account).

B. Prepaid (Deferred) Expenses

1. **Prepaid Expenses** are items *paid for* in advance of receiving their benefits. Prepaid expenses are assets. When the assets are used, their costs become expenses.

2. Common prepaid items are prepaid insurance, supplies, and other prepaid expenses.

3. Adjusting entries for prepaids involve increasing (debiting) expenses and decreasing (crediting) assets (with the exception of depreciation on plant and equipment assets).

4. A special category of prepaid expenses is plant assets. **Plant assets** are long-term tangible assets used to produce and sell products and services; they are expected to provide benefits for more than one period.

5. **Depreciation** is the process of allocating the cost of plant and equipment assets over their expected useful lives. **Straight-line depreciation** allocates equal amounts of the assets' net cost to depreciation during its useful life.

6. Adjusting entries for depreciation expense involve increasing (debiting) expenses and increasing (crediting) a special account called Accumulated Depreciation. Accumulated depreciation is a contra asset account. A **contra account** is an account linked with another account, and having an opposite normal balance.

7. Accumulated depreciation is reported as a subtraction from the related plant asset account balance in the balance sheet.

8. **Book value** is a term used to describe the asset less its contra-asset (accumulated depreciation).

    C. Unearned (Deferred) Revenues

        1. **Unearned Revenues** are liabilities created by cash received in advance of providing products or services. The company has an obligation to provide the service or product. As they are provided unearned revenues (liabilities) become *earned* revenues (revenues).

        2. Adjusting entries for unearned revenues involve increasing (crediting) revenues and decreasing (debiting) unearned revenues.

    D. Accrued Expenses

        1. **Accrued expenses** refer to costs that are incurred in a period but are both unpaid and unrecorded.

        2. Common accrued expenses are salaries, interest, rent, and taxes.

        3. Adjusting entries for recording accrued expenses involve increasing (debiting) expenses and increasing (crediting) liabilities. (The liability is a payable.)

        4. Future payment of accrued expenses generally results in cash payments in the next period. Debit the payable for amount accrued and credit cash for the full amount paid. If the amount paid exceeds the amount accrued, the difference is an expense in the current period.

    E. Accrued Revenues

        1. **Accrued revenues** refer to revenues earned in a period that are both unrecorded and not yet received in cash (or other assets).

        2. Accrued revenues commonly result from services, products, interest, and rent.

        3. Adjusting entries for recording accrued revenues involve increasing (debit) assets and increasing (credit) revenues. (The asset is a receivable.)

        4. Accrued revenues at the end of one accounting period result in cash receipts in a future period. Debit cash for the full amount received and credit the receivable for the amount accrued.

        5. If the amount received exceeds the amount accrued, the difference is an additional amount earned to be credited to revenue.

    F. Links to Financial Statements

        The process of adjusting accounts is intended to bring an asset or liability account balance to its correct amount. It also updates a related expense or revenue account. Each adjusting entry affects one or more income statement accounts *and* one or more balance sheet accounts. Failure to make a necessary adjustment will result in misstatements of amounts on each of the financial statements. (See Exhibit 3-12 for a summary of adjustments.)

G. Adjusted Trial Balance

An **unadjusted trial balance** is a list of accounts and balances prepared *before* adjustments are recorded. An **adjusted trial balance** is a list of accounts and balances prepared *after* adjusting entries have been recorded and posted to the ledger.

III. **Preparing Financial Statements**

Financial statements are prepared directly from information in the *adjusted* trial balance:

A. Revenue and expense balances are transferred from the adjusted trial balance to the income statement.

B. The net income, retained earnings, and dividends are then used to prepare the statement of retained earnings.

C. Asset, liability, and common stock balances on the adjusted trial balance are transferred to the balance sheet; the ending retained earnings is determined on the statement of retained earnings and transferred to the balance sheet.

D. Financial statements are usually prepared in the following order: income statement, statement of retained earnings, balance sheet, and statement of cash flows.

IV. **Closing Process**

The **closing process** is an important step at the end of the accounting period *after* financial statements have been completed. It prepares accounts for recording the transactions and the events of the *next* period.

A. Steps in closing process:

1. Identify accounts for closing.

2. Record and post closing entries.

3. Prepare a post-closing trial balance.

B. Purpose of closing process:

1. Resets revenue, expense, and dividend account balances to zero at the end of each period so that these accounts can properly measure income and dividends for the next period.

2. Helps in summarizing a period's revenues and expenses.

C. Temporary and Permanent Accounts

1. **Temporary (or nominal) accounts** accumulate data related to one accounting period; they include all income statement accounts, the dividends account, and the Income Summary account. The closing process applies only to temporary accounts.

2. **Permanent (or real) accounts** report on activities related to one or more future accounting periods. They carry their ending balances into the next period and generally consist of all balance sheet accounts. Real accounts are not closed.

D. Recording Closing Entries

1. To record and post **closing entries** is to transfer the end-of-period balances in revenue, expense, and dividends accounts to retained earnings.

2. To close these accounts, transfer their balances first to a temporary account (used only for the closing process) called **Income Summary**. Its balance equals net income or net loss and is transferred to Retained Earnings.

3. The four steps necessary to close temporary accounts are:

   a. Close credit balances in revenue (and gain) accounts to Income Summary; bring accounts with credit balances to zero by debiting them.

   b. Close debit balances in expense (and loss) accounts to Income Summary; bring accounts with debit balances to zero by crediting them.

   c. Close the Income Summary account to the Retained Earnings account; after the first two steps, the balance of the Income Summary account is equal to the period's net income. If a net loss occurred, the third entry is reversed: debit Retained Earnings and credit Income Summary.

   d. Close the Dividends account to the Retained Earnings account; bring the Dividends account, which has a debit balance, to zero by crediting it.

E. Post-Closing Trial Balance.

1. A **post-closing trial balance** is a list of permanent accounts and their balances from the ledger after all closing entries have been journalized and posted.

2. The aim is to verify that (1) total debits equal total credits for permanent accounts, and (2) all temporary accounts have zero balances.

F. Accounting Cycle Summary

The term **accounting cycle** refers to the steps in preparing financial statements; it is a cycle because all steps are repeated each reporting period. Exhibit 3.19 shows the ten steps in the cycle:

1. Analyze transactions

2. Journalize

3. Post

4. Prepare unadjusted trial balance

5. Adjust

6. Prepare adjusted trial balance

7. Prepare statements

8. Close

9. Prepare post-closing trial balance

10. Reverse (optional; explained in Appendix 3C).

V. **Classified Balance Sheet**—organizes assets and liabilities into subgroups that provide more useful information to decision makers:

A. Classification Structure

1. One of the more important classifications is the separation between current and noncurrent assets and liabilities.

2. Current items are expected to come due (both collected and owed) within one year or the company's *operating cycle*, whichever is longer.

3. The **operating cycle** is the time span from when cash is used to acquire goods and services until cash is received from the sale of those goods and services. Most operating cycles are less than one year; a few companies have an operating cycle *longer* than one year.

B. Classification Categories

1. **Current Assets**—cash or other assets that are expected to be sold, collected, or used within one year or the company's operating cycle, whichever is longer. Examples: cash, short-term investments, accounts receivable, short-term notes receivable, goods for sale (called *merchandise* or *inventory*), and prepaid expenses.

2. **Long-Term Investments**—assets that are expected to be held for more than the longer of one year or the operating cycle. Examples: notes receivable, investments in stocks, and land held for future expansion.

3. **Plant Assets**—tangible, long-lived assets that are both *long-lived* and *used to produce or sell products and services*. Examples: equipment, machinery, buildings, and land that are used to produce or sell products and services.

4. **Intangible Assets**—long-term resources that benefit business operations. They usually lack physical form and have uncertain benefits. Examples: patents, trademarks, copyrights, franchises, and goodwill.

5. **Current Liabilities**—obligations due to be paid or settled within one year or the operating cycle, whichever is longer. Examples: accounts payable, notes payable, wages payable, taxes payable, interest payable, and unearned revenues. Any portion of a long-term liability due to be paid within one year or the operating cycle, whichever is longer, is a current liability.

6. **Long-Term Liabilities**—obligations *not* due within one year or the operating cycle, whichever is longer. Examples: notes payable, mortgages payable, bonds payable, and lease obligations.

7. **Equity**—owners' claim on assets; divided into two main subsections: common stock and retained earnings.

VI. **Decision Analysis—Profit Margin and Current Ratio**

A. Profit Margin

1. **Profit margin** (also called *return on sales*) is a useful measure of a company's operating results.

2. It is calculated as net income divided by net sales.

3. It is interpreted as reflecting the portion of profit in each dollar of sales.

B. Current Ratio

1. The **current ratio** is an important measure of a company's ability to pay its short-term obligations.

2. It is calculated as total current assets divided by total current liabilities.

VII. **Alternative Accounting for Prepayments (Appendix 3A)**

A. Recording the Prepayment of Expenses in Expense Accounts
Prepaid expenses may originally be recorded with debits to expense accounts (instead of to asset accounts). If so, then adjusting entries must transfer the cost of the unused portions from expense accounts to prepaid expense (asset) accounts.

B. Recording the Prepayment of Revenues in Revenue Accounts
Unearned revenues may originally be recorded with credits to revenue accounts (instead of to liability accounts).
If so, then adjusting entries must transfer the unearned portions from revenue accounts to unearned revenue (liability) accounts.

C. Note that the financial statements are identical under either procedure, but the adjusting entries are different.

VIII. **Work Sheet as a Tool (Appendix 3B)**

A. Working papers are internal documents. One widely used working paper is the work sheet, which is a useful tool for preparers in working with accounting information. It is usually not available to external decision makers.

B. Use of a Work Sheet

Preparing a work sheet has five important steps:

1. Enter the unadjusted trial balance in the first two columns.

2. Enter the adjustments in the third and fourth columns. Total columns to verify debit adjustments equal credit adjustments.

3. Prepare the Adjusted Trial Balance. This is done by combining the unadjusted trial balance and adjustment columns. Total Adjusted Trial Balance columns to verify debits equal credits.

4. Sort the adjusted trial balance amounts to the appropriate financial statement columns.

5. Total statement columns, compute net income or loss, and balance the columns by adding net income or loss.

IX. **Reversing Entries (Appendix 3C)**

A. **Reversing entries** are optional; they are recorded in response to accrued assets and accrued liabilities that were created by adjusting entries at the end of a reporting period.

B. Accounting *without* Reversing Entries—the disadvantage of this approach is the slightly more complex entry required when the cash subsequently changes hands (i.e., when cash is received for the asset that was originally accrued or when cash is paid for the liability that was originally accrued).

C. Accounting *with* Reversing Entries

1. A reversing entry is the exact opposite of an adjusting entry.

2. Reversing entries are prepared after closing entries and dated the first day of the new period.

3. Procedure is to transfer accrued asset and liability account balances to related revenue and expense accounts creating abnormal balances in these accounts.

4. The full subsequent cash receipts (and payments) are recorded as increases in revenue (and expense) accounts creating a net balance equal to the amount earned or incurred in that period.

ACCRUAL BASIS ACCOUNTING

(Follows GAAP)

<u>requires</u> that the

Income Statement (for a period)

reports

GAAP Revenue Recognition

ALL REVENUES EARNED in period (Collected or Not)

<u>Minus ALL EXPENSES INCURRED in period (Paid or Not)</u>

<u>Equals Net Income or Net Loss for the period</u>

GAAP Matching

ACCOUNTS MUST BE ADJUSTED TO FOLLOW PRINCIPLES

DEFERRALS

The converse of statements in Visual #3-1 also applies.

Revenue not earned or expense not incurred results in
Deferrals*

UNEARNED = LIABILITY *

A REVENUE not earned cannot be shown, even if collected.

An EXPENSE not incurred cannot be shown, even if paid.

PREPAID = ASSET *

*We defer or postpone the reporting of the collected revenues
(as revenues) and prepaid expenses (as expenses) until the
revenue is earned and the expense is incurred.

ADJUSTMENTS

TYPE	GENERALIZED* ENTRY	AMOUNT
1. Prepaid items or supplies a) initially recorded as assets	Dr. _____ Expense Cr. The Asset* acct.	Amount used, or consumed, or expired
b) initially recorded as expenses (alternate treatment)	Dr. the Asset** acct. Cr. _____ Expense	Amount left, or not consumed, or unexpired
2. Accrued expenses (expenses <u>incurred</u> but not yet recorded)	Dr. _____ Expense Cr. _____ Payable	Amount accrued
3. Accrued revenues (revenues <u>earned</u> but not yet recorded)	Dr. _____ Receivable Cr. The Revenue** acct.	Amount accrued
4. Long-term assets that are depreciable	Dr. Depreciation Expense Cr. Accumulated Depreciation	Portion of cost allocated to this period as depreciation
5. Unearned revenues (received in advance) a) record initially as liability (unearned account)	Dr. Unearned _____ Cr. The Revenue** acct.	Amount earned to date
b) initially recorded as a revenue (alternate treatment)	Dr. the Revenue** acct. Cr. Unearned_____	Amount still <u>not</u> earned

* Note: (1) Each adjustment affects a Balance Sheet Account and an Income Statement Account (2) <u>CASH</u> <u>NEVER</u> appears in an adjustment.
** Title or account name varies.

VISUAL #3-4

THE ACCOUNTING CYCLE

STEPS	PURPOSE	TIMING
1. Analyze transactions	Analyze transactions to prepare for journalizing.	During the period
2. Journalize	Record accounts, including debits and credits, in a journal.	During the period
3. Post	Transfer debits and credits from the journal to the ledger.	During the period
4. Prepare unadjusted trial balance	Summarize unadjusted ledger accounts and amounts.	End of period
5. Adjust	Record adjustments to bring account balances up to date; journalize and post adjusting entries.	End of period
6. Prepared adjusted trial balance	Summarize adjusted ledger accounts and amounts.	End of period
7. Prepare statements	Use adjusted trial balance to prepare financial statements.	End of period
8. Close	Journalize and post entries to close temporary accounts.	End of year
9. Prepare post-closing trial balance	Test clerical accuracy of the closing procedures.	End of year
10. Reverse (Optional)	Reverse certain adjustments in the next period (See Appendix 3C)	Beginning of next year

MUSIC WORLD
BALANCE SHEET
DECEMBER 31, 20XX

Assets

Current Assets

Cash		$30,360	
Short-Term Investments		2,000	
Notes Receivable		8,000	
Accounts Receivable		35,300	
Merchandise Inventory		60,400	
Prepaid Insurance		6,600	
Supplies		1,696	
Total Current Assets			$144,356

Investments

Land Held for Future Use			13,950

Property, Plant, and Equipment

Land		$ 4,500	
Building	$20,650		
Less Accumulated Depreciation	8,640	12,010	
Office Equipment	$ 8,600		
Less Accumulated Depreciation	5,000	3,600	
Total Property, Plant, and Equipment			20,110

Intangible Assets

Trademark			500
Total Assets			$178,916

Liabilities

Current Liabilities

Notes Payable	$15,000	
Accounts Payable	25,683	
Salaries Payable	2,000	
Current Portion of Mortgage Payable	10,200	
Total Current Liabilities		$ 52,883

Long-Term Liabilities

Mortgage Payable		27,600
Total Liabilities		$ 80,483

Equity

Common Stock		40,000
Retained Earnings		58,433
Total Liabilities and Equity		$178,916

On July 1, 20×9, Howard M. Tenant, Inc., rents office space from John Q. Landlord for two years, starting immediately, at a rate of $100 per month, or $2,400 in total. The full $2,400 was paid on this date.

Required:

Record the original transaction on 7/1 and the appropriate adjusting entries at the end of years in 20X9, 20X10, and 2011 from the point of view of Tenant and Landlord.

(If this alternative demonstration problem is not covered in class, see your instructor for the solution.)

Problem I

The following statements are either true or false. Place a (T) in the parentheses before each true statement and an (F) before each false statement.

1. ( ) The effect of a debit to an unearned revenue account and a corresponding credit to a revenue account is to transfer the earned portion of the fee from the liability account to the revenue account.

2. ( ) If the accountant failed to make the end-of-period adjustment to remove from the Unearned Fees account the amount of fees earned, the omission would cause an overstatement of assets.

3. ( ) The financial effect of a revenue generally occurs when it is earned, not when cash is received.

4. ( ) Under the cash basis of accounting, revenues are recognized when they are earned and expenses are matched with revenues.

5. ( ) After all closing entries are posted at the end of an accounting period, the Income Summary account balance is zero.

6. ( ) Throughout the current period, one could refer to the balance of the Income Summary account to determine the amount of net income or loss that was earned in the prior accounting period.

Problem II

You are given several words, phrases, or numbers to choose from in completing each of the following statements or in answering the following questions. In each case select the one that best completes the statement or answers the question and place its letter in the answer space provided.

_____ 1. Time periods covered by statements are called:
    a. seasonal periods.
    b. fiscal years.
    c. operating cycles of a business.
    d. accounting periods.
    e. natural business years.

_____ 2. X Company has four employees who are each paid $40 per day for a five-day work week. The employees are paid every Friday. If the accounting period ends on Wednesday, X Company should make the following entry to accrue wages:

    a. Salaries Expense 800
           Salaries Payable.. 800
    b. Salaries Expense 800
           Cash 800
    c. Salaries Expense 480
           Salaries Payable.. 480
    d. Salaries Expense 320
           Salaries Payable.. 320
    e. No entry should be made until the salaries are actually paid.

3. Lori Teach owns a sole proprietorship. During April of 20X8, Lori's business received $250 cash in advance for future services. The following entry should be made when the money is received:

a. Cash...250

    Accounts Receivable   250

b. Accounts Receivable...250

    Unearned Revenue...   250

c. Cash...250

    Unearned Revenue...   250

d. Unearned Revenue..250

    Services Revenue...   250

e. No entry should be made until services are actually rendered.

4. On December 1, B & B Security Service collected three months' fees of $6,000 in advance of providing services and credited Unearned Security Service Fees.
They provided the monthly service from that date forward. The December 31st adjustment will require that Unearned Security Service Fees be:

a. Credited for $ 2,000.

b. Debited for $ 6,000.

c. Credited for $ 6,000.

d. Debited for $ 4,000.

e. Debited for $ 2,000.

5. The GreenTree Restaurant prepares monthly financial statements. On January 31 the balance in the Supplies account was $1,600. During February, $2,960 of supplies were purchased and debited to Supplies. Assuming a February 28 inventory showed that $1,300 of supplies were on hand, the company should record the following adjusting entry as of February 28:

a. Supplies Expense 300

    Supplies...   300

b. Supplies..300

    Supplies Expense   300

c. Supplies..3,260

    Cash...   3,260

d. Supplies Expense 3,260

    Supplies...   3,260

6. ABC Company's financial statements show the following:

Net income $195,000

Total revenues...850,000

Total expenses...655,000

ABC's profit margin is:

a. 22.9 %
b. 29.8 %
c. 435.9 %
d. 129.8 %
e. 77.1 %

_____ 7. Based on the following T-accounts and their end-of-period balances, what will be the balance of the Retained Earnings account after the closing entries are posted?

Retained Earnings	Dividends	Income Summary
Dec. 31 7,000	Dec. 31 9,600	

Revenue	Rent Expense	Salaries Expense
Dec. 3129,700	Dec. 31 3,600	Dec. 31 7,200

Insurance Expense	Depr. Expense, Equipment
Dec. 31 920	Dec. 31 500

a. $12,880 Debit.
b. $12,880 Credit.
c. $24,480 Credit.
d. $14,880 Credit.
e. $10,480 Debit.

_____ 8. The following information is available from the financial statements of Harvard Company:

Current assets	$ 195,000
Total assets	850,000
Current liabilities	113,500
Total liabilities	441,500
Stockholder's Equity	408,500

Harvard's current ratio is:

a. 1.9
b. 2.1
c. 1.7
d. 1.5
e. 5.8

Problem III

Many of the important ideas and concepts discussed in Chapter 3 are reflected in the following list of key terms. Test your understanding of these terms by matching the appropriate definitions with the terms. Record the number identifying the most appropriate definition in the blank space next to each term.

_____ Accounting cycle	_____ Interim financial statements
_____ Accounting period	_____ Long-term investments
_____ Accrual basis accounting	_____ Long-term liabilities
_____ Accrued expenses	_____ Matching principle
_____ Accrued revenues	_____ Natural business year
_____ Adjusted trial balance	_____ Operating cycle
_____ Adjusting entry	_____ Permanent accounts
_____ Annual financial statements	_____ Plant assets
_____ Book value	_____ Post-closing trial balance
_____ Cash basis accounting	_____ Prepaid expenses
_____ Classified balance sheet	_____ Profit margin
_____ Closing entries	_____ Pro forma financial statements
_____ Closing process	_____ Reversing entries**
_____ Contra account	_____ Straight-line depreciation method
_____ Current assets	_____ Temporary accounts
_____ Current liabilities	_____ Time-period principle
_____ Current ratio	_____ Unadjusted trial balance
_____ Depreciation	_____ Unclassified balance sheet
_____ Fiscal year	_____ Unearned revenues
_____ Income Summary	_____ Working papers
_____ Intangible assets	_____ Work sheet*

Key term discussed in Appendix 3B.
**Key term discussed in Appendix 3C.*

1. Costs incurred in a period that are both unpaid and unrecorded; adjusting entries for recording accrued expenses involve increasing (debiting) expenses and increasing (crediting) liabilities.

2. Ratio of a company's net income to net sales; the percent of income in each dollar of revenue.

3. Allocates equal amounts of an asset's cost (less any salvage value) to depreciation expense during its useful life.

4. List of accounts and balances prepared after adjustments are recorded and posted.

5. Revenues earned in a period that are both unrecorded and not yet received in cash (or other assets); adjusting entries for recording accrued revenues involve increasing (debiting) assets and increasing (crediting) revenues.

6. List of accounts and balances prepared before adjustments have been recorded and posted.

7. Assumes an organization's activities can be divided into specific time periods such as months, quarters, or years.

8. Consecutive 12-month (or 52 week) period chosen as the organization's annual accounting period.

9. Expense created by allocating the cost of plant and equipment to the periods in which they are used.

10.   Cash (or other assets) received in advance of providing products or services; a liability.

11.   Journal entry at the end of an accounting period to bring an asset or liability account to its proper amount and update the related revenue or expense account.

12.   Requires expenses to be reported in the same period as the revenues that were earned as a result of the expenses.

13.   The 12-month period that ends when a company's sales activities are at their lowest point.

14.   Balance sheet that broadly groups the assets, liabilities and equity accounts.

15.   Accounting system that recognizes revenues when cash is received and records expenses when cash is paid.

16.   Accounting system that recognizes revenues when earned and expenses when incurred; the basis for GAAP.

17.   Account linked with another account and having the opposite normal balance; reported as a subtraction from the other account's balance.

18.   Length of time covered by periodic financial statements; also called *reporting period.*

19.   Necessary steps to prepare the accounts for recording the transactions of the next period.

20.   Financial statements covering periods of less than one year; usually based on one- or three- or six-month periods.

21.   Financial statements covering a one-year period; often based on a calendar year, but any consecutive 12-month (or 52-week) period is acceptable.

22.   Items paid for in advance of receiving their benefits; classified as assets.

23.   An asset's acquisition costs less its accumulated depreciation.

24.   Assets such as notes receivable or investments in stocks and bonds that are held for more than the longer of one year or the operating cycle.

25.   List of permanent accounts and their balances from the ledger after the closing entries are journalized and posted.

26.   Recurring steps performed each accounting period, starting with analyzing transactions and continuing through the post-closing trial balance (or reversing entries).

27.   Balance sheet that presents the assets and liabilities in relevant subgroups.

28.   Accounts used to record revenues and expenses; they are closed at the end of the period; also called *nominal accounts.*

29.   Analyses and other informal reports prepared by accountants when organizing information for formal reports and financial statements.

30.   Accounts used to report activities related to one or more future periods; balance sheet accounts whose balances are not closed; also called *real accounts.*

31.   Temporary account used only in the closing process to which the balances of revenues and expenses are transferred; its balance is transferred to the retained earnings account.

32.   Optional entries recorded at the beginning of a new period that prepare the accounts for the usual journal entries as if adjusting entries had not occurred.

33.   Entries recorded at the end of each accounting period to transfer end-of-period balances in revenue and expense accounts to retained earnings.

©The McGraw-Hill Companies, Inc., 2009

34. Spreadsheet used to draft an unadjusted trial balance, adjusting entries, adjusted trial balance, and financial statements; an optional step in accounting.

35. Statements that show the effects of the proposed transactions as if they occurred.

36. Long-term assets used to produce or sell products or services; they usually lack physical form and their benefits are uncertain.

37. Cash or other assets that are expected to be sold, collected, or used within one year or the company's operating cycle, whichever is longer.

38. Obligations due to be paid or settled within one year or the operating cycle, whichever is longer.

39. Ratio used to evaluate a company's ability to pay its short-term obligations; calculated by dividing current assets by current liabilities.

40. Obligations that are not due to be paid within one year or the operating cycle, whichever is longer.

41. Tangible long-lived assets used to produce or sell products and services; also called *property, plant and equipment* or fixed assets.

42. Normal time between paying cash for merchandise or employee services and receiving cash from customers.

Problem IV

Complete the following by filling in the blanks.

1. Under the cash basis of accounting, revenues are reported as being earned in the accounting period in which _____, expenses are charged to the period in which _____, and net income for the period is the difference between _____ and _____.

2. Under the accrual basis of accounting, revenues are credited to the period in which _____, expenses are _____ with revenues, and no consideration is given as to when cash is received or disbursed.

3. Revenue accounts have credit balances; consequently, to close a revenue account and make it show a zero balance, the revenue account is _____ , and the Income Summary account is _____ for the amount of the balance.

4. Expense accounts have debit balances; therefore, expense accounts are _____ , and the Income Summary account is _____ in closing the expense accounts.

5. Only balance sheet accounts should have balances appearing on the post-closing trial balance because the balances of all temporary accounts are reduced to _____ in the closing procedure.

6. Closing entries are necessary because if at the end of an accounting period the revenue and expense accounts are to show only one period's revenues and expenses, they must begin the period with _____ balances, and closing entries cause the revenue and expense accounts to begin a new period with _____ balances.

7. Closing entries accomplish two purposes: (1) they cause all _____ accounts to begin the new accounting period with zero balances, and (2) they transfer the net effect of the past period's _____ and _____ transactions to the Retained Earnings account.

Problem V

On October 1 of the current year, Harold Lloyd incorporated a business to perform services as a public stenographer. During the month he completed the following transactions:

10/01   Invested $3,000 in the business.
10/01   Paid three months' rent in advance on the office space, $1,245.
10/01   Purchased office equipment for cash, $925.50.
10/02   Purchased on credit office equipment, $700, and office supplies, $75.50.
10/31   Completed stenographic work during the month and collected cash, $1,725.
10/31   Declared and paid a dividend in the amount of $725.

After these transactions were journalized and posted, the company's accounts were as follows:

GENERAL LEDGER

Cash   Account No. 101

DATE	EXPLANATION	P.R.	DEBIT				CREDIT				BALANCE			
Oct. 1		G-1	3	0 0 0	00						3	0 0 0	00
1		G-1					1	2 4 5	00		1	7 5 5	00
1		G-1						9 2 5	50			8 2 9	50
31		G-2	1	7 2 5	00						2	5 5 4	50
31		G-2						7 2 5	00		1	8 2 9	50

Office Supplies   Account No. 124

DATE	EXPLANATION	P.R.	DEBIT			CREDIT			BALANCE		
Oct. 2		G-1		7 5	50					7 5	50

Prepaid Rent   Account No. 131

DATE	EXPLANATION	P.R.	DEBIT			CREDIT			BALANCE		
Oct. 1		G-1	1	2 4 5	00				1	2 4 5	00

Office Equipment   Account No. 163

DATE	EXPLANATION	P.R.	DEBIT			CREDIT			BALANCE		
Oct. 1		G-1		9 2 5	50					9 2 5	50
2		G-1		7 0 0	00				1	6 2 5	50

Accumulated Depreciation, Office Equipment   Account No. 164

DATE	EXPLANATION	P.R.	DEBIT			CREDIT			BALANCE		

Accounts Payable   Account No. 201

DATE	EXPLANATION	P.R.	DEBIT	CREDIT	BALANCE
Oct. 2		G-1		7 7 5 50	7 7 5 50

Common Stock   Account No. 301

DATE	EXPLANATION	P.R.	DEBIT	CREDIT	BALANCE
Oct. 1		G-1		3 0 0 0 00	3 0 0 0 00

Dividends   Account No. 303

DATE	EXPLANATION	P.R.	DEBIT	CREDIT	BALANCE
Oct. 31		G-2	7 2 5 00		7 2 5 00

Stenographic Services Revenue   Account No. 403

DATE	EXPLANATION	P.R.	DEBIT	CREDIT	BALANCE
Oct. 31		G-2		1 7 2 5 00	1 7 2 5 00

Depreciation Expense, Office Equipment   Account No. 612

DATE	EXPLANATION	P.R.	DEBIT	CREDIT	BALANCE

Rent Expense   Account No. 640

DATE	EXPLANATION	P.R.	DEBIT	CREDIT	BALANCE

Office Supplies Expense   Account No. 650

DATE	EXPLANATION	P.R.	DEBIT	CREDIT	BALANCE

On October 31, Harold Lloyd gathered the following information in preparation for adjusting the company's books and preparing its balance sheet and an income statement.

a. One month's rent had expired.
b. An inventory of office supplies showed $40 of unused office supplies.
c. The office equipment had depreciated $35 during October.

Required:

1. Prepare and post journal entries to record the adjustments.

2. After posting the adjusting entries, complete the adjusted trial balance.

3. Using the adjusted trial balance, prepare an income statement and statement of retained earnings for the month of October and a <u>classified</u> balance sheet as of the end of October.

GENERAL JOURNAL   Page 2

DATE	ACCOUNT TITLES AND EXPLANATION	P.R.	DEBIT	CREDIT

HAROLD LLOYD, INC.

Adjusted Trial Balance

October 31, 20—

	Cash				
	Office supplies				
	Prepaid rent				
	Office equipment				
	Accumulated depreciation, office equipment				
	Accounts payable				
	Common stock				
	Dividends				
	Stenographic services revenue				
	Depreciation expense, office equipment				
	Rent expense				
	Office supplies expense				
	Totals				

HAROLD LLOYD, INC.

Income Statement

For Month Ended October 31, 20—

HAROLD LLOYD, INC.

Statement of Retained Earnings

For Month Ended October 31, 20—

HAROLD LLOYD, INC.

Balance Sheet

October 31, 20—

Financial Accounting Fundamentals

Problem VI

Blade Company has one employee who earns $72.50 per day. The company operates with monthly accounting periods, and the employee is paid each Friday night for a workweek that begins on Monday. Assume the calendar for October appears as shown below:

OCTOBER						
S	M	T	W	T	F	S
	1	2	3	4	5	6
7	8	9	10	11	12	13
14	15	16	17	18	19	20
21	22	23	24	25	26	27
28	29	30	31			

Required:

1. Enter the four $362.50 weekly wage payments directly in the T-accounts below. Then enter the adjustment for the wages earned but unpaid on October 31 directly in the T-accounts.

Cash	Wages Payable	Wages Expense

2. Blade Company's October income statement should show $_____ of wages expense, and its October 31 balance sheet should show a $_____ liability for wages payable. The wages earned by its employee but unpaid on October 31 are an example of an _____ expense.

3. Prepare the journal entry to record payment of a full week's wages to the Blade Company employee on November 2.

GENERAL JOURNAL   Page 1

DATE	ACCOUNT TITLES AND EXPLANATION	P.R.	DEBIT	CREDIT

Problem VII

Riverview Properties operates an apartment building. On December 31, at the end of an annual accounting period, its Rent Earned account had a $335,500 credit balance, and the Unearned Rent account had a $3,600 credit balance. The following information was available for the year-end adjustments: (a) the credit balance in the Unearned Rent account resulted from a tenant paying his rent for six months in advance beginning on November 1; (b) also, a tenant in temporary financial difficulties had not paid his rent for the month of December. The amount due was $475.

Required:

1. Enter the necessary adjustments directly in the T-accounts below.

Rent Receivable	Unearned Rent	Rent Earned
	Nov. 1 3,600	Bal. 335,500

2. After the adjustments described above are entered in the accounts, the company's Rent Earned account has a balance of $_____ which will appear on its income statement as revenue earned during the year. Its Unearned Rent account has a balance of $_____, which will appear on the company's balance sheet as a _____. Likewise, the company's Rent Receivable account has a $_____ balance, and this should appear on its balance sheet as a(n) _____.

Problem VIII

The adjusted trial balance of Homer's Home Shop, Inc. appears below:

HOMER'S HOME SHOP, INC.
Adjusted Trial Balance
December 31, 20__

Cash...	$ 2,875	....
Accounts receivable	2,000	....
Shop supplies..	725	....
Shop equipment..	5,125	....
Accumulated depreciation, shop equipment...................................	....	$ 1,200
Accounts payable	....	575
Wages payable..	....	388
Common stock..	....	5,500
Retained earnings	30,000	....
Repair services revenue...	....	55,785
Wages expense	18,638	....
Rent expense...	2,500	....
Shop supplies expense..	1,037	....
Depreciation expense, shop equipment..	475	....
Miscellaneous expense	73	....
Totals..	$63,448	$63,448

Required:

1. Prepare the entries required to close the company's accounts.
2. Prepare a post-closing trial balance.

GENERAL JOURNAL   Page 2

DATE	ACCOUNT TITLES AND EXPLANATION	P.R.	DEBIT	CREDIT

HOMER'S HOME SHOP, INC.

Post-Closing Trial Balance

December 31, 20__

Solutions for Chapter 3

Problem I

1. T
2. F
3. T
4. F
5. T
6. F

Problem II

1. D
2. C
3. C
4. E
5. D
6. A
7. D
8. C

Problem III

26	Accounting cycle		20	Interim financial statements
18	Accounting period		24	Long-term investments
16	Accrual basis accounting		40	Long-term liabilities
1	Accrued expenses		12	Matching principle
5	Accrued revenues		13	Natural business year
4	Adjusted trial balance		42	Operating cycle
11	Adjusting entry		30	Permanent accounts
21	Annual financial statements		41	Plant assets
23	Book value		25	Post-closing trial balance
15	Cash basis accounting		22	Prepaid expenses
27	Classified balance sheet		2	Profit margin
33	Closing entries		35	Pro forma financial statements
19	Closing process		32	Reversing entries**
17	Contra account		3	Straight-line depreciation method
37	Current assets		28	Temporary accounts
38	Current liabilities		7	Time-period principle
39	Current ratio		6	Unadjusted trial balance
9	Depreciation		14	Unclassified balance sheet
8	Fiscal year		10	Unearned revenues
31	Income Summary		29	Working papers
36	Intangible assets		34	Work sheet*

Problem IV

1. they are received in cash; they are paid; revenue receipts; expense disbursements

2. earned; matched

3. debited; credited

4. credited; debited

5. zero

6. zero; zero

7. temporary; revenue; expense

Problem V

1.

Oct. 31	Rent Expense	415.00	
	Prepaid Rent		415.00
31	Office Supplies Expense	35.50	
	Office Supplies		35.50
31	Depreciation Expense, Office Equipment	35.00	
	Accumulated Depreciation, Office Equipment		35.00

Cash

Date	Debit	Credit	Balance
Oct 1	3,000.00		3,000.00
1		1,245.00	1,755.00
1		925.50	829.50
31	1,725.00		2,554.50
31		725.00	1,829.50

Office Supplies

Oct. 2	75.50		75.50
31		35.50	40.00

Prepaid Rent

Oct. 1	1,245.00		1,245.00
31		415.00	830.00

Office Equipment

Oct. 1	925.50		925.50
2	700.00		1,625.50

Accumulated Depr., Office Equipment

Oct. 31		35.00	35.00

Accounts Payable

Date	Debit	Credit	Balance
Oct. 2		775.50	775.50

Common Stock

Oct. 1		3,000.00	3,000.00

Dividends

Oct. 31	725.00		725.00

Stenographic Services Revenue

Oct. 31		1,725.00	1,725.00

Depr. Expense, Office Equipment

Oct. 31	35.00		35.00

Rent Expense

Oct. 31	415.00		415.00

Office Supplies Expense

Oct. 31	35.50		35.50

2.

HAROLD LLOYD, INC.
Adjusted Trial Balance
October 31, 20__

Cash	$1,829.50	
Office supplies	40.00	
Prepaid rent	830.00	
Office equipment	1,625.50	
Accumulated depreciation, office equipment		$ 35.00
Accounts payable		775.50
Common stock		3,000.00
Retained earnings	725.00	
Stenographic services revenue		1,725.00
Depreciation expense, office equipment	35.00	
Rent expense	415.00	
Office supplies expense	35.50	
Totals	$5,535.50	$5,535.50

3.

HAROLD LLOYD, INC.
Income Statement
For Month Ended October 31, 20__

Revenue:		
Stenographic services revenue		$1,725.00
Operating expenses:		
Depreciation expense, office equipment	$ 35.00	
Rent expense	415.00	
Office supplies expense	35.50	
Total operating expenses		485.50
Net income		$1,239.50

HAROLD LLOYD, INC.
Statement of Retained Earnings
For Month Ended October 31, 20__

Retained earnings, October 1, 20---		$ 0.00
October net income	$1,239.50	
Less dividends	725.00	
Excess of income over dividends		514.50
Retained earnings, October 31, 20---		$514.50

HAROLD LLOYD, INC.
Balance Sheet
October 31, 20___
Assets

Current assets
Cash.. $1,829.50
Office supplies... 40.00
Prepaid rent... 830.00
Total current assets 2,699.50
Plant assets
Office equipment.. $1,625.50
Less accumulated depreciation... 35.00
Total plant assets 1,590.50
Total assets $4,290.00

Liabilities

Current liabilities
Accounts payable .... $ 775.50

Equity

Common stock... 3,000.00
Retained earnings 514.50
Total liabilities and equity.. $4,290.00

Problem VI

1.

	Cash			Wages Expense	
	Oct. 5	362.50	Oct. 5	362.50	
	12	362.50	12	362.50	
	19	362.50	19	362.50	
	26	362.50	26	362.50	
			31	217.50	

Wages Payable		
	Oct. 31	217.50

2. $1,667.50; $217.50; accrued

3. Nov. 2   Wages Expense.. 145.00
              Wages Payable.. 217.50
              Cash.. 362.50

Problem VII

1.

Rent Receivable				Unearned Rent			
Dec. 31	475			Dec. 31	1,200	Nov. 1	3,600

Rent Earned		
	Bal.	335,500
	Dec. 31	1,200
	31	475

2. Rent Earned; $337,175; Unearned Rent; $2,400, liability; Rent Receivable; $475, asset.

Problem VIII

1.

Dec. 31	Repair Services Revenue	55,785	
	Income Summary		55,785

Dec. 31	Income Summary	22,723	
	Wages Expense		18,638
	Rent Expense		2,500
	Shop Supplies Expense		1,037
	Depreciation Expense, Shop Equipment		475
	Miscellaneous Expense		73

Dec. 31	Income Summary	33,062	
	Retained Earnings		33,062

2.

HOMER'S HOME SHOP, INC.
Post-Closing Trial Balance
December 31, 20__

Cash	$ 2,875	....
Accounts receivable	2,000	....
Shop supplies	725	....
Shop equipment	5,125	....
Accumulated depreciation, shop equipment	....	$ 1,200
Accounts payable	....	575
Wages payable	....	388
Common stock	....	5,500
Retained earnings (33,062 – 30,000)	....	3,062
Totals	$10,725	$10,725

CHAPTER 4
ACCOUNTING FOR
MERCHANDISING OPERATIONS

Learning Objective C1:

Describe merchandising activities and identify income components for a merchandising company.

Merchandisers buy products and resell them. Examples of merchandisers include Wal-Mart, Home Depot, The Limited, and Barnes & Noble. A merchandiser's costs on the income statement include an amount for cost of goods sold. Gross profit, or gross margin, equals sales minus cost of goods sold.

Learning Objective C2:

Identify and explain the inventory asset of a merchandising company.

The current asset section of a merchandising company's balance sheet includes *merchandise inventory*, which refers to the products a merchandiser sells and are available for sale at the balance sheet date.

Learning Objective C3:

Describe both perpetual and periodic inventory systems.

A perpetual inventory system continuously tracks the cost of goods available for sale and the cost of goods sold. A periodic system accumulates the cost of goods purchased during the period and does not compute the amount of inventory or the cost of goods sold until the end of a period.

Learning Objective C4:

Analyze and interpret cost flows and operating activities of a merchandising company.

Cost of merchandise purchases flows into Merchandise Inventory and from there to Cost of Goods Sold on the income statement. Any remaining inventory is reported as a current asset on the balance sheet.

Learning Objective A1:

Compute the acid-test ratio and explain its use to assess liquidity.

The acid-test ratio is computed as quick assets (cash, short-term investments, and current receivables) divided by current liabilities. It indicates a company's ability to pay its current liabilities with its existing quick assets. An acid-test ratio equal to or greater than 1.0 is often adequate.

Learning Objective A2:

Compute the gross margin ratio and explain its use to assess profitability.

The gross margin ratio is computed as gross margin (net sales minus cost of goods sold) divided by net sales. It indicates a company's profitability before considering other expenses.

Learning Objective P1:

Analyze and record transactions for merchandise purchases using a perpetual system.

For a perpetual inventory system, purchases of inventory (net of trade discounts) are added to the Merchandise Inventory account. Purchase discounts and purchase returns and allowances are subtracted from Merchandise Inventory, and transportation-in costs are added to Merchandise Inventory.

Learning Objective P2:

Analyze and record transactions for merchandise sales using a perpetual system.

A merchandiser records sales at list price less any trade discounts. The cost of items sold is transferred from Merchandise Inventory to Cost of Goods Sold. Refunds or credits given to customers for unsatisfactory merchandise are recorded in Sales Returns and Allowances, a contra account to Sales. If merchandise is returned and restored to inventory, the cost of this merchandise is removed from Cost of Goods Sold and transferred back to Merchandise Inventory. When cash discounts from the sales price are offered and customers pay within the discount period, the seller records Sales Discounts, a contra account to Sales.

Learning Objective P3:

Prepare adjustments and close accounts for a merchandising company.

With a perpetual system, it is often necessary to make an adjustment for inventory shrinkage. This is computed by comparing a physical count of inventory with the Merchandise Inventory balance. Shrinkage is normally charged to Cost of Goods Sold. Temporary accounts closed to Income Summary for a merchandiser include Sales, Sales Discounts, Sales Returns and Allowances, and Cost of Goods Sold.

Learning Objective P4:

Define and prepare multiple-step and single-step income statements.

Multiple-step income statements include greater detail for sales and expenses than do single-step income statements. They also show details of net sales and report expenses in categories reflecting different activities.

Learning Objective P5 (Appendix 4A):

Record and compare merchandising transactions using both periodic and perpetual inventory systems.

Transactions involving the sale and purchase of merchandise are recorded and analyzed under both the periodic and perpetual inventory systems. Adjusting and closing entries for both inventory systems are illustrated and explained.

I.   **Merchandising Activities**
         Products that a company acquires to resell to customers are referred
         to as **merchandise** (also called *goods*). A **merchandiser** earns net
         income by buying and selling merchandise. A **wholesaler** is an
         intermediary that buys products from manufacturers or other
         wholesalers and sells them to retailers or other wholesalers.

   A.   Reporting Income for a Merchandiser
         Revenue (*net sales*) from selling merchandise minus the **cost of
         goods sold** (the expense of buying and preparing the
         merchandise) to customers is called **gross profit** (also called
         gross margin). This amount minus expenses (generally called
         operating expenses) determines the net income or loss for the
         period.

   B.   Reporting Inventory for a Merchandiser
         1.   A merchandiser's balance sheet is the same as a service
              business with the exception of one additional current asset,
              merchandise inventory, or simply *inventory*.

         2.   The cost of this asset includes the cost incurred to buy the
              goods, ship them to the store, and make them ready for sale.

   C.   Operating Cycle for a Merchandiser
         A merchandising company's operating cycle begins by
         purchasing merchandise and ends by collecting cash from selling
         the merchandise. Companies try to keep their operating cycles
         short because assets tied up in inventory and receivables are not
         productive.

   D.   Inventory Systems
         1.   Merchandise available for sale consists of beginning
              inventory and what it purchases (net purchases). The
              merchandise available is either sold (cost of goods sold) or
              kept for future sales (ending inventory).

         2.   Two alternative inventory systems are used to collect
              information about cost of goods sold and the cost of
              inventory:

              a.   **Perpetual inventory system**—continually updates
                   accounting records for merchandise transactions,
                   specifically, for those records of inventory available for
                   sale and inventory sold.

              b.   **Periodic inventory system**—updates the accounting
                   records for merchandise transactions only at the *end* of a
                   period.

              c.   Some companies use a hybrid system where the
                   perpetual system is used for tracking units available and
                   the periodic system is used to compute cost of sales.

The following sections of this outline use the perpetual inventory system. Appendix 4A uses the period system (with perpetual results on the side). An instructor can choose to cover either one or both inventory systems.

II. Accounting for Merchandise Purchases
The invoice serves as a *source document* for this event.

A. Trade Discounts

1. In catalogs, each item has a **list price** or catalog price. An item's intended selling price equals list price minus a given percent called a **trade discount**.

2. A buyer records the net amount of list price minus trade discount.

B. Purchases Discounts
Credit terms for a purchase include the amounts and timing of payments from a buyer to a seller. The amount of time before full payment is due is called the **credit** period.

1. Sellers can grant a **cash discount** to encourage the buyer to pay earlier. A seller views a cash discount as a **sales discount** and a buyer views a cash discount as a **purchase discount.** This reduced payment applies only for the **discount period**.

2. Example: *credit terms*, 2/10 n/30, offers a 2 % discount if the invoice is paid within 10 days of invoice date.

3. Entry for buyer for purchase of merchandise on credit: debit Merchandise Inventory, credit Accounts Payable.

4. Entry for buyer to record payment within discount period: debit Accounts Payable (full invoice amount), credit Cash (amount paid = invoice – discount), credit Merchandise Inventory (amount of discount).

C. Purchase Returns and Allowances

1. *Purchase returns* refer to merchandise a buyer acquires but then returns to the seller.

2. A *purchase allowance* is a reduction in the cost of defective or unacceptable merchandise that a buyer acquires.

3. The buyer issues a **debit memorandum** to inform the seller of a debit made to the supplier's account.

4. Entry for buyer to record purchase return or allowance: debit Accounts Payable or Cash (if refund given) and credit Merchandise Inventory.

5. When goods are returned, a buyer can take a purchase discount on only the remaining balance of the invoice.

D. Transportation Costs and Ownership Transfer
The buyer and seller must agree on who is responsible for paying any freight costs and who bears the risk of loss during transit for merchandising transactions. The point of transfer is called the **FOB** (*free on board*) point.

1. FOB shipping point—buyer accepts ownership when goods depart sellers' place of business; buyer pays shipping costs.

    a. Shipping costs increase the cost of merchandise acquired (cost principle).

    b. Entry for buyer to record shipping costs: Debit Merchandise Inventory, credit Cash or Accounts Payable (if to be paid with merchandise later).

2. FOB destination—ownership of goods transfers to buyer when goods arrive at buyer's place of business; seller pays shipping costs.

    a. Shipping costs are an operating (selling) expense for seller

    b. Entry for seller to record shipping costs: Debit Delivery Expense (or Transportation-Out or Freight-Out), credit Cash.

III. **Accounting for Merchandise Sales**
A. Sales of Merchandise
Each sales transaction involves two parts:

1. Recognize revenue—entry for seller to record: debit Accounts Receivable (or cash), credit Sales (for the invoice amount).

2. Recognize cost— entry for seller to record: debit Cost of Goods Sold, credit Merchandise Inventory (for the cost of the merchandise sold).

B. Sales Discounts
Sales discounts are usually not recorded until a customer actually pays with the discount period.

1. Entry for seller to record collection after discount period— Debit Cash, Credit Accounts Receivable (full invoice amount).

2. Entry for seller to record collection within discount period— debit Cash (invoice amount less discount), debit Sales Discounts (discount amount), credit Accounts Receivable (invoice amount).

3. Sales Discounts is a contra-revenue account; it is subtracted from Sales when computing a company's net sales.

4. Sales discounts are monitored to assess the effectiveness and cost of its discount policy.

    C. Sales Returns and Allowances

       1. *Sales returns*—merchandise that a customer returns to the seller after a sale.

       2. *Sales allowances*—reductions in the selling price of merchandise sold to customers (usually for damaged or defective merchandise that a customer is willing to keep at a reduced price).

       3. Entry for seller to record sales returns or allowances: debit Sales Returns and Allowances and credit Accounts Receivable; additional entry if returned merchandise is salable: debit Merchandise Inventory, credit Cost of Goods Sold.

       4. Seller prepares a **credit memorandum** to inform buyer of the seller's credit to the buyer's Accounts Receivable (on the seller's books).

IV.   **Completing the Accounting Cycle**

    A. Adjusting Entries for Merchandisers
Generally same as discussed in chapter 3 for a service business.

       1. Additional adjustment needed to update inventory to reflect any loss of merchandise, including theft and deterioration, is referred to as **shrinkage**.

       2. Shrinkage is determined by comparing a physical count of the inventory with recorded quantities.

       3. Entry to record shrinkage: debit Cost of Goods Sold, credit Merchandise Inventory.

    B. Preparing Financial Statements
The financial statement for a merchandiser are similar to those for a service company described in chapters 2 and 3.

       1. The income statement mainly differs by the inclusion of *cost of goods sold* and *gross profit*. Net sales is affected by discounts, returns, and allowances, and some additional expenses are possible such as delivery expense and loss from defective merchandise.

       2. The balance sheet mainly differs by the inclusion of *merchandise inventory* as part of current assets.

    C. Closing Entries
Closing entries are similar to a service business except that some new temporary accounts that arise from merchandising activities must be closed (e.g., Sales Discount, Sales Returns and Allowances, and Cost of Goods Sold). These debit balance accounts are closed with the expense accounts to Income Summary.

V.   Financial Statement Formats—No specific format is required in practice. Two common income statement formats:

A. Multiple-Step Income Statement

1. A **multiple-step income statement** has three main parts:

a. *Gross profit*—net sales minus cost of goods sold),

b. *Income from operations*—gross profit less operating expenses, and

c. *Net income*—income from operations adjusted for nonoperating items.

2. Operating expenses are classified into two sections:

a. **Selling expenses**—the expenses of promoting sales, making sales, and delivering goods to customers, and

b. **General and administrative expenses**—expenses related to accounting, human resource management, and financial management.

3. *Nonoperating activities*—consist of other expenses, revenues, losses, and gains that are unrelated to a company's operations; reported in two sections:

a. *Other revenues and gains*—interest revenue, dividend revenue, rent revenue, and gains from asset disposals.

b. *Other expenses and losses*—interest expense, losses from asset disposals, and casualty losses.

B. Single-Step Income Statement
A **single-step income statement** includes cost of goods sold as an operating expense and shows only one subtotal for total expenses, one subtraction to arrive at net income.

C. Classified Balance Sheet
The merchandiser's classified balance sheet reports merchandise inventory as a current asset, usually after accounts receivable.

VI.   Decision Analysis—Acid-Test and Gross Margin Ratios

A. Acid-Test Ratio

1. The **acid-test ratio** is used to assess the company's liquidity or ability to pay its current debts; it differs from the current ratio by excluding less liquid current assets.

2. It is calculated by dividing *quick assets* by current liabilities; quick assets are cash, short-term investments, and current receivables.

3. Rule of thumb is that the acid-test ratio should have a value of at least 1.0 to conclude that a company is unlikely to face near-term liquidity problems.

    B. Gross Margin Ratio

      1. The **gross margin ratio** (also called gross profit ratio) is used to assess a company's profitability before considering operating expenses.

      2. It is calculated by dividing *gross margin* (net sales – cost of goods sold) by net sales.

VII. Periodic Inventory System (Appendix 4A)

    A. Records merchandise acquisitions, discounts and returns in temporary accounts (Purchases, Purchase Returns, Purchases Discounts) rather than the merchandise inventory account.

    B. Records only the revenue aspect of sales-related events; updates inventory and determines cost of goods sold only at the end or the accounting period.

    C. The Merchandise Inventory account can be updated as part of the adjusting or closing process.

    D. Requires closing additional temporary accounts.

VIII. Work Sheet—Perpetual System (Appendix 4B)
Differs slightly from the work sheet layout for a service company in Chapter 3; includes additional accounts used by a merchandiser: Merchandise Inventory, Sales, Sales Returns and Allowances, Sales Discounts, and Cost of Goods Sold.

COMPONENTS OF NET INCOME (FROM OPERATIONS)

	Steps:
(a) Net Sales	X
(b) – Cost of Goods Sold*	– X
(c) Gross Profit on Sales	X
(d) – Operating Expenses	– X
(e) Net Income (Loss) from Operations	X

COMPONENTS OF COST OF GOODS SOLD

	Steps:
(a) Merchandise Inventory, Beginning of Period	X
(b) + Total Cost of Merchandise Purchases	+ X
(c) Merchandise Available for Sale	X
(d) – Merchandise Inventory, End of Period	– X
(e) Cost of Goods Sold	X

COMPONENTS COST OF GOODS PURCHASED

		Steps:
(a) Purchases		X
(b) – Purchase Returns & Allowances and Purchases Discounts	X + X	– X
(c) Net Purchases		X
(d) + Transportation-In		+ X
(e) Total Cost of Merchandise Purchases		X

* Perpetual inventory systems have a cost of goods sold account that continuously accumulates costs as items are sold. In a periodic inventory system this amount is calculated at the end of period.

VISUAL #4-2

THE OUTDOOR STORE
Income Statement
For the Year Ended December 31, 20xx

Sales revenues			
Sales		$700,000	
Less: Sales returns and allowances	$ 5,000		
Sales discounts	3,000	8,000	
Net sales......................................			$692,000
Cost of goods sold			
Merchandise inventory, January 1		40,300	
Purchases......................................	462,000		
Less: Purchase discounts........... $12,000			
Purchase returns and			
Allowances.................... 6,400	18,400		
Net purchases...................................	443,600		
Add: Freight-in.................................	3,600		
Total cost of merchandise purchased..........		447,200	
Goods available for sale		487,500	
Merchandise inventory, December 31..........		70,000	
Cost of goods sold			417,500
Gross profit			274,500
Operating expenses			
Selling expenses			
Sales salaries expense	76,000		
Sales commission expense..............	14,500		
Depreciation expense - Display equip.	13,300		
Utilities expense..........................	6,600		
Insurance expense........................	4,320		
Total selling expenses		114,720	
General and administrative expenses			
Office salaries expense..................	32,000		
Depreciation expense – building.......	10,400		
Property tax expense....................	4,800		
Utilities expense........................	4,400		
Insurance expense......................	2,880		
Total administrative expenses		54,480	
Total operating expenses...............			169,200
Income from operations.............................			105,300
Other revenues and gains			
Interest revenue		4,000	
Other expenses and losses			
Interest expense		11,000	7,000
Net income			$ 98,300

The following data was taken from ledger account balances and supplementary data for the Whisk Company for the year ended December 31, 20XX:

Merchandise inventory, 1/1/20XX	$ 20,000
Merchandise inventory, 12/31/20XX	23,000
Purchases	215,000
Purchases discounts	6,000
Purchases returns and allowances	3,000
Sales	400,000
Sales discounts	3,200
Sales returns and allowances	1,800
Transportation-in	10,000

Required:

1. Compute the total cost of merchandise purchases.

2. Compute the cost of goods sold.

3. Prepare a multiple-step income statement (only through the gross profit line) for the year ended December 31, 20XX.

(If this alternative demonstration problem is not covered in class, see your instructor for the solution.)

Note: Problems I through VI assume the use of a perpetual inventory system. Problem VII (appendix 4A) assumes a periodic inventory system.

Problem I

The following statements are either true or false. Place a (T) in the parentheses before each true statement and an (F) before each false statement.

1. (　) Sales returns and allowances or discounts are not included in the calculation of net sales.

2. (　) On a multiple-step income statement, ending inventory is subtracted from the cost of goods available for sale to determine cost of goods sold.

3. (　) Net sales minus cost of goods sold equals gross profit on sales.

4. (　) The balance sheet for a merchandising business is generally the same as for a service business with the exception of the addition of one account.

5. (　) Quick assets include cash, short-term investments, receivables, and merchandise inventory.

6. (　) A perpetual inventory system may require updating the inventory at the end of every fiscal period.

7. (　) Cash discounts on merchandise purchased are debited to the inventory account.

8. (　) Transportation costs on merchandise purchased are debited to the inventory account.

9. (　) A debit or credit memorandum may originate with either party to a transaction, but the memorandum gets its name from the action of the selling party exclusively.

10. (　) Recording the purchase of merchandise on account requires a debit to the inventory account and a credit to accounts payable.

Problem II

You are given several words, phrases, or numbers to choose from in completing each of the following statements or in answering the following questions. In each case select the one that best completes the statement or answers the question and place its letter in the answer space provided.

_____1.　A method of accounting for inventories in which cost of goods sold is recorded each time a sale is made and an up-to-date record of goods available is maintained is called a:
a. product inventory system.
b. perpetual inventory system.
c. periodic inventory system.
d. parallel inventory system.
e. principal inventory system.

_____2.　What is the effect on the income statement at the end of an accounting period in which the ending inventory of the prior period was understated and carried forward incorrectly?
a. Cost of goods sold is overstated and net income is understated.
b. Cost of goods sold is understated and net income is understated.
c. Cost of goods sold is understated and net income is overstated.
d. Cost of goods sold is overstated and net income is overstated.
e. The errors of the prior period and the current period offset each other, so there is no effect on the income statement.

_____ 3. Based on the following information, calculate the missing amounts.

Sales	$28,800	Cost of goods sold.........	?
Beginning inventory	?	Gross profit	$10,800
Purchases.............................	18,000	Expenses.......................	?
Ending inventory....................	12,600	Net income	3,600

a. Beginning inventory, $16,200; Cost of goods sold, $12,600; Expenses, $1,800.
b. Beginning inventory, $23,400; Cost of goods sold, $10,800; Expenses, $7,200.
c. Beginning inventory, $9,000; Cost of goods sold, $14,400; Expenses, $3,600.
d. Beginning inventory, $12,600; Cost of goods sold, $18,000; Expenses, $7,200.
e. Beginning inventory, $19,800; Cost of goods sold, $25,200; Expenses, $14,400.

_____ 4. The following information is taken from a single proprietorship's income statement. Calculate ending inventory for the business.

Sales	$165,250	Purchase returns	$ 390
Sales returns	980	Purchase discounts	1,630
Sales discounts	1,960	Transportation-in...........	700
Beginning inventory	16,880	Gross profit	58,210
Purchases.............................	108,380	Net income	17,360

a. $19,840.
b. 22,080.
c. $21,160.
d. 44,250.
e. Some other amount.

_____ 5. On July 18, Aught Company sold $1,800 of merchandise on credit, terms 2/10, n/30. On July 21, Aught issued a $180 credit memorandum to the customer who returned a portion of the merchandise purchased. In addition to the journal entry that debits inventory and credits cost of goods sold, what other journal entry is necessary to record the July 21 transaction?

a.	Accounts Receivable	180.00	
	Sales..		180.00
b.	Sales Returns and Allowances..............................	180.00	
	Accounts Receivable.......................................		180.00
c.	Accounts Receivable	900.00	
	Sales Returns and Allowances..............................	180.00	
	Sales..		1,080.00
d.	Sales	180.00	
	Accounts Receivable.......................................		180.00
e.	Sales Returns and Allowances..............................	180.00	
	Sales..		180.00

©The McGraw-Hill Companies, Inc., 2009

_____6. The following information is available from the balance sheet of Foster Company:

Cash	$22,300
Short-term investments	10,500
Accounts receivable	47,360
Merchandise inventory	52,100
Accounts payable	66,800
J. Foster, capital	57,300

Foster's acid-test ratio is:

a. 0.5
b. 1.2
c. 2.0
d. 1.4
e. 2.3

Problem III

Many of the important ideas and concepts discussed in Chapter 4 are reflected in the following list of key terms. Test your understanding of these terms by matching the appropriate definitions with the terms. Record the number identifying the most appropriate definition in the blank space next to each term.

_____ Acid-test ratio
_____ Cash discount
_____ Cost of goods sold
_____ Credit memorandum
_____ Credit period
_____ Credit terms
_____ Debit memorandum
_____ Discount period
_____ EOM
_____ FOB
_____ General and administrative expenses
_____ Gross margin
_____ Gross margin ratio
_____ Gross profit
_____ Inventory
_____ List price

_____ Merchandise
_____ Merchandise inventory
_____ Merchandiser
_____ Multiple-step income statement
_____ Periodic inventory system
_____ Perpetual inventory system
_____ Purchases discount
_____ Retailer
_____ Sales discount
_____ Selling expenses
_____ Shrinkage
_____ Single-step income statement
_____ Supplementary records
_____ Trade discount
_____ Wholesaler

1. Net sales minus cost of goods sold; also called *gross profit*.

2. Method that maintains continuous records of the cost of inventory available and the cost of goods sold.

3. Reduction from a list or catalog price that can vary for wholesalers, retailers, and consumers.

4. Term used by a seller to describe a cash discount granted to customers for paying within the discount period.

5. Notification that the sender has debited the recipient's account kept by the sender.

6. Merchandise a company owns and expects to sell in its normal operations.

7. Abbreviation for *end of month;* used to describe credit terms for some transactions.

8. Catalog price of an item before any trade discount is deducted.

9. Products that a company owns and expects to sell to customers; also called *merchandise inventory.*

10. Description of the amounts and timing of payments that a buyer agrees to make in the future.

11. Time period that can pass before a customer's payment is due.

12. Ratio used to assess a company's ability to settle its current debts with its most liquid assets; defined as quick assets (cash, short-term investments, and current receivables) over current liabilities.

13. Term used by a purchaser to describe a cash discount granted to the purchaser for paying within the discount period.

14. Notification that the sender has credited the recipient's account kept by the sender.

15. Method that records the cost of inventory purchased but does not track the quantity available or sold to customers; records are updated at the end of each period to reflect the physical count of goods available.

16. Time period in which a cash discount is available and the buyer can make a reduced payment.

17. Income statement format that includes cost of goods sold as an expense and shows only one subtotal for total expenses.

18. Reduction in the price of merchandise granted by a seller to a buyer when payment is made within the discount period.

19. Expenses of promoting sales, such as displaying and advertising merchandise, making sales, and delivering goods to customers.

20. Products that a company owns and expects to sell to their customers; also called *merchandise.*

21. Expenses that support the operating activities of a business.

22. Abbreviation for *free on board;* the point at which ownership of goods passes to the buyer; *FOB shipping point* (or *factory*) means the buyer pays shipping costs and accepts ownership of the goods at the seller's place of business; *FOB destination* means the seller pays shipping costs and buyer accepts ownership of the goods at the buyer's place of business;

23. Income statement format that shows subtotals between sales and net income and details of net sales and expenses.

24. Inventory losses that occur as a result of theft or deterioration.

25. Cost of inventory sold to customers during a period.

26. Gross margin (net sales minus cost of goods sold) divided by net sales; also called *gross profit ratio.*

27. Entity that earns net income by buying and selling merchandise.

28. Intermediary that buys products from manufacturers or other wholesalers and sells them to retailers or other wholesalers.

29. Information outside the usual accounting records.

30. Intermediary that buys products from manufacturers or wholesalers and sells them to customers.

31. Net sales minus cost of goods sold; also called *gross margin.*

Problem IV

The following amounts appeared on the adjusted trial balance of Valentine Variety Store, Inc. as of December 31, 2009, the end of its fiscal year:

	Debit	Credit
Cash	$ 4,000	
Merchandise inventory	15,000	
Other assets	8,000	
Liabilities		$ 4,000
Common stock		5,000
Retained earnings		7,300
Sales		80,000
Sales returns and allowances	600	
Cost of goods sold	47,700	
General and administrative expenses	8,000	
Selling expenses	13,000	
Totals	$96,300	$96,300

On December 31, 2008, the company's merchandise inventory amounted to $13,000. *Supplementary records* of merchandising activities during the 2009 year disclosed the following:

Invoice cost of merchandise purchases	$48,500
Purchase discounts received	900
Purchase returns and allowances received	400
Cost of transportation-in	2,500

Required:

Using the data above, complete the Income Statement for Valentine Variety Store, Inc. for December 31, 20X9. Use the form provided below.

VALENTINE VARIETY STORE, INC.

Income Statement

For the Year Ended December 31, 2009

Problem V

Refer to the adjusted trial balance for Valentine Variety Store, Inc. that is presented above in Problem IV.

Required:

Prepare the closing entries for Valentine Variety Store, Inc. Explanations are not necessary.

GENERAL JOURNAL   Page 1

DATE	ACCOUNT TITLES AND EXPLANATION	P.R.	DEBIT	CREDIT

Problem VI

1. If a company determines cost of goods sold by counting the inventory at the end of the period and subtracting the inventory from the cost of goods available for sale, the system of accounting for inventories is called a(n) _____.

2. Trade discounts _____ (are, are not) credited to the Inventory account.

3. A reduction in a payable that is granted if it is paid within the discount period is a _____ discount.

4. A store received a credit memorandum from a wholesaler for unsatisfactory merchandise that the store sent back for credit. The store should record the memorandum with a _____ (debit, credit) to its Inventory account and a _____ (debit, credit) to its Accounts Payable account.

5. The two common systems of accounting for merchandise inventories are the _____ inventory system and the _____ inventory system. Before the availability of computers, the _____ inventory system was most likely used in stores that sold a large volume of relatively low-priced items.

Problem VII (Appendix 4A)

The trial balance that follows was taken from the ledger of Sporthaus Lindner, Inc. at the end of its annual accounting period. Fritz Lindner, the owner of Sporthaus Lindner, Inc. did not make additional investments in the business during 20×9.

SPORTHAUS LINDNER, INC.
Unadjusted Trial Balance
December 31, 20X9

Cash...	$ 1,840	
Accounts receivable	2,530	
Merchandise inventory..	3,680	
Store supplies	2,070	
Accounts payable		$ 4,370
Salaries payable..	---	---
Common stock...		2,000
Retained earnings		2,600
Sales		14,260
Sales returns and allowances..	1,150	
Purchases...	5,750	
Purchase discounts		920
Transportation-in..	1,150	
Salaries expense	4,370	
Rent expense	1,610	
Store supplies expense..	---	---
Totals...	$24,150	$24,150

Required:

Prepare adjusting journal entries and closing journal entries for Sporthaus Lindner using the following information:

    a.   Ending store supplies inventory, $1,150.

    b.   Accrued salaries payable, $690.

    c.   Ending merchandise inventory, $4,830.

Record the adjusting journal entries and closing journal entries in the general journal below.

DATE	ACCOUNT TITLES AND EXPLANATION	P.R.	DEBIT			CREDIT		

Solutions for Chapter 4

Problem I

1. F
2. T
3. T
4. T
5. F
6. F
7. F
8. T
9. F
10. T

Problem II

1. B
2. C
3. D
4. A
5. B
6. B

Problem III

12	Acid-test ratio		9	Merchandise
18	Cash discount		20	Merchandise inventory
25	Cost of goods sold		27	Merchandiser
14	Credit memorandum		23	Multiple-step income statement
11	Credit period		15	Periodic inventory system
10	Credit terms		2	Perpetual inventory system
5	Debit memorandum		13	Purchases discount
16	Discount period		30	Retailer
7	EOM		4	Sales discount
22	FOB		19	Selling expenses
21	General and administrative expenses		24	Shrinkage
1	Gross margin		17	Single-step income statement
26	Gross margin ratio		29	Supplementary records
31	Gross profit		3	Trade discount
6	Inventory		28	Wholesaler
8	List price			

Problem IV

VALENTINE VARIETY STORE, INC.
Income Statement
For the Year Ended December 31, 2009

Revenue:...			
Sales...		$80,000	
Less: Sales returns and allowances.............................		600	
Net sales..			$79,400
Cost of goods sold:..			
Merchandise inventory, December 31, 20X8..................		$13,000	
Purchases...	$48,500		
Less: Purchases returns and allowances.....................	$400		
Purchase discounts	900	1,300	
Net purchases..		47,200	
Add: Transportation-in...		2,500	
Cost of goods purchases.......................................		49,700	
Goods available for sale...		62,700	
Merchandise inventory, December 31, 20X9..................		15,000	
Cost of goods sold..			47,700
Gross profit from sales			31,700
Operating expenses:			
General and administrative expenses..........................		8,000	
Selling expenses..		13,000	
Total operating expenses......................................			21,000
Net income			$10,700

Problem V

Dec. 31	Sales...	80,000	
	Income Summary...		80,000
31	Income Summary..	69,300	
	Sales Returns and Allowances.............................		600
	Cost of Goods Sold...		47,700
	General and Administrative Expenses.....................		8,000
	Selling Expenses...		13,000
31	Income Summary...	10,700	
	Retained Earnings..		10,700

Problem VI

1. periodic inventory system

2. are not

3. cash

4. credit, debit

5. periodic, perpetual (these first two answers are interchangeable), periodic

Problem VII (Appendix 4A)

Adjusting Entries

Dec. 31	Store Supplies Expense	920	
	Store Supplies		920
31	Salaries Expense	690	
	Salaries Payable		690

Closing Entries

Dec. 31	Sales	14,260	
	Merchandise Inventory	4,830	
	Purchase Discounts	920	
	Income Summary		20,010
31	Income Summary	19,320	
	Sales Returns and Allowances		1,150
	Merchandise Inventory		3,680
	Purchases		5,750
	Transportation-in		1,150
	Salaries Expense		5,060
	Rent Expense		1,610
	Store Supplies Expense		920
31	Income Summary	690	
	Retained Earnings		690

CHAPTER 5
ACCOUNTING FOR INVENTORIES

Learning Objective C1:

Identify the items making up merchandise inventory.

Merchandise inventory refers to goods owned by a company and held for resale. Three special cases merit our attention. Goods in transit are reported in inventory of the company that holds ownership rights. Goods on consignment are reported in the consignor's inventory. Goods damaged or obsolete are reported in inventory at their net realizable value.

Learning Objective C2:

Identify the costs of merchandise inventory.

Costs of merchandise inventory include expenditures necessary to bring an item to a salable condition and location. This includes its invoice cost minus any discount plus any added or incidental costs necessary to put it in a place and condition for sale.

Learning Objective A1:

Analyze the effects of inventory methods for both financial and tax reporting.

When purchase costs are rising or falling, the inventory costing methods are likely to assign different costs to inventory. Specific identification exactly matches costs and revenues. Weighted average smooths out cost changes. FIFO assigns an amount to inventory closely approximating current replacement cost. LIFO assigns the most recent costs incurred to cost of goods sold and likely better matches current costs with revenues.

Learning Objective A2:

Analyze the effects of inventory errors on current and future financial statements.

An error in the amount of ending inventory affects assets (inventory), net income (cost of goods sold), and equity for that period. Since ending inventory is next period's beginning inventory, an error in ending inventory affects next period's cost of goods sold and net income. Inventory errors in one period are offset in the next period.

Learning Objective A3:

Assess inventory management using both inventory turnover and days' sales in inventory.

We prefer a high inventory turnover, provided that goods are not out of stock and customers are not turned away. We use days' sales in inventory to assess the likelihood of goods being out of stock. We prefer a small number of days' sales in inventory if we can serve customer needs and provide a buffer for uncertainties.

Learning Objective P1:

Compute inventory in a perpetual system using the methods of specific identification, FIFO, LIFO, and weighted average.

Costs are assigned to the cost of goods sold account each time a sale occurs in a perpetual system. Specific identification assigns a cost to each item sold by referring to its actual cost (for example, its net invoice cost). Weighted average assigns a cost to items sold by dividing the current balance in the inventory account by the total items available for sale to determine cost per unit. We then multiply the number of units sold by this cost per unit to get the cost of each sale. FIFO assigns cost to items sold assuming that the earliest units purchased are the first units sold. LIFO assigns cost to items sold assuming that the most recent units purchased are the first units sold.

Learning Objective P2:

Compute the lower of cost or market amount of inventory.

Inventory is reported at market cost when market is lower than recorded cost, called the lower of cost or market (LCM) inventory. Market is typically measured as replacement cost. Lower of cost or market can be applied separately to each item, to major categories of items, or to the entire inventory.

Learning Objective P3 (Appendix 5A):

Compute inventory in a periodic system using the methods of specific identification, FIFO, LIFO, and weighted average.

Periodic inventory systems allocate the cost of goods available for sale between cost of goods sold and ending inventory at the end of a period. Specific identification and FIFO give identical results whether the periodic or perpetual system is used. LIFO assigns costs to cost of goods sold assuming the last units purchased for the period are the first units sold. The weighted average cost per unit is computed by dividing the total cost of beginning inventory and net purchases for the period by the total number of units available. Then, it multiplies cost per unit by the number of units sold to give cost of goods sold.

Learning Objective P4 (Appendix 5B):

Apply both the retail inventory and gross profit methods to estimate inventory. The retail inventory method involves three steps: (1) goods available at retail minus net sales at retail equals ending inventory at retail, (2) goods available at cost divided by goods available at retail equals the cost-to-retail ratio, and (3) ending inventory at retail multiplied by the cost-to-retail ratio equals estimated ending inventory at cost. The gross profit method involves two steps: (1) net sales at retail multiplied by 1 minus the gross profit ratio equals estimated cost of goods sold, and (2) goods available at cost minus estimated cost of goods sold equals estimated ending inventory at cost.

I.   **Inventory Basics**

    A.   Determining Inventory Items

       Merchandise inventory includes all goods that a company owns and holds for sale. The following inventory items require special attention:

       1.   Goods in Transit

          If ownership has passed to the purchaser, the goods are included in the purchaser's inventory. Ownership is determined by reviewing the shipping terms.

       2.   Goods on Consignment—goods shipped by the owner, called the **consignor**, to another party, the **consignee**.

          a.   A consignee sells goods for the owner.

          b.   The consignor continues to own the consigned goods and reports them in its inventory.

       3.   Goods Damaged or Obsolete

          a.   Damaged and obsolete (and deteriorated) goods are not counted in inventory if they cannot be sold.

          b.   If these goods can be sold at a reduced price, they are included in inventory at their **net realizable value**, the sales price minus the cost of making the sale.

    B.   Determining Inventory Costs

       1.   The cost of an inventory item includes its invoice cost minus any discount, plus any incidental costs (such as import duties, freight, storage, and insurance necessary to put it in place and condition for sale).

       2.   The *matching principle* states that inventory costs should be recorded against revenue in the period when inventory is sold. Some companies use the *materiality constraint (cost-to-benefit constraint)* to avoid assigning those incidental costs to inventory. Instead, they expense them when incurred.

    C.   Internal Controls and Taking a Physical Count

       1.   The Inventory account under a perpetual system is updated for each purchase and sale, but events (such as theft, loss, damage, and errors) can cause the inventory account balance to differ from the actual inventory on hand.

       2.   Nearly all companies take a *physical count of inventory* at least once a year; the physical count is used to adjust the Inventory account balance to the actual inventory on hand.

       3.   Internal controls when taking a physical count of inventory include:

          a.   *Prenumbered inventory tickets*; each ticket must be accounting for.

          b.   Those responsible for the inventory do not count the inventory.

    c. Counters confirm the validity of inventory, including its existence, amount, and quality.

    d. A second count is taken by a different counter.

    e. A manager confirms that all inventories are ticketed once, and only once.

II. **Inventory Costing under a Perpetual System**
Major goal is to properly match costs with sales. The *matching principle* is used to decide how much of the cost of goods available for sale is deducted from sales (on the income statement) and how much is carried forward as inventory (on the balance sheet). One of the most important issues in accounting for inventory is determining the per unit cost assigned to inventory items.

  A. Inveztory Cost Flow Assumption
Four methods are commonly used to assign costs to inventory and cost of goods sold. Each method assumes a particular pattern for how costs flow through inventory. **Physical flow and cost flow need not be the same.**

    1. First-in, first-out (FIFO)—assumes costs flow in the order incurred.

    2. Last-in, first-out (LIFO)—assumes costs flow in the reverse order occurred.

    3. Weighted average—assumes costs flow in an average of the costs available.

    4. Specific identification—each item can be identified with a specific purchase and invoice. Specific identification is usually only practical for companies with expensive, custom-made inventory.

Note: The following sections assume the use of a perpetual system, the assignment of costs to inventory using a periodic system is described in Appendix 5A.

  B. Inventory Costing Illustration

    1. Specific identification—As sales occur, cost of goods sold is charged with the actual or invoice cost, leaving actual costs of inventory on hand in the inventory account.

    2. First-in, first-out (FIFO)—As sales occur, FIFO charges costs of the earliest units acquired to cost of goods sold, leaving costs of the most recent purchases in inventory.

    3. Last-in, first-out (LIFO)—As sales occur, LIFO charges costs of the most recent purchase to cost of goods sold, leaving costs of the earliest purchases in inventory.

    4. Weighted average—As sales occur, weighted average computes the average cost per unit of inventory at the time of sale and charges this cost per unit sold to cost of goods sold leaving average cost per unit on hand in inventory. Weighted average equals cost of goods available for sale divided by the units available.

C. Financial Statement Effects of Costing Methods

   1. When purchase prices do not change, each inventory costing method assigns the same amounts to inventory and to cost of goods sold. When purchase prices are different, the methods assign different cost amounts. When purchase costs *regularly rise:*

     a. FIFO assigns the lowest amount to cost of goods sold resulting in the highest gross profit and the highest net income. Advantage: Inventory on the balance sheet approximates its current replacement cost; it also mimics the actual flow of goods for most businesses.

     b. LIFO assigns the highest amount to cost of goods sold resulting in the lowest gross profit and the lowest net income. Advantage: Better match of current costs with revenues in computing gross margin.

     c. Weighted average method yields results between FIFO and LIFO. Advantage: Smoothing out of price changes.

     d. Specific identification always yields results that depend on which units are sold. Advantage: Exactly matches costs and revenues.

   When costs *regularly decline*, the reverse occurs for FIFO and LIFO.

D. Tax Effects of Costing Methods
Since inventory costs affect net income, they have potential tax effects.

   1. Financial reporting often differs from the method used for tax reporting.

   2. Exception: LIFO may only be used for tax purposes if it is also used for financial reporting.

E. Consistency in Using Costing Methods

   1. **Consistency concept** requires the use of the same accounting methods period after period so the financial statements are comparable across periods.

   2. Method change is acceptable if it will improve financial reporting. *The full-disclosure principle* requires statement notes report type of change, its justification, and its effect on income.

   3. Different methods may be consistently applied to different categories of inventory.

III. **Valuating Inventory at LCM and the Effects of Inventory Errors**

A. Lower of Cost or Market
Accounting principles require that inventory be reported on the balance sheet at the **lower of cost or market (LCM)**.

   1. Market is the current replacement cost of purchasing the same inventory items in the usual manner.

2. When the recorded cost of inventory is higher than the replacement cost, a loss is recognized; when the recorded cost is lower, no adjustment is made.

3. Lower of cost or market pricing is applied in one of three ways to:

    a. Each individual item separately,

    b. Major categories of items, or

    c. To the entire inventory.

4. Accounting rules require that inventory be adjusted to market when market is less than cost, but inventory normally cannot be written up to market when market exceeds cost. The **conservatism constraint** prescribes the use of the less optimistic amount when more than one estimate of the amount to be received or paid exists and these estimates are about equally likely.

B. Financial Statement Effects of Inventory Errors
    An inventory error causes misstatements in cost of goods sold, gross profit, net income, current assets, and equity. It also causes misstatements in the next period's financial statements because ending inventory of one period is the beginning inventory of the next.

    1. Income statement effects:

        a. If ending inventory is understated, cost of goods sold is overstated and net income is understated.

        b. If beginning inventory is understated, cost of goods sold is understated and net income is overstated.

        c. If ending inventory is overstated, cost of goods sold is understated and net income is overstated.

        d. If beginning inventory is overstated, cost of goods sold is overstated and net income is understated.

    2. Balance sheet effects:

        a. If ending inventory is understated, assets and equity are understated.

        b. If ending inventory is overstated, assets and equity are overstated.

        c. Errors in beginning inventory do not yield misstatements in the end-of-period balance sheet, but they do affect current period's income statement (see 1 above).

IV. **Decision Analysis—Inventory Turnover and Days' Sales in Inventory**

A. Inventory Turnover

    1. **Inventory turnover** is used to measure a company's ability to pay short-term obligations can depend on how quickly inventory is sold.

      2. It is calculated by dividing cost of goods sold by average inventory.

      3. It measures the number of *times* a company's average inventory was sold during an accounting period.

  B. Days' Sales in Inventory

      1. **Day's sales in inventory** measures how much inventory is available in terms of the number of days' sales.

      2. It is calculated by dividing ending inventory by cost of goods sold, and then multiplying the result by 365.

      3. It estimates how many days it will take to convert inventory at the end of a period into accounts receivable or cash.

  C. Analysis of Inventory Management
      Inventory management is a major emphasis for most merchandisers; they must both plan and control inventory purchases and sales. We prefer a high inventory turnover.

V.   **Inventory Costing under a Periodic System (Appendix 5A)**

    Results of periodic vs. perpetual by method:

  A. Specific identification—same results as perpetual.

  B. First-in, first-out (FIFO)—same results as perpetual.

  C. Last-in, first-out (LIFO)—results differ from perpetual because timing of cost assignment changes what is identified as the last cost.

  D. Weighted average—results differ from perpetual because timing of cost assignment changes what costs are averaged.

VI.   **Inventory Estimation Methods (Appendix 5B)**

    Inventory sometimes requires estimation for two reasons. First, companies often require interim financial statements, but only take an annual physical count of inventory. Second, companies may require an inventory estimate if some casualty makes taking a physical count impossible. Estimates are usually only required for companies that use the periodic system.

  A. Retail Inventory Method
      The **retail inventory method** estimates the cost of ending inventory for interim statements in a periodic inventory when a physical count is taken only annually. Steps include:

      1. Subtract sales (general ledger amount) from goods available measured at retail price (retail data in supplementary records) to get ending inventory at retail.

      2. Find cost ratio by dividing total of goods available at cost by total of goods available at retail.

      3. Apply cost ratio to ending inventory at retail to convert to ending inventory at cost.

    Note: The cost ratio is also used to convert a physical inventory taken using retail price to cost. Shrinkage can be measured by comparing converted to estimated inventory.

C. Gross Profit Method

The **gross profit method** estimates the cost of ending inventory by applying the gross profit ratio to net sales (at retail). This type of estimate is often used for insurance claims when inventory is destroyed, lost or stolen. Steps include:

1. Determine the normal gross profit percentage from recent years.

2. Find the cost of goods percentage (100% less gross profit percentage).

3. Multiply actual sales by the cost of goods sold percentage to get estimated cost of goods sold.

4. Subtract estimated cost of goods sold from the actual amount of cost of goods available for sale to get estimated ending inventory at cost.

Schedule of Cost of Goods Available

	Units		Cost		Total
Jan. 1 Beginning Inventory	60	@	$10	=	$ 600
Mar. 27 Purchase	90	@	11	=	990
Aug. 15 Purchase	100	@	13	=	1,300
Nov. 6 Purchase	50	@	16	=	800
	300				$3,690

Cost of goods available for sale $3,690

Methods of Assigning Cost to Units in Ending Inventory

(1) **Specific Identification** - requires that each item in an inventory be assigned its <u>actual</u> invoice cost.

(2) **Weighted Average** - a weighted average cost per unit is determined based on total cost and units of goods available for sale. This cost is assigned to units in the ending inventory.

(3) **First-in, First-out (FIFO)** - assumes the first units acquired (beginning inventory) are the first to be sold and that additional sales flow is in the order purchased. Therefore, the costs of the last items received are assigned to the ending inventory.

(4) **Last-in, First-out (LIFO)** - assumes the last units acquired (most recent purchase) are the first units sold. Therefore, the cost of the first items acquired (starting with beginning inventory) are assigned to the ending inventory.

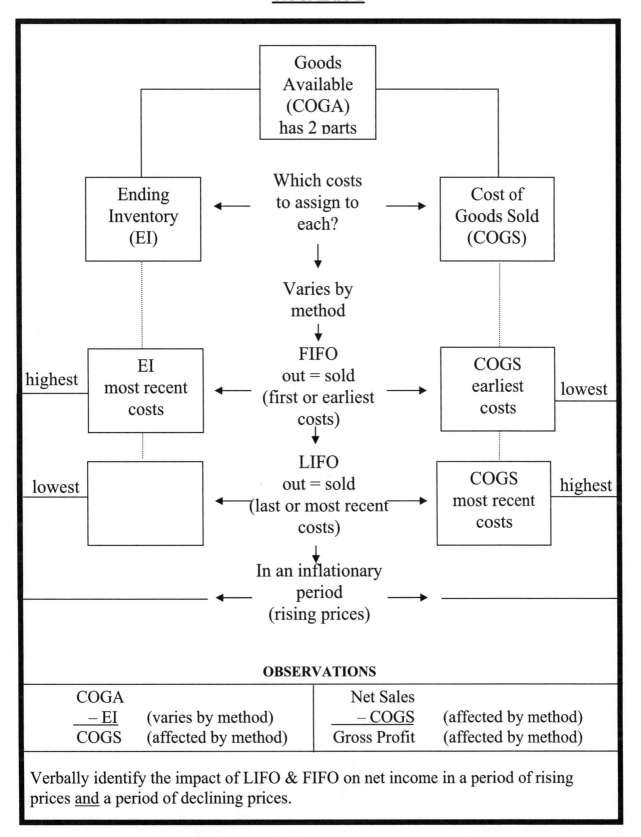

OBSERVATIONS

COGA		Net Sales	
– EI	(varies by method)	– COGS	(affected by method)
COGS	(affected by method)	Gross Profit	(affected by method)

Verbally identify the impact of LIFO & FIFO on net income in a period of rising prices <u>and</u> a period of declining prices.

Chapter Five – Alternate Demonstration Problem #1

The ABC Company had the following inventory record for the month of January:

Date	Description	# of Items	Unit Price	Item
1/1	Beginning inventory	5	$20	Z1 - Z5
1/5	Sale	2		Z2, Z5
1/11	Purchase	9	12	Z6 - Z14
1/28	Sale	7		Z1, Z3, Z6, Z7, Z8, Z9, Z14

Required:

Assuming a perpetual system is in use, determine the cost of goods sold and the ending inventory using each of the following methods:

1. FIFO

2. LIFO

3. Weighted average

4. Specific identification

(If this alternative demonstration problem is not covered in class, see your instructor for the solution.)

Problem I

The following statements are either true or false. Place a (T) in the parentheses before each true statement and an (F) before each false statement.

1. ( ) The merchandise inventory of a business includes goods sold FOB destination if they are not yet delivered.

2. ( ) When a perpetual inventory system is used, the dollar amount of ending inventory is determined by counting the units of product on hand, multiplying the count for each product by each product's cost, and adding the costs for all products.

3. ( ) If prices of goods purchased remain unchanged, then all four methods of assigning costs to goods in the ending inventory would yield the same cost figures.

4. ( ) When first-in, first-out inventory pricing is used in a perpetual inventory system, as sales occur the costs of the first items purchased are assigned to cost of goods sold.

5. ( ) If prices are rising, then using the LIFO method of pricing inventory will result in the highest net income.

6. ( ) The conservatism principle supports the lower of cost or market rule.

7. ( ) A misstatement of ending inventory will carry forward and cause misstatements in the succeeding period's cost of goods sold, gross profit, and net income.

8. ( ) The perpetual inventory system uses a Purchases account to record items purchased.

9. ( ) Using FIFO, the perpetual and periodic inventory systems do not result in the same amounts of sales, cost of goods sold, and end-of-period merchandise inventory.

10. ( ) Lower of cost or market may be applied separately to each product, to major categories of products, or to the merchandise inventory as a whole.

Problem II

You are given several words, phrases, or numbers to choose from in completing each of the following statements or in answering the following questions. In each case select the one that best completes the statement or answers the question and place its letter in the answer space provided.

_____ 1. Cisco Company's ending inventory consists of the following:

Product	Units on Hand	Unit Cost	Replacement Cost per Unit
X	100	$10	$ 8
Y	90	15	14
Z	75	8	10

Replacement cost is determined to be the best measure of market. Lower of cost or market for the inventory applied separately to each product is:

a. $2,950

b. $2,810

c. $2,660

d. $3,100

e. Cannot be determined from the information given.

The following information is to be used for questions 2 to 5:

Serese Co. made purchases of a particular product in the current year (20×9) as follows:

Jan.	1	Beginning inventory...	120 units	@	$5.00	=	$ 600
Mar.	7	Purchased	250 units	@	$5.60	=	1,400
July	28	Purchased	500 units	@	$5.80	=	2,900
Oct.	3	Purchased	450 units	@	$6.00	=	2,700
Dec.	19	Purchased	100 units	@	$6.20	=	620
		Total	1,420 units				$8,220

Serese Co. made sales on the following dates at $15 a unit:

Jan.	10	70 units
Mar.	15	125 units
Oct.	5	600 units
Total		795 units

The business uses a perpetual inventory system, and the ending inventory consists of 625 units, 500 from the July 28 purchase and 125 from the Oct. 3 purchase.

_____ 2. Using the specific identification cost assignment method, the amounts to be assigned to cost of goods sold and ending inventory respectively are:
  a. $4,465, $3,755
  b. $4,537.50, $3,682.50
  c. $4,570, $3,650
  d. $4,620, $3,600
  e. None of the above.

_____ 3. Using the LIFO cost assignment method, the amounts to be assigned to cost of goods sold and ending inventory respectively are:
  a. $4,465, $3,755
  b. $4,537.50, $3,682.50
  c. $4,570, $3,650
  d. $4,620, $3,600
  e. None of the above.

_____ 4. Using the FIFO cost assignment method, the amounts to be assigned to cost of goods sold and ending inventory respectively are:
  a. $4,465, $3,755
  b. $4,537.50, $3,682.50
  c. $4,570, $3,650
  d. $4,620, $3,600
  e. None of the above.

_____5. Using the weighted average cost assignment method, the amounts to be assigned to cost of goods sold and ending inventory respectively are:

a. $4,465, $3,7550

b. $4,537.50, $3,682.50

c. $4,570, $3,650

d. $4,620, $3,600

e. None of the above.

_____6. Atlantis Company uses a periodic inventory system and made an error at the end of year 1 that caused its year 1 ending inventory to be understated by $5,000. What effect does this error have on the company's financial statements?

a. Net income is understated; assets are understated.

b. Net income is understated; assets are overstated.

c. Net income is overstated; assets are understated.

d. Net income is overstated; assets are overstated.

e. Net income is overstated; assets are correctly stated.

_____7. Trador Company's ending inventory at December 31, 20×9 and 20×8, was $210,000 and $146,000, respectively. Cost of goods sold for 20×9 was $832,000 and $780,000 for 20×8. Calculate Trador's merchandise turnover for 20×9.

a. 4.7 times.

b. 4.5 times.

c. 4.0 times.

d. 3.8 times.

e. Cannot be determined from the information given.

_____8. Refer to the information presented in question 7. Calculate Trador's days' stock on hand for 20×9.

a. 78.1 days.

b. 80.6 days.

c. 66.1 days.

d. 92.1 days.

e. 68.3 days

Note: Questions 9 – 12 relate to Appendix 5A.

_____ 9. Magnum Company began a year and purchased merchandise as follows:

Jan.	1	Beginning inventory	40 units	@ $17.00
Feb.	4	Purchased...	80 units	@ $16.00
May	12	Purchased...	80 units	@ $16.50
Aug.	9	Purchased...	60 units	@ $17.50
Nov.	23	Purchased...	100 units	@ $18.00

The company uses a periodic inventory system and the ending inventory consists of 60 units, 20 from each of the last three purchases. Determine ending inventory assuming costs are assigned on the basis of FIFO.

a. $1,040

b. $1,000

c. $1,069

d. $1,080

e. $1,022

_____ 10. Linder Company began a year and purchased merchandise as follows:

Jan.	1	Beginning inventory	40 units	@ $17.00
Feb.	4	Purchased...	80 units	@ $16.00
May	12	Purchased...	80 units	@ $16.50
Aug.	9	Purchased...	60 units	@ $17.50
Nov.	23	Purchased...	100 units	@ $18.00

The company uses a periodic inventory system and the ending inventory consists of 60 units, 20 from each of the last three purchases. Determine ending inventory assuming costs are assigned on the basis of LIFO.

a. $1,040

b. $1,000

c. $1,022

d. $980

e. $1,080.

_____ 11. Box Company began a year and purchased merchandise as follows:

Jan.	1	Beginning inventory	40 units	@ $17.00
Feb.	4	Purchased...	80 units	@ $16.00
May	12	Purchased...	80 units	@ $16.50
Aug.	9	Purchased...	60 units	@ $17.50
Nov.	23	Purchased...	100 units	@ $18.00

The company uses a periodic inventory system and the ending inventory consists of 60 units, 20 from each of the last three purchases. Determine ending inventory assuming costs are assigned on the basis of specific invoice prices.

a. $1,000

b. $1,022

c. $1,040

d. $1,080

e. $990

_____ 12. Crow Company began a year and purchased merchandise as follows:

Jan.	1	Beginning inventory..........................	40 units	@ $17.00
Feb.	4	Purchased...	80 units	@ $16.00
May	12	Purchased...	80 units	@ $16.50
Aug.	9	Purchased...	60 units	@ $17.50
Nov.	23	Purchased...	100 units	@ $18.00

The company uses a periodic inventory system and the ending inventory consists of 60 units, 20 from each of the last three purchases. Determine ending inventory assuming costs are assigned on a weighted average basis.

a. $1,022.00

b. $1,040.00

c. $1,080.00

d. $1,000.00

e. $1,042.50

_____ 13. (Appendix 5B) Sanders Company wants to prepare interim financial statements for the first quarter of 20X9. The company uses a periodic inventory system and has an average gross profit rate of 30%. Based on the following information, use the gross profit method to prepare an estimate of the March 31 inventory.

January 1, beginning inventory	$ 97,000
Purchases	214,000
Purchases returns	2,000
Transportation-in	4,000
Sales..	404,000
Sales returns..	5,000

a. $ 33,700.

b. $193,300.

c. $119,700.

d. $179,900.

e. $ 26,700.

Problem III

Many of the important ideas and concepts discussed in Chapter 5 are reflected in the following list of key terms. Test your understanding of these terms by matching the appropriate definitions with the terms. Record the number identifying the most appropriate definition in the blank space next to each term.

_____ Average cost	_____ Interim statements
_____ Conservatism constraint	_____ Inventory turnover
_____ Consignee	_____ Last-in, first-out (LIFO)
_____ Consignor	_____ Lower of cost or market (LCM)
_____ Consistency concept	_____ Net realizable value
_____ Days' sales in inventory	_____ Retail inventory method*
_____ First-in, first-out (FIFO)	_____ Specific identification
_____ Gross profit method*	_____ Weighted average

*   Key term discussed in Appendix 5B

Financial Accounting Fundamentals

1. Required method to report inventory at market when market replacement cost is lower than recorded cost.

2. Method to assign cost to inventory that assumes items are sold in the order acquired; earliest items purchased are the first sold.

3. Method to assign cost to inventory where the cost of goods available for sale is divided by number of units available to get per unit cost that is multiplied by the units in inventory.

4. Number of times a company's average inventory is sold during a period; computed by dividing cost of goods sold by the average inventory; also called *merchandise turnover*.

5. Principle encouraging the use of the same accounting methods over time so that the financial statements are comparable across periods

6. Estimate of days needed to convert inventory into receivables or cash; equals the ending inventory divided by cost of goods sold and multiplying by 365; also called *days' stock on hand*.

7. Expected selling price of an item minus the cost of making the sale.

8. Owner of goods who ships them to another party who will sell them for the owner.

9. Procedure to estimate inventory when the past gross profit rate is used to estimate cost of goods sold, which is then subtracted from the cost of goods available for sale.

10. Method to assign cost to inventory when the purchase cost of each item in inventory is identified and used to compute the cost of inventory.

11. Another name for weighted average cost.

12. Method to assign cost to inventory that assumes costs for the most recent items purchased are sold first and charged to cost of goods sold.

13. Principle that seeks to select the less optimistic estimate when two estimates are about equally likely.

14. Financial statements prepared for periods of less than one year.

15. Method to estimate ending inventory based on the ratio of the amount of goods for sale at cost to the amount of goods for sale at retail.

16. One who receives and holds goods owned by another for purposes of selling the goods for the owner.

Problem IV

Complete the following by filling in the blanks.

1. Consistency in the use of an inventory costing method is particularly important if there is to be

   _____ .

2. If a running record is maintained for each inventory item of the number of units received as units are received, the number of units sold as units are sold, and the number of units remaining after each receipt or sale, the inventory system is called

   _____ .

3. When a company changes its accounting procedures, the _____ principle requires that the nature of the change, justification for the change, and the effect of the change on _____ be disclosed in the notes accompanying the financial statements.

4. With a periodic inventory system, an error in taking an end-of-period inventory will cause a misstatement of periodic net income for _____ (one, two) accounting periods because _____ .

5. When identical items are purchased during an accounting period at different costs, a problem arises as to which costs apply to the ending inventory and which apply to the goods sold. There are at least four commonly used ways of assigning costs to inventory and to goods sold. They are:

    a. _____ ;

    b. _____ ;

    c. _____ ;

    d. _____ ;

6. A major objective of accounting for inventories is the proper determination of periodic net income through the process of matching _____ and _____ . The matching process consists of determining how much of the cost of the goods that were for sale during an accounting period should be deducted from the period's _____ and how much should be carried forward as _____ , to be matched against a future period's revenues.

7. Although changing back and forth from one inventory costing method to another might allow management to report the incomes it would prefer, the accounting concept of _____ requires a company to use the same pricing method period after period unless it can justify the change.

8. In separating cost of goods available for sale into cost of goods sold and cost of goods unsold, the procedures for assigning a cost to the ending inventory are also the means of determining _____ because whatever portion of the cost of goods available for sale is assigned to ending inventory, the remainder goes to _____

9. Use of the lower-of-cost-or-market rule places an inventory on the balance sheet at a _____ figure. The argument in favor of this rule provides that any loss should be _____ in the year the loss occurs.

10. When recording a sale of merchandise using a _____ (perpetual, periodic) inventory system, two journal entries must be made. One entry records the revenue received for the sale and the second entry debits the _____ account.

11. (Appendix 5B) In the gross profit method of estimating an ending inventory, an average _____ _____ rate is used to determine estimated cost of goods sold, and the ending inventory is then estimated by subtracting estimated _____ from the cost of goods available for sale.

Problem V

A company uses a perpetual inventory system and during a year had the following beginning inventory, purchases, and sales of Product Z:

Jan.	1	Inventory	200 units	@	$0.50	=	$100
Mar.	15	Purchased	400 units	@	0.50	=	200
Apr.	1	Sold	300 units	@			
June	3	Purchased	300 units	@	0.60	=	180
July	1	Sold	200 units	@			
Oct.	8	Purchased	600 units	@	0.70	=	420
Nov.	1	Sold	500 units	@			
Dec.	15	Purchased	500 units	@	0.80	=	400

In the spaces below show the cost that should be assigned to the ending inventory and to the goods sold under the following assumptions:

	Portions Assigned to—	
	Ending Inventory	Cost of Goods Sold
1. A first-in, first-out basis was used to price the ending inventory	$	$
2. A last-in, first-out basis was used to price the ending inventory	$	$

Problem VI (Appendix 5B)

The following end-of-period information about a store's beginning inventory, purchases, and sales is available.

	At Cost	At Retail
Beginning inventory	$ 9,600	$13,000
Net purchases	54,400	69,100
Transportation-in	1,680	
Net sales		69,000

1. Use the above information to estimate the store's ending inventory by the retail method by completing the table below.

    a. The store had goods available for sale during the year calculated as follows:

	At Cost	At Retail
Beginning inventory	$	$
Net purchases		
Transportation-in		
Goods available for sale	$	$

    b. The store's cost ratio was: ....

      $_____ / $_____ x 100 = _____

c. Of the goods the store had available for sale at retail
    prices during the year, the following is gone because
    of sales at retail ....
    Which left the store an estimated ending inventory at
    retail .... $ _____

d. And when the store's cost ratio is applied to this
    estimated ending inventory at retail, the estimated
    ending inventory at cost is .... $ _____

2. The store took a physical inventory and counted only $12,850 of merchandise on hand (at retail).
    Calculate the inventory shortage at cost.

Solutions for Chapter 5

Problem I

1. T
2. F
3. T
4. T
5. F
6. T
7. T
8. F
9. F
10. T

Problem II

1. C
2. C
3. D
4. A
5. B
6. A
7. A
8. A
9. D
10. B
11. C
12. A
13. A

Problem III

11	Average cost	14	Interim statements
13	Conservatism constraint	4	Inventory turnover
16	Consignee	12	Last-in, first-out (LIFO)
8	Consignor	1	Lower of cost or market (LCM)
5	Consistency concept	7	Net realizable value
6	Days' sales in inventory	15	Retail inventory method*
2	First-in, first-out (FIFO)	10	Specific identification
9	Gross profit method*	3	Weighted average

*   *Key term discussed in Appendix 5B*

Problem IV

1. comparability in the financial statements prepared period after period

2. a perpetual inventory system

3. full-disclosure; net income

4. two; the ending inventory of one period becomes the beginning inventory of the next

5. (a) specific invoice prices; (b) weighted average cost; (c) first-in, first-out; (d) last-in, first-out

6. costs; revenues; revenues; merchandise inventory

7. consistency

8. cost of goods sold; cost of goods sold

9. conservative; recognized

10. perpetual; cost of goods sold

11. gross profit; cost of goods sold

Problem V

	Portions Assigned to	
	Ending Inventory	Cost of Goods Sold
1.	$750	$550
2.	680	620

Problem VI (Appendix 5B)

1. Estimate of store's ending inventory using the retail method:

			At Cost	At Retail
a.	Goods for sale			
	Beginning inventory		$ 9,600	$13,000
	Net purchases...		54,400	69,100
	Transportation-in...		1,680	
	Goods available for sale................................		$65,680	82,100
b.	Cost ratio: $65,680/$82,100 x 100 = 80 %.....			
c.	Less net sales at retail....................................			69,000
	Ending inventory at retail..............................			$13,100
d.	Ending inventory at cost ($13,100 x 80 %)....		$10,480	

2. Inventory shortage at cost:

$13,100 − $12,850 = $250
$250 × 80%   = $200

CHAPTER 6
ACCOUNTING FOR
CASH AND INTERNAL CONTROLS

Learning Objective C1:

Define internal control and identify its purpose and principles.

An internal control system consists of the policies and procedures managers use to protect assets, ensure reliable accounting, promote efficient operations, and urge adherence to company policies. It can prevent avoidable losses and help managers both plan operations and monitor company and human performance. Principles of good internal control include establishing responsibilities, maintaining adequate records, insuring assets and bonding employees, separating recordkeeping from custody of assets, dividing responsibilities for related transactions, applying technological controls, and performing regular independent reviews.

Learning Objective C2:

Define cash and cash equivalents and explain how to report them.

Cash includes currency, coins, and amounts on (or acceptable for) deposit in checking and savings accounts. Cash equivalents are short-term, highly liquid investment assets readily convertible to a known cash amount and sufficiently close to their maturity date so that market value is not sensitive to interest rate changes. Cash and cash equivalents are liquid assets because they are readily converted into other assets or can be used to pay for goods, services, or liabilities.

Learning Objective C3:

Identify control features of banking activities.

Banks offer several services that promote the control and safeguarding of cash. A bank account is a record set up by a bank permitting a customer to deposit money for safekeeping and to draw checks on it. A bank deposit is money contributed to the account with a deposit ticket as proof. A check is a document signed by the depositor instructing the bank to pay a specified amount of money to a designated recipient.

Learning Objective A1:

Compute the days' sales uncollected ratio and use it to assess liquidity.

Many companies attract customers by selling to them on credit. This means that cash receipts from customers are delayed until accounts receivable are collected. Users want to know how quickly a company can convert its accounts receivable into cash. The days' sales uncollected ratio, one measure reflecting company liquidity, is computed by dividing the ending balance of receivables by annual net sales, and then multiplying by 365.

Learning Objective P1:

Apply internal control to cash receipts and disbursements.

Internal control of cash receipts ensures that all cash received is properly recorded and deposited. Attention focuses on two important types of cash receipts: over-the-counter and by mail. Good internal control for over-the-counter cash receipts includes use of a cash register, customer review, use of receipts, a permanent transaction record, and separation of the custody of cash from its recordkeeping. Good internal control for cash receipts by mail includes at least two people assigned to open mail and a listing of each sender's name, amount, and explanation.

Learning Objective P2:

Explain and record petty cash fund transactions.

Petty cash disbursements are payments of small amounts for items such as postage, courier fees, minor repairs, and supplies. A company usually sets up one or more petty cash funds. A petty fund cashier is responsible for safekeeping the cash, making payments from this fund, and keeping receipts and records. A Petty Cash account is debited only when the fund is established or increased in amount. When the fund is replenished, petty cash disbursements are recorded with debits to expense (or asset) accounts and a credit to cash.

Learning Objective P3:

Prepare a bank reconciliation.

A bank reconciliation proves the accuracy of the depositor's and the bank's records. The bank statement balance is adjusted for items such as outstanding checks and unrecorded deposits made on or before the bank statement date but not reflected on the statement. The book balance is adjusted for items such as service charges, bank collections for the depositor, and interest earned on the account.

Learning Objective P4 (Appendix 6A):

Describe the use of documentation and verification to control cash disbursements.

A voucher system is a set of procedures and approvals designed to control cash disbursements and acceptance of obligations. The voucher system of control relies on several important documents, including the voucher and its supporting files. A key factor in this system is that only approved departments and individuals are authorized to incur certain obligations.

I.   **Internal Control**

   A. Purpose of Internal Control
      A properly designed internal control system is a key part of
      system design, analysis, and performance. Internal controls do
      not provide guarantees, but they lower the company's risk of
      loss. An **internal control system** consists all policies and
      procedures managers use to:

      1. Protect assets.

      2. Ensure reliable accounting.

      3. Promote efficient operations.

      4. Urge adherence to company policies.

      The **Sarbanes-Oxley Act (SOX)** requires manager and auditors
      of public companies to document and certify that company's
      system of internal controls.

   B. Principles of Internal Control
      Certain fundamental internal control principles apply to all
      companies. Internal control procedures increase the reliability
      and accuracy of accounting records. The **principles of internal
      control** are to:

      1. Establish responsibilities.

      2. Maintain adequate records.

      3. Insure assets and bond key employees.

      4. Separate recordkeeping from custody of assets.

      5. Divide responsibility for related transactions.

      6. Apply technological controls.

      7. Perform regular and independent reviews.

   C. Technology and Internal Control
      Technology provides rapid access to large quantities of data.
      Examples of technological impacts on internal control:

      1. Reduced processing errors.

      2   More extensive testing of records.

      3. Limited evidence of processing.

      4. Crucial separation of duties.

   D. Limitations of Internal Control

      1. Internal control policies and procedures are applied by people;
         the human element creates several potential limitations:

         a. Human error—resulting from negligence, fatigue,
            misjudgment, or confusion.

         b. Human fraud—involves intent by people to defeat
            internal controls, such as *management override*, for
            personal gain.

      2. Cost-benefit principle—the costs of internal controls must
         not exceed their benefits.

II. **Control of Cash**

Basic guidelines for control of cash include: handling of cash must be separate from recordkeeping of cash, cash receipts are promptly deposited in a bank, and disbursements of cash are made by check.

A. Cash, Cash Equivalents, and Liquidity

1. **Liquidity** refers to a company's ability to pay for its near-term obligations. Cash and similar assets are called **liquid assets** because they can be readily used to settle such obligations.

2. **Cash** includes currency and coins, deposits in bank and checking accounts, many savings accounts, and items that are acceptable for deposit in those accounts.

3. **Cash equivalents** are short-term, highly liquid investment assets meeting two criteria. (Note: only investments purchased within three months of their maturity dates usually satisfy these criteria.)

   a. Readily convertible to a known cash amount.

   b. Sufficiently close to their maturity date so that their market value is not sensitive to interest rate changes.

B. Cash management

1. Companies must plan both cash receipts and cash payments. The goals of cash management are to plan cash receipts to meet cash payments when due and to keep the minimum level of cash necessary to operate.

2. Effective cash management involves the following principles:

   a. Encourage collection of receivables.

   b. Delay payment of liabilities.

   c. Keep only necessary levels of assets.

   d. Plan expenditures.

   e. Invest excess cash.

C. Control of Cash Receipts

Internal control of cash receipts ensures that cash is properly recorded and deposited.

1. Over-the-counter cash receipts:

   a. Record on a cash register at time of sale.

   b. Separate custody from recordkeeping.

2. Cash Over and Short

Sometimes errors in making change are discovered from differences between the cash in a cash register and the record of the amount of cash receipts.

   a. Record any petty cash shortages/overages in the **Cash Over and Short** account.

   b. Entry to record cash sales with an overage: debit Cash, credit Cash Over and Short, credit Sales.

    c. Entry to record cash sales with a shortage: debit Cash, debit Cash Over and Short, credit Sales.

    d. Report balance of cash over and short account, an income statement account; as part of *miscellaneous expenses* if it has a debit balance or as part of *miscellaneous revenues* if it has a credit balance.

  3. Cash receipts by mail:

    a. Preferably, two people should open the mail and prepare a list of cash received; copies should be sent to cashier, recordkeeper in accounting area, and clerks who open mail.

    b. The cashier deposits the money in a bank.

    c. The recordkeeper records the amounts received in the accounting records.

    d. Bank account should be reconciled by another person (see below).

D. Control of Cash Disbursements

To safeguard against theft—require all expenditures be made by check (except for small payments made from petty cash fund) and deny access to the accounting records to anyone, other than the owner, who has authority to sign checks.

  1. A **voucher system** is a set of procedures and approvals designed to control cash disbursements and the acceptance of obligations. The voucher system includes procedures for:

    a. Verifying, approving, and recording obligations for eventual cash disbursements.

    b. Issuing checks for payment of verified, approved, and recorded obligations.

    c. Key factors in a voucher system:

      i. Only approved departments and individuals are authorized to incur such obligations.

      ii. Several business documents (purchase requisition, purchase order, invoice, receiving report, and check) are accumulated in a **voucher**, which is an internal document (or file) used to accumulate information to control cash disbursements.

  2. Use a **petty cash** system of control as follows:

    a. Write and cash a check to establish petty cash fund. Entry to record establishment: debit Petty Cash, credit Cash.

    b. A petty cash fund is used to pay for small items such as postage, courier fees, minor repairs, and low-cost supplies.

    c.   Assign a petty cashier (custodian) to account for the amounts expended and keep receipts.

    d.   Entry to record reimbursement: debit the related expense and/or asset accounts for the amounts paid for with petty cash, credit Cash for the amount reimbursed to the petty cash fund.

    e.   Sometimes, the petty cash payments reported plus the cash remaining will not total to the fund balance.

       i.   A shortage is recorded as an expense in the reimbursing entry with a debit to the Cash Over and Short account.

      ii.   An overage is recorded with a credit to the Cash Over and Short account in the reimbursing entry.

III.   **Banking Activities as Controls**

  A. Basic Bank Services

    Bank accounts permit depositing money for safeguarding and help control withdrawals.

    1. A *bank account* is a record set up by a bank for a customer. To limit access, all persons authorized to write **checks,** documents instructing the bank to pay a specified amount of money to a designated recipient, sign a **signature card**. Each bank deposit is supported by a **deposit ticket**.

    2. Electronic Funds Transfer (EFT) is the electronic communication transfer of cash from one party to another.

  B. Bank Statement

    Once a month, the bank sends each depositor a **bank statement** showing activities in the bank account.

  C. Bank Reconciliation

    1. A **bank reconciliation** is a report explaining any differences between the checking account balance according to the depositor's records and the balance reported on the bank statement.

    2. The balance reported on the bank statement rarely equals the balance in the depositor's accounting records; this is usually due to information that one party has that the other does not. Factors causing the bank statement balance to differ from the depositor's book balance are:

    a. Outstanding checks.

    b. Deposits in transit.

    c. Deductions for uncollectible items and for services

    d. Additions for collections and for interest.

    e. Errors.

3. Steps in preparing the bank reconciliation:
   a. Identify the bank statement balance of the cash account (*balance per bank*).
   b. Identify and list any unrecorded deposits and any bank errors understating the bank balance. Add them to the bank balance.
   c. Identify and list any outstanding checks and any bank errors overstating the bank balance. Deduct them from the bank balance.
   d. Compute the *adjusted bank balance*, also called corrected or reconciled balance.
   e. Identify the company's balance of the cash account (*balance per book*).
   f. Identify and list any unrecorded credit memoranda from the bank, interest earned, and errors understating the book balance. Add them to the book balance.
   g. Identify and list any unrecorded debit memoranda from the bank, service charges, and errors overstating the book balance. Deduct them from the book balance.
   h. Compute the *adjusted book balance*, also called corrected or reconciled balance.
   i. Verify the two adjusted balances from steps d and h are equal. If so, they are reconciled. If not, check for mathematical accuracy and missing data to achieve reconciliation.

4. A bank reconciliation often identifies unrecorded items that need recording. Only the items reconciling the book balance require adjustment.
   a. All reconciling additions to book balance are debits to cash. Credit depends on reason for addition.
   b. All reconciling subtractions from book balance are credits to cash. Debit depends on reason for subtraction.

IV. **Decision Analysis—Days' Sales Uncollected**
   A. One measure of the receivables' nearness to cash is the **days' sales uncollected** ratio (also called *days' sales in receivables*).
   B. It is calculated by dividing accounts receivable by net sales and multiplying the result by 365.
   C. It is used to estimate how much time is likely to pass before the current amount of accounts receivable is received in cash.

Chapter Outline   **Notes**

V. **Documentation and Verification (Appendix 6A)**
   A. Purchase Requisition

    B. Purchase Order

    C. Invoice

    D. Receiving Report

    E. Invoice Approval

    F. Voucher

VI.   **Controls of Purchases Discounts (Appendix 6B)**

It is very important for a company to take advantage of purchases discounts.

A. Recording inventory purchases using net method provides more control than the gross method, which was described in Chapter 4.

B. The **gross method** of recording purchases initially records the invoice at its *gross* amount ignoring any cash discount.

C. The **net method** records the invoice at its *net* amount of any cash discount. The net method gives management an advantage in controlling and monitoring cash payments involving purchase discounts. Any discounts not taken advantage of are recorded in a **Discounts Lost** expense account. Entries to record the:

    1. Purchase of inventory on credit: debit Merchandise Inventory, credit Accounts Payable (for the amount of the invoice net of the discount).

    2. Payment of the invoice within the discount period: debit Accounts Payable, credit Cash (for the amount of the invoice net of the discount).

    3. Payment of the invoice after the discount period has expired:

        a. As of the date corresponding to the end of the discount period: debit Discounts Lost, credit Accounts Payable (for the amount of the discount).

        b. As of the date of payment: debit Accounts Payable, credit Cash (for the amount of the payment, which is the gross amount of the invoice).

BANK RECONCILIATION

Reasons for differences
between bank statement
and checkbook balance:

Handle as follows:

Reason	Handle as follows
Unrecorded deposits	Add to Bank Balance
Outstanding checks	Deduct from Bank Balance
Bank service charges	Deduct from Book Balance
Debit memos	Deduct from Book Balance
Credit memos	Add to Book Balance
NSF checks	Deduct from Book Balance
Interest	Add to Book Balance
Errors	Must analyze individually (bank errors affect bank balance and book errors affect book balance)

The Betsy Dough Company wants to prepare a bank reconciliation for the month of June. When the bank statement for the month of June arrives from the bank, the following steps are performed:

1. The deposits to the bank account, as recorded on the bank statement, are compared to the deposit slips retained by the company. It is noted that the last deposit, of $400, occurred after banking hours on the day of the bank statement and therefore has not been recorded by the bank on this bank statement.

2. Checks returned with the bank statement are compared to the checks written and listed in checkbook. This comparison shows that there are checks outstanding amounting to $1,456.

3. The ending balances on the statement and in the company's books are determined. The ending bank statement balance is exactly $10,129 whereas the books show $9,000.

4. Other information contained on the bank statement, not previously known to the company, is determined. This includes the following: (a) a note from a customer for $200 has been collected by the bank and credited to our account; (b) a check from Frank Ony for $120 previously deposited has been returned for lack of sufficient funds; (c) the bank charged $25 for its services (this includes a $10 fee for the NSF check).

5. A bank reconciliation is prepared; it does not balance! The difference is $18, so a transposition error is looked for (whenever the difference is a multiple of 9, there is a very good chance that there has been an inadvertent exchange of two digits (for example, writing 29 when it should have been 92). An error is found. Check number 141 was written for $235 and cleared the bank for $235, but was recorded in the company records as $253.

Required:

Prepare a bank reconciliation for the Betsy Dough Company at June 30, 20X9.

(If this alternative demonstration problem is not covered in class, see your instructor for the solution.)

Problem I

The following statements are either true or false. Place a (T) in the parentheses before each true statement and an (F) before each false statement.

1. ( )   One of the fundamental principles of internal control states that the person who has access to or is responsible for an asset should not maintain the accounting record for that asset.

2. ( )   Procedures for controlling cash disbursements are as important as those for cash receipts.

3. ( )   When a voucher system is used, duplication of procedures among several departments is instrumental in maintaining control over cash disbursements.

4. ( )   In order to approve an invoice for payment for the purchase of assets, the accounting department of a large company should require copies of the purchase requisition, purchase order, invoice, and receiving report.

5. ( )   After the petty cash fund is established, the Petty Cash account is not debited or credited again unless the size of the fund is changed.

6. ( )   The Cash Over and Short account is usually shown on the income statement as part of miscellaneous revenues if it has a credit balance at the end of the period.

7. ( )   If 20 canceled checks are listed on the current month's bank statement, then no less than 20 checks could have been issued during the current month.

8. ( )   When the net method of recording invoices is used, cash discounts lost are reported as an expense in the income statement; when the gross method is used, cash discounts taken are deducted from purchases in the income statement.

Problem II

You are given several words, phrases, or numbers to choose from in completing each of the following statements or in answering the following questions. In each case select the one that best completes the statement or answers the question and place its letter in the answer space provided.

_____   1.   A voucher system:

 a. Permits only authorized individuals to incur obligations that will result in cash disbursements.
 b. Establishes procedures for incurring such obligations and for their verification, approval, and recording.
 c. Permits checks to be issued only in payment of properly verified, approved, and recorded obligations.
 d. Requires that every obligation be recorded at the time it is incurred and every purchase be treated as an independent transaction, complete in itself.
 e. Does all of the above.

_____ 2. Liquidity is:

    a. The portion of a corporation's equity that represents investments in the corporation by its stockholders.

    b. Cash or other assets that are reasonably expected to be realized in cash or be sold or consumed within one year or one operating cycle of the business.

    c. A characteristic of an asset indicating how easily the asset can be converted into cash or used to buy services or satisfy obligations.

    d. Obligations that are due to be paid or liquidated within one year or one operating cycle of the business.

    e. Economic benefits or resources without physical substance, the value of which stems from the privileges or rights that accrue to their owner.

_____ 3. A voucher is:

    a. An internal business paper (or folder) used to accumulate other papers and information needed to control cash disbursements and to ensure that the transaction is properly recorded.

    b. A business form used within a business to ask the purchasing department of the business to buy needed Hems.

    c. A document, prepared by a vendor, on which are listed the items sold, the sales prices, the customer's name, and the terms of sale.

    d. A form used within a business to notify the proper persons of the receipt of goods ordered and of the quantities and condition of the goods.

    e. A document on which the accounting department notes that it has performed each step in the process of checking an invoice and approving it for recording and payment.

_____ 4. Each of the following items would cause Brand X Sales Company's book balance of cash to differ from its bank statement balance.

    A. A service charge made by the bank.

    B. A check listed as outstanding on the previous month's reconciliation and that is still outstanding.

    C. A customer's check returned by the bank marked "NSF."

    D. A deposit which was mailed to the bank on the last day of November and is unrecorded on the November bank statement.

    E A check paid by the bank at its correct $422 amount but recorded in error in the General Journal at $442.

    F. An unrecorded credit memorandum indicating the bank had collected a note receivable for Brand X Sales Company and deposited the proceeds in the company's account.

    G. A check written during November and not yet paid and returned by the bank.

Which of the above items require entries on the books of Brand X Sales Company?

    a. A., B., C., and E.

    b. A., C., E., and F.

    c. A., B., D., and F.

    d. A., B., D., E., and G.

    e. C., D., E., and F.

_____ 5. A company reported net sales for 2009 and 2010 of $560,000 and $490,000 respectively. The year-end balances of accounts receivable were $34,000 and $31,000. Days' sales uncollected for 2010 is:

    a. 6 days

    b. 20.2 days

    c. 15.8 days

    d. 23.1 days

    e. 24.2 days

Problem III

Many of the important ideas and concepts discussed in Chapter 6 are reflected in the following list of key terms. Test your understanding of these terms by matching the appropriate definitions with the terms. Record the number identifying the most appropriate definition in the blank space next to each term.

_____ Bank reconciliation		_____ Invoice approval*
_____ Bank statement		_____ Liquid assets
_____ Canceled checks		_____ Liquidity
_____ Cash		_____ Net method**
_____ Cash equivalents		_____ Outstanding checks
_____ Cash Over and Short		_____ Petty cash
_____ Check		_____ Principles of internal control
_____ Days' sales uncollected		_____ Purchase order*
_____ Deposit ticket		_____ Purchase requisition*
_____ Deposits in transit		_____ Receiving report*
_____ Discounts Lost**		_____ Signature card
_____ Electronic funds transfer (EFT)		_____ Vendee
_____ Gross method**		_____ Vendor*
_____ Internal control system		_____ Voucher
_____ Invoice		_____ Voucher system

  * *Key term discussed in Appendix 6A*
** *Key term discussed in Appendix 6B*

1. Form used to report that ordered goods are received and to describe their quantity and condition.

2. Company's ability to pay for its short-term obligations.

3. Expense resulting from failing to take advantage of cash discounts on purchases.

4. Checks written and recorded by the depositor but not yet paid by the bank at the bank statement date.

5. Seller of goods or services.

6. Itemized record of goods prepared by the vendor that lists the customer's name, the items sold, the sales prices, and the terms of sale.

7. Internal file used to store documents and information to control cash disbursements and to ensure that a transaction is properly recorded.

8. Method of recording purchases at the full invoice price without deducting any cash discounts.

9. Resources such as cash that are easily converted into other assets or used to pay for goods, services, or liabilities.

10. Checks that the bank has paid and deducted from the depositor's account.

11. Document containing a checklist of steps necessary for approving an invoice for recording and payment; also called *check authorization*.

12. Document listing merchandise needed by a department and requesting it be purchased.

13. Income statement account used to record cash overages and cash shortages arising from missing petty cash receipts or simple errors.

14. All policies and procedures used to protect assets, ensure reliable accounting, promote efficient operations, and urge adherence to company policies.

15. Procedures and approvals designed to control cash disbursements and acceptance of obligations.

16. Document used by the purchasing department to place an order with a seller (vendor).

17. Report that explains the difference between the book balance of cash and the balance reported on the bank statement.

18. Measure of the liquidity of receivables computed by dividing the current balance of receivables and dividing by the annual (or net) sales, and then multiplying by 365; also called *days' sales in receivables*.

19. Method of recording purchases at the full invoice price less any cash discounts.

20. Buyer or purchaser of goods or services.

21. Short-term, investment assets that are readily convertible into a known cash amount and sufficiently close to their maturity date so that market value is not sensitive to interest rate changes.

22. Includes the signatures of each person authorized to sign checks on the account.

23. Principles requiring management to establish responsibility, maintain records, insure assets, separate recordkeeping from custody of assets, divide responsibility for related transactions, apply technological controls, and perform reviews.

24. Use of electronic communication to transfer cash from one party to another.

25. Lists items such as currency, coins, and checks deposited and their corresponding dollar amounts.

26. Document signed by the depositor instructing the bank to pay a specified amount to a designated recipient.

27. Includes currency, coins, and amounts on deposit in bank checking or savings accounts.

28. Deposits recorded by the company but not yet by its bank.

29. Bank report on the depositor's beginning and ending cash balances, and a listing of its changes for a period.

30. Small amount of cash in a fund to pay minor expenses; accounted for using an imprest system.

Problem IV

Complete the following by filling in the blanks.

1. A (n) _____ form is used by the accounting department in checking and approving an invoice for recording and payment.

2. If the size of the petty cash fund remains unchanged, the Petty Cash account _____ (is, is not) debited in the entry to replenish the petty cash fund.

3. Control of a small business is commonly gained through the direct supervision and active participation of the _____ in the affairs and activities of the business. However, as a business grows, it becomes necessary for the manager to delegate responsibilities and rely on _____ rather than personal contact in controlling the affairs and activities of the business.

4. A properly designed internal control system encourages adherence to prescribed managerial policies; and it also (a) _____,
    (b) _____,
    and (c) _____.

5. A good system of internal control for cash requires a _____ of duties so that the people responsible for handling cash and for its custody are not the same people who _____. It also requires that all cash receipts be deposited in the bank _____ and that all payments, except petty cash payments, be made by _____.

6. A bank reconciliation is prepared to account for the difference between the _____ and the _____.

7. An accounting system used to control the incurrence and payment of obligations requiring the disbursement of cash is a _____.

8. A _____ is commonly used by a selling department to notify the purchasing department of items that the selling department wishes the purchasing department to purchase.

9. The business form commonly used by the purchasing department of a large company to order merchandise is called a(n) _____.

10. Good internal control follows certain broad principles, including:

    (a) Responsibilities should be clearly established, and, in every situation, _____ should be made responsible for each task.

    (b) Adequate records should be maintained since they provide an important means of protecting _____.

    (c) Assets should be _____ and employees _____.

    (d) Recordkeeping for assets and _____ of assets should be separated.

    (e) Responsibility for related transactions should be _____ so that the work of one department or individual may act as a check on the work of others.

    (f) Mechanical devices _____ where practicable.

    (g) Regular and independent _____ of internal control procedures should be conducted.

11. After preparing a bank reconciliation, journal entries _____ (should, should not) be made to record those items listed as outstanding checks.

12. Days' sales uncollected is used in evaluating the _____ of a company.

Problem V

On November 5 of the current year Cullen Company drew Check No. 23 for $50 to establish a petty cash fund.

Required:

1. Prepare the journal entry to record the establishment of the fund. Do not provide an explanation.

DATE	ACCOUNT TITLES AND EXPLANATION	P.R.	DEBIT	CREDIT

After making a payment from petty cash on November 25, the petty cashier noted that there was only $2.50 cash remaining in the fund. The cashier prepared the following list of expenditures from the fund and requested that the fund be replenished.

Nov. 9	Express freight on merchandise purchased	$ 9.75
12	Miscellaneous expense to clean office	10.00
15	Office supplies	3.50
18	Delivery of merchandise to customer	8.00
23	Miscellaneous expense for collect telegram	3.25
25	Express freight on merchandise purchased	13.00

Check No. 97 in the amount of $47.50 was drawn to replenish the fund.

2. Prepare the journal entry to record the check replenishing the petty cash fund. Do not provide an explanation.

DATE	ACCOUNT TITLES AND EXPLANATION	P.R.	DEBIT	CREDIT

Problem VI

Information about the following eight items is available to prepare Verde Company's December 31 bank reconciliation.

Two checks (1) No. 453 and (2) No. 457 were outstanding on November 30. Check No. 457 was returned with the December bank statement but Check No. 453 was not. (3) Check No. 478, written on December 26, was not returned with the canceled checks; and (4) Check No. 480 for $96 was incorrectly entered in the Cash Disbursements Journal and posted as though it were for $69. (5) A deposit placed in the bank's night depository after banking hours on November 30 appeared on the December bank statement, but (6) one placed there after hours on December 31 did not. (7) Enclosed with the December bank statement was a debit memorandum for a bank service charge and (8) a check received from a customer and deposited on December 27 but returned by the bank marked "Not Sufficient Funds."

Required:

1. If an item in the above list should not appear on the December 31 bank reconciliation, ignore it. However, if an item should appear, enter its number below in the appropriate set of parentheses to show where it should be added or subtracted in preparing the reconciliation.

VERDE COMPANY
Bank Reconciliation
December 31, 20___

Book balance of cash...............	$X,XXX	Bank statement balance..................	$X,XXX
Add:		Add:	
( )		( )	
( )		( )	
( )		( )	
Deduct:		Deduct:	
( )		( )	
( )		( )	
( )		( )	
Reconciled balance..................	$X,XXX	Reconciled balance........................	$X,XXX

2. Certain of the above items require entries on Verde Company's books. Place the numbers of these items within the following parentheses:

   ( ), ( ), ( ), ( ), ( ), ( )

Problem VII

The bank statement dated September 30, 2009, for the Smith Company showed a balance of $2,876.35 which differs from the $1,879.50 book balance of cash on that date. In attempting to reconcile the difference, the accountant noted the following facts:

1. The bank recorded a service fee of $15 that was not recorded on the books of Smith Company.

2. A deposit of $500 was made on the last day of the month but was not recorded by the bank.

3. A check for $176 had been recorded on the Smith Company books as $167. The bank paid the correct amount.

4. A check was written during September but has not been processed by the bank. The amount was $422.85.

5. A check for $1,000 is still outstanding from August.

6. A check for $100 deposited by Smith Company was returned marked "Not Sufficient Funds."

7. A credit memorandum stated that the bank collected a note receivable of $200 for Smith Company and charged Smith a $2 collection fee. Smith Company had not previously recorded the collection.

Required:

Prepare, in good form, a bank reconciliation which shows the correct cash balance on September 30, 2009

Problem VIII (Appendix 6B)

The records of ABC Company, which records all purchases at gross amounts, included the following transactions.

June 1	Received shipment of merchandise having $2,000 invoice price, terms 2/10, n/30.
June 2	Received shipment of merchandise having $500 invoice price, terms 1/10, n/60.
June 7	Paid for merchandise received on June 1.
July 30	Paid for merchandise received on June 2.

Required:

1. Prepare the journal entries to record the following transactions. Do not provide explanations. Skip a line between entries.

DATE	ACCOUNT TITLES AND EXPLANATION	P.R.	DEBIT	CREDIT

2. Prepare the appropriate journal entries for the ABC Company assuming that the company instead records purchases at net amounts. You may need to use the Discount Lost account. Do not provide explanations. Skip a line between entries.

DATE	ACCOUNT TITLES AND EXPLANATION	P.R.	DEBIT	CREDIT

Solutions for Chapter 6

Problem I

1. T
2. T
3. F
4. T
5. T
6. T
7. F
8. T

Problem II

1. E
2. C
3. A
4. B
5. D

Problem III

17	Bank reconciliation
29	Bank statement
10	Canceled checks
27	Cash
21	Cash equivalents
13	Cash Over and Short
26	Check
18	Days' sales uncollected
25	Deposit ticket
28	Deposits in transit
3	Discounts Lost**
24	Electronic funds transfer (EFT)
8	Gross method**
14	Internal control system
6	Invoice*
11	Invoice approval*
9	Liquid assets
2	Liquidity
19	Net method**
4	Outstanding checks
30	Petty cash
23	Principles of internal control
16	Purchase order*
12	Purchase requisition*
1	Receiving report*
22	Signature card
20	Vendee
5	Vendor*
7	Voucher
15	Voucher system

* Key term discussed in Appendix 6A
** Key term discussed in Appendix 6B

Problem IV

1. invoice approval
2. is not
3. owner-manager; a system of internal control
4. (a) promotes operational efficiencies; (b) protects the business assets from waste, fraud, and theft; and (c) ensures accurate and reliable accounting data
5. separation; keep the cash records; intact each day, check
6. book balance of cash; bank statement balance
7. voucher system
8. purchase requisition
9. purchase order
10. one person; (b) assets; (c) insured, bonded; (d) custody; (e) divided; (f) should be used; (g) reviews
11. should not
12. liquidity

Problem V

1. Nov. 5	Petty Cash...	50.00	
	Cash...		50.00
	Established a petty cash fund.		

2. Nov. 25	Transportation-In (or Inventory if Perpetual system is used)..	22.75	
	Miscellaneous Expenses..	13.25	
	Office Supplies..	3.50	
	Delivery Expense	8.00	
	Cash...		47.50
	Reimbursed the petty cash fund.		

Problem VI

1. Book balance of cash...............	$X,XXX		Bank statement balance	$X,XXX
Add:			Add:	
( )			(6)	
Deduct:			Deduct:	
(4)			(1)	
(7)			(3)	
(8)			( )	

2. (4), (7), (8)

Problem VII

SMITH COMPANY
Bank Reconciliation
September 30, 2009

Book balance of cash	$1,879.50	Bank statement balance	$2,876.35
Add:		Add:	
Proceeds of note less			
Collection fee	198.00	Deposit on 9/30/X8	500.00
	2,077.50		3,376.35
Deduct:		Deduct:	
NSF check $100.00		Outstanding checks:	
Service fee 15.00		August $1,000.00	
Recording error 9.00	124.00	September 422.85	1,422.85
Reconciled balance	$1,953.50	Reconciled balance	$1,953.50

Problem VIII (Appendix 6B)

1.	June 1	Merchandise Inventory...	2,000.00	
		Accounts Payable		2,000
	2	Merchandise Inventory...	500.00	
		Accounts Payable		500.00
	7	Accounts Payable..	2,000.00	
		Merchandise Inventory....................................		40.00
		Cash...		1,960.00
	July 30	Accounts Payable..	500.00	
		Cash...		500.00
2.	June 1	Merchandise Inventory ($2,000 × 98%)	1,960.00	
		Accounts Payable		1,960.00
	2	Merchandise Inventory ($500 × 99%)	495.00	
		Accounts Payable		495.00
	7	Accounts Payable..	1,960.00	
		Cash...		1,960.00
	12	Discounts Lost..	5.00	
		Accounts Payable		5.00
	July 30	Accounts Payable..	500.00	
		Cash		500.00

©The McGraw-Hill Companies, Inc., 2009

Learning Objective C1:

Describe accounts receivable and how they occur and are recorded.

Accounts receivable are amounts due from customers for credit sales. A subsidiary ledger lists amounts owed by each customer. Credit sales arise from at least two sources: (1) sales on credit and (2) credit card sales. *Sales on credit* refers to a company's granting credit directly to customers. Credit card sales involve customers' use of third-party credit cards.

Learning Objective C2:

Describe a note receivable and the computation of its maturity date and interest.

A note receivable is a written promise to pay a specified amount of money at a definite future date. The maturity date is the day the note (principal and interest) must be repaid. Interest rates are normally stated in annual terms. The amount of interest on the note is computed by expressing time as a fraction of one year and multiplying the note's principal by this fraction and the annual interest rate.

Learning Objective C3:

Explain how receivables can be converted to cash before maturity.

Receivables can be converted to cash before maturity in three ways. First, a company can sell accounts receivable to a factor, who charges a factoring fee. Second, a company can borrow money by signing a note payable that is secured by pledging the accounts receivable. Third, notes receivable can be discounted at (sold to) a financial institution.

Learning Objective A1:

Compute accounts receivable turnover and use it to help assess financial condition.

Accounts receivable turnover is a measure of both the quality and liquidity of accounts receivable. The accounts receivable turnover measure indicates how often, on average, receivables are received and collected during the period. Accounts receivable turnover is computed as net sales divided by average accounts receivable.

Learning Objective P1:

Apply the direct write-off and allowance methods to account for accounts receivable.

The direct write-off method charges Bad Debts Expense when accounts are written off as uncollectible. This method is acceptable only when the amount of bad debts expense is immaterial. Under the allowance method, bad debts expense is recorded with an adjustment at the end of each accounting period that debits the Bad Debts Expense account and credits the Allowance for Doubtful Accounts. The uncollectible accounts are later written off with a debit to the Allowance for Doubtful Accounts.

Learning Objective P2:

Estimate uncollectibles using methods based on sales and accounts receivable.

Uncollectibles are estimated by focusing on either (1) the income statement relation between bad debts expense and credit sales or (2) the balance sheet relation between accounts receivable and the allowance for doubtful accounts. The first approach emphasizes the matching principle using the income statement. The second approach emphasizes realizable value of accounts receivable using the balance sheet.

Learning Objective P3:

Record the receipt of a note receivable.

A note received is recorded at its principal amount by debiting the Notes Receivable account. The credit amount is to the asset, product, or service provided in return for the note.

Learning Objective P4:

Record the honoring and dishonoring of a note and adjustments for interest.

When a note is honored, the payee debits the money received and credits both Notes Receivable and Interest Revenue. Dishonored notes are credited to Notes Receivable and debited to Accounts Receivable (to the account of the maker in an attempt to collect), and Interest Revenue is recorded for interest earned for the time the note is held.

I.   **Accounts Receivable**

A *receivable* is an amount due from another party. **Accounts Receivable** are amounts due from customers for credit sales.

A. Recognizing Accounts Receivable

Accounts Receivable occur from credit sales to customers.

1. **Sales on Credit**

Credit sales are recorded by increasing (debiting) Accounts Receivable.

a. The General Ledger continues to keep a single Accounts Receivable account.

b. A supplementary record, called the *accounts receivable ledger*, is created to maintain a separate account for each customer that tracks the balance of each customer.

c. The sum of the individual accounts in the accounts receivable ledger equals the debit balance of the Accounts Receivable account in the general ledger.

d. Entry to record credit sale: debit Accounts Receivable— Customer Name, credit Sales. The debit is posted to the Accounts Receivable account in the general ledger and to the customer account in the accounts receivable ledger.

e. Many larger retailers maintain their own credit cards to grant credit to preapproved customers and to earn interest on unpaid balances. The entries are the same as in d. above except for the possibility of added interest revenue; entry to record interest: debit Interest Receivable, credit Interest Revenue.

2. **Credit Card Sales** (examples: Visa, MasterCard, American Express)

Sellers allow customers to use third-party credit and debit cards for several reasons:

a. The seller does not have to evaluate each customer's credit standing.

b. The seller avoids the risk of extending credit to customers who may not pay.

c. The seller typically receives cash from the credit card company sooner than had it granted credit directly to customers.

d. A variety of credit options for customers offers a potential increase in sales volume.

       e.   Entry for credit card sales when cash is received upon deposit of sales receipt: debit Cash (for the amount of sale less the credit card charge), debit Credit Card Expense (for the fee), credit Sales (for the full invoice amount).

       f.   Entry if company must remit the credit card sales receipts to the credit card company and wait for the cash payment: debit Accounts Receivable (for full invoice less the fee), debit Credit Card Expense (for the fee), credit Sales. Entry when payment is received: debit Cash, credit Accounts Receivable.

   3. **Installment Sales and Receivables** – amounts owed by customers from credit sales where payments are made in periodic amounts over an extended time period. The customer is usually charged interest. Classified as current assets.

B. Valuing Accounts Receivable – Direct Write-Off Method Accounts of customers who do not pay what they promised are uncollectible accounts, commonly called **bad debts**. The total amount of uncollectible accounts is an expense of selling on credit. Two methods are used to account for uncollectible accounts: the direct write-off method and the allowance method.

   1. **Recording and Writing Off Bad Debts** – The **direct write-off method** records the loss from an uncollectible account receivable when it is determined to be uncollectible. Entry to write off uncollectible and recognize loss: debit Bad Debt Expense, credit Accounts Receivable.

   2. **Recovering a Bad Debt** – sometimes, an account which was written off is later collected. This results in two journal entries. First a reversal of the write off (see above) and second, a normal collection of account entry.

   3. **Assessing the Direct Write-Off Method** – companies must weigh at least two accounting concepts when considering the use of the direct write-off method including the following:

       a.   The **matching principle** requires expenses to be reported in the same accounting period as the sales they helped produce; the direct write-off method usually does <u>not</u> best match sales and expenses because the related expense is not recorded until an account becomes uncollectible, which may be in the next accounting period.

       b.   The **materiality constraint** states that an amount can be ignored if its effect on the financial statements is unimportant to users' business decision,; it permits the use of the direct write-off method when bad debts expenses are very small in relation to a company's other financial statement items.

C. Valuing Accounts Receivable – Allowance Method. The allowance method matches the *estimated loss* from uncollectibles against the sales they helped produce. At the end of each accounting period, bad debts expense is *estimated* and recorded in an adjusting entry. Advantages include that it records bad debt expense when the related sales are recorded and it reports accounts receivable on the balance sheet at the estimated amount of cash to be collected.

1. **Recording bad debts expense.** The allowance method estimates bad debts expense at the end of the accounting period and records it with an adjusting entry. Entry to record estimate of bad debt expense: debit Bad Debts Expense, credit **Allowance for Doubtful Accounts**, a contra-asset account. (This contra account is used instead of Accounts Receivable because, at the time of the adjusting entry, the company does not know which customers will not pay.) **Realizable value** is the expected proceeds from converting an asset into cash; in the balance sheet, the Allowance for Doubtful Accounts is subtracted from Accounts Receivable to show the amount expected to be collected.

2. **Writing off a bad debt.** When a specific account is identified as uncollectible, it is written off against the Allowance for Doubtful Accounts. Entry to write off a bad debt: debit Allowance for Doubtful Accounts, credit Accounts Receivable. (Note that the write-off does not affect the realizable value of accounts receivable.)

3. **Recovering a bad debt.** Recovering of a bad debt requires two journal entries. The first entry is a reversal of the write-off (see iv above) and effectively reinstates the customer's account. The second entry records the collection of the reinstated account.

D. Estimating Bad Debts – Percent of Sales Method
The allowance method requires an estimate of bad debts expense to prepare an adjusting entry at the end of the accounting period.

The **percent of sales method**—also referred to as the *income statement method,* uses income statement relations to estimate bad debts.

1. Based on experience, company estimates what percentage of credit sales will be uncollectible.

2. Bad debts expense is calculated as the estimated percentage times sales for the period.

3. The amount calculated is the estimated bad debt expense for the period; this amount is used in the adjusting entry. The allowance account ending balance rarely equals the bad debt expense because the allowance account was not likely to be zero prior to adjustment.

Chapter Outline

Notes

E. Estimating Bad Debts—Percent of Receivables Method—the *accounts receivable method* uses balance sheet relations to estimate bad debts.

1. Goal of the bad debts adjusting entry for these methods is to make the Allowance for Doubtful Accounts balance equal to the portion of accounts receivable that is estimated to be uncollectible. The estimated balance for the allowance account is obtained in one of two ways.

2. The **percent of accounts receivables method** assumes that a given percentage of a company's receivables is uncollectible.

F. Estimating Bad Debts—Aging of Receivables Method. The **aging of accounts receivable method** uses both past and current receivables information to estimate the allowance amount. See Exhibit 7.11 for an example. Specifically:

1. Each receivable is classified by how long it is past its due date,

2. Experience is used to estimate the percent of each uncollectible class (the longer an amount is past due, the more likely it is to be uncollectible),

3. The percents are applied to each class and then totaled to get the estimated balance in the Allowance for Doubtful Accounts.

G. Estimating Bad Debts—Summary of Methods. Exhibit 7.13 summarizes the principles for all three estimation methods. Percent of sales is focused on the income statement and matches bad debts expense with sales. The accounts receivables methods are balance sheet focused and report accounts receivable at realizable value.

II. **Notes Receivable**

A **promissory note** is a written promise to pay a specified amount of money *(the **principal** of the note)* usually with **interest** (the cost for borrowing money) either on demand or at a definite future date. Promissory notes are notes payable to the **maker** (person promising to pay) and notes receivable to the **payee** (person to be paid). Sellers sometimes ask for a note to replace an accounts receivable when a customer requests an extension to pay their account.

A. Computing Maturity and Interest

1. The **maturity date** is the day the note must be repaid.

a. When the time of the note is expressed in days, its maturity date is the specified number of days after the note's date.

b. When months are used, the note matures and is payable in the month of its maturity on the *same day of the month* as its original date.

2. Interest Computation:
   Principal of note times the annual interest rate times the time expressed in years. Note that a year has 360 days for interest computations (*the banker's rule*).

B. Recognizing Notes Receivable: debit Notes Receivable for principal or face amount of note; credit will vary (depends on reason note is received). Note that interest is not recorded until earned.

C. Valuing and Settling Notes
   The principal and interest of a note are due on its maturity date.

   1. Recording an Honored Note. The maker of the notes usually *honors* the note and pays it in full; entry (by the payee) to record: debit Cash, credit Notes Receivable, credit Interest Revenue. When a note is dishonored, we remove it from Notes Receivable and charge it back to an Account Receivable.

   2. Recording a Dishonored Note. When the maker does not pay at maturity, the note is *dishonored*; entry (by payee) to record: debit Accounts Receivable (for the principal and interest due), credit Note Receivable (for principal), credit Interest Revenue.

   3. Recording End-of-Period Interest Adjustment. When notes receivable are outstanding at the end of a period, any accrued interest earned is computed and recorded. Entry (by payee) to record: debit Interest Receivable, credit Interest Revenue.

   4. Entry to record honoring of a note if interest has been accrued: debit Cash (for full amount received), credit Interest Receivable (amount previously accrued), credit Interest Revenue (amount earned since accrual date), credit Notes Receivable (face amount of note).

III.   Disposing of Receivables
       Companies can convert receivables to cash before they are due. Reasons for this include the need for cash or a desire to not be involved in collection activities.

A. Selling Receivables
   A company can sell all or a portion of its receivables to a finance company or a bank.

   1. Buyer, called a *factor*, charges the seller a *factoring fee* and then takes ownership of the receivables and receives cash when come due.

   2. Entry (by seller of receivables): debit Cash, debit Factoring Fee Expense, credit Account Receivable.

B. Pledging Receivables
    A company can pledge its receivables as security for a loan.

    1. Borrower retains ownership of the receivables.

    2. If borrower defaults on the loan, the lender has the right to be paid from the cash receipts of collections on accounts receivable.

    3. The borrower's financial statements must disclose the pledging of the receivables.

V. **Decision Analysis—Accounts Receivable Turnover**

    A. The **accounts receivable turnover ratio** measures both the quality (refers to the likelihood of collection without loss) and liquidity of accounts receivable; it indicates how often the average accounts receivable balance was converted to cash during the year.

    B. It is calculated by dividing net sales by average accounts receivable.

    C. A high turnover in comparison with competitors suggests that management should consider using more liberal credit terms to increase sales. A low turnover suggests management should consider stricter credit terms and more aggressive collection efforts.

VISUAL #7-1
METHODS OF ACCOUNTING FOR BAD DEBTS

	DIRECT WRITE-OFF METHOD	ALLOWANCE METHOD
	Bad debts expense is recorded at the time a account is determined to be uncollectible.	Bad debts expense is estimated and recorded at the end of each accounting period.
Year-end	No adjusting entry	Adjusting entry required: **Bad Debt Expense** XXX **Allowance for Uncollectible Accounts** XXX (The amount is an estimate based on a percentage of sales or a percentage of outstanding accounts receivable. If the estimate is based on sales, the full estimate is used in the adjusting entry. If the estimate is based on accounts receivable the allowance account balance is brought to the amount of the estimate.)

When an account is determined to be uncollectible	Write-off entry required:
	Bad Debts Expense XXX
	   Accounts Receivable/Customer XXX
	(The amount is the balance of the uncollectible account.)
		Write-off entry required:
		Allowance for Uncollectible Accounts XXX
		   Accounts Receivable/Customer XXX
		(The amount is the balance of the uncollectible account.)

When an account previously written off is recovered	1. Reinstate account *by reversing write-off:*
	Accounts Receivable/Customer XXX
	   Bad Debts Expense XXX
	(Amount is the account balance that was written off.)
	2. Record collection on account normally:
	Cash XXX
	   Accounts Receivable/Customer XXX
	(Amount is the amount collected.)
		1. Reinstate account *by reversing write-off:*
		Accounts Receivable/Customer XXX
		   Allowance for Uncollectible Accounts XXX
		(Amount is the account balance that was written off.)
		2. Record collection on account normally:
		Cash XXX
		   Accounts Receivable/Customer XXX
		(Amount is the amount collected.)

Advantages:	• **Does not require adjusting entry.** • **Does not require year-end estimating of uncollectibles.**	• Matches expense against related revenues. • Reports the net realizable accounts receivable on the balance sheet (a more accurate reporting of assets).
Disadvantages:	• **Violates matching, therefore only allowed if qualified under materiality principle. (May be used by a business that anticipates an immaterial amount of uncollectibles.)**	• Requires adjusting entry. • Requires year-end estimating of uncollectibles.

PROMISSORY NOTE

(6) ──► $2,000.00   April 15, 20X8 ◄── (1)
        Amount   **Date**

For value received, I promise to pay to the order of
Plexi-Plus Supply Co. ◄────────── (2)
Tobay, New York

(7) ──► Two thousand and no/100 ------------------Dollars
                on_____ June 14, 20X8◄────── (3)
        plus interest at the annual rate of 9 percent.◄───── (4)

                        _____Scott Cooke ◄──── (5)
                        for Tobay Surfer Inc.

Chapter Seven – Alternate Demonstration Problem #1

At the end of the year, the M. I. Wright Company showed the following selected account balances:

Sales (all on credit) $300,000

Accounts Receivable 800,000

Allowance for Doubtful Accounts 38,000

Required:

1. Assume the company estimates that 1% of all credit sales will not be collected.

    a. Prepare the proper journal entry to recognize the expense involved.

    b. Present the balances in Accounts Receivable and Allowance for Doubtful Accounts as they would appear on the balance sheet.

    Also show the net realizable Accounts Receivable.

2. Assume the company estimates that 5% of its accounts receivable will never be collected.

    a. Prepare the proper journal entry to recognize the expense involved.

    b. Present the balances in Accounts Receivable and Allowance for Doubtful Accounts as they would appear on the balance sheet. Also show the net realizable Accounts Receivable.

3. Under each of the two assumptions (described in #1 and #2 above), prepare the proper journal entry for the following event:

    June 3   John Shifty, who owes us $500, informs us that he is broke and cannot pay. We believe him.

(If this alternative demonstration problem is not covered in class, see your instructor for the solution.)

Problem I

The following statements are either true or false. Place a (T) in the parentheses before each true statement and an (F) before each false statement.

1. ( ) If cash from credit card sales is received immediately when the credit card receipts are deposited at the bank, the credit card expense is recorded at the time the sale is recorded.

2. ( ) Businesses with credit customers must maintain a separate account for each customer.

3. ( ) After all entries are posted, the sum of the balances in the Accounts Receivable Ledger should be equal to the balance of the Accounts Receivable account in the General Ledger.

4. ( ) Under the allowance method of accounting for bad debts, accounts receivable are reported on the balance sheet at the amount of cash proceeds expected from their collection.

5. ( ) At the time an adjusting entry to record estimated bad debts expense is made, the credit side of the entry is to Accounts Receivable.

6. ( ) When an account deemed uncollectible is written off against Allowance for Doubtful Accounts, the estimated realizable amount of Accounts Receivable is decreased.

7. ( ) The income statement approach to estimating bad debts is based on the idea that some percentage of credit sales will be uncollectible.

8. ( ) The balance sheet approach to estimating bad debts is based on the idea that some particular percentage of a company's credit sales will become uncollectible.

9. ( ) Aging of accounts receivable requires the review of each account in the accounts receivable ledger.

10. ( ) A 90-day note, dated August 17, matures on November 16.

11. ( ) Although the direct write-off method of accounting for bad debts usually mismatches revenues and expenses, it may be allowed in cases where bad debt losses are immaterial in relation to total net sales and net income.

12. ( ) When a note receivable is discounted without recourse, the bank does not assume the risk of a bad debt loss.

13. ( ) When a note receivable is discounted with recourse, the company that discounts the note has a contingent liability.

14. ( ) A company that pledges its accounts receivable as security for a loan should disclose the fact in the notes to the financial statements.

Problem II

You are given several words, phrases, or numbers to choose from in completing each of the following statements or in answering the following questions. In each case select the one that best completes the statement or answers the question and place its letter in the answer space provided.

_____ 1. Orion Company has decided to write off the account of Jack Irwin against the Allowance for Doubtful Accounts. The $2,100 balance in Irwin's account originated with a credit sale in July of last year. What is the general journal entry to record this write-off?

a.	Allowance for Doubtful Accounts...........................	2,100
	Accounts Receivable—Jack Irwin	2,100
b.	Accounts Receivable	2,100
	Allowance for Doubtful Accounts	2,100
c.	Bad Debts Expense..	2,100
	Allowance for Doubtful Accounts	2,100
d.	Accounts Receivable	2,100
	Accounts Receivable—Jack Irwin	2,100
e.	Bad Debts Expense..	2,100
	Accounts Receivable.......................................	2,100

_____ 2. Hitech Corporation had credit sales of $3,000,000 in 20×9. Before recording the December 31, 20×9, adjustments, the company's Allowance for Doubtful Accounts had a credit balance of $1,400. A schedule of the December 31,20×9, accounts receivable by age is summarized as follows:

December 31, 20×9 Accounts Receivable	Age of Accounts Receivable	Uncollectible Percent Expected
$285,000	Not due	1.5
87,000	1-45 days past due	8.2
34,000	46-90 days past due	37.0
8,000	over 90 days past due	70.0

Calculate the amount that should appear on the December 31, 20X9, balance sheet as allowance for doubtful accounts.

a. $28,189.
b. $5,600.
c. $25,314.
d. $30,989.
e. $29,589.

_____ 3. Based on the information given in problem 4, what is the general journal entry to record bad debts expense for 20X9?
    a. Debit Bad Debts Expense; credit Allowance for Doubtful Accounts.
    b. Debit Accounts Receivable; credit Allowance for Doubtful Accounts.
    c. Debit Bad Debts Expense; credit Accounts Receivable.
    d. Debit Allowance for Doubtful Accounts; credit Bad Debts Expense.
    e. Debit Accounts Receivable; credit Bad Debts Expense.

_____4.   MBC Company discounts a $25,000 note receivable, with recourse, and receives proceeds of $25,250. MBC's entry to record the transaction would include the following:

a. $25,000 debit to Cash.
b. $250 debit to Interest Expense.
c. $250 credit to Interest Revenue.
d. $25,250 credit to Notes Receivable.
e. None of the above.

_____5.   Westing Company had net sales of $500,000 and $400,000 for 2010 and 2009, respectively. Accounts receivable at December 31, 2010 and 2009, were $45,000 and $55,000. What is Westing's accounts receivable turnover for 2010?

a. 11.1 times.
b. 10.0 times.
c. 20.0 times.
d. 9.0 times.
e. None of the above.

Problem III

Many of the important ideas and concepts discussed in Chapter 7 are reflected in the following list of key terms. Test your understanding of these terms by matching the appropriate definitions with the terms. Record the number identifying the most appropriate definition in the blank space next to each term.

_____ Accounts receivable
_____ Accounts receivable turnover
_____ Aging of accounts receivable
_____ Allowance for Doubtful Accounts
_____ Allowance method
_____ Bad debts
_____ Direct write-off method
_____ Interest

_____ Maker of a note
_____ Matching principle
_____ Materiality constraint
_____ Maturity date of a note
_____ Payee of a note
_____ Principal of a note
_____ Promissory note (or note)
_____ Realizable value

1.   Measure of both the quality and liquidness of accounts receivable; indicates how often receivables are received and collected during the period; computed by dividing net sales by average accounts receivable.

2.   Entity who signs a note and promises to pay it at maturity.

3.   Procedure that (1) estimates and matches bad debts expense with its sales for the period and (2) reports accounts receivable at estimated realizable value.

4.   Entity to whom a note is made payable.

5.   Method that records the loss from an uncollectible accounts receivable at the time it is determined to be uncollectible; no attempt is made to estimate bad debts.

6.   Implies an amount can be ignored if its effect on financial statements is unimportant to users.

7.   Accounts of customers who do not pay what they have promised to pay; an expense of selling on credit; also called *uncollectible accounts*.

8.   Requires expenses to be reported in the same period as the sales they helped produce.

9. Expected proceeds from converting an asset into cash.

10. Contra asset account with a balance approximating uncollectible accounts receivable; also called *Allowance for Uncollectible Accounts*.

11. Date when principal and interest of a note are due.

12. Process of classifying accounts receivable by how long they are past due for purposes of estimating uncollectible accounts.

13. Amounts due from customers for credit sales.

14. Written promise to pay a specified amount either on demand or at a definite future date.

15. Charge for using money (or assets) until repaid at a future date.

16. Amount that the signer of a note agrees to pay back when it matures, not including interest.

Problem IV

On December 12, Lark Company received from Guy Hall, a customer, $300 in cash and a $1,500, 12%, 60-day note dated December 11 in granting a time extension on Hall's past-due account. On December 31, Lark Company recorded the accrued interest on the note, and Guy Hall paid the note and its interest on the following February 9. Prepare the journal entries to record these transactions.

DATE	ACCOUNT TITLES AND EXPLANATION	P.R.	DEBIT		CREDIT	
Dec. 12						
	Received cash and a note in granting a time extension					
	On a past-due account.					
31						
	To record accrued interest on a note receivable.					
Feb 9						
	Received payment of a note and interest.					

Problem V

On March 1, Lark Company accepted a $1,200, 12%, 60-day note dated that day from a customer, Mary Dale, in granting a time extension on the customer's past-due account. When Lark Company presented the note for payment on April 30, it was dishonored, and on December 20 Lark Company wrote off the debt as uncollectible. Prepare the journal entries to record the dishonor and the write-off against the company's Allowance for Doubtful Accounts.

DATE	ACCOUNT TITLES AND EXPLANATION	P.R.	DEBIT		CREDIT	
Apr 30						
	To charge the account of Mary Dale for her					
	dishonored $1,200, 12%, 60-day note.					
Dec. 20						
	To write off the uncollectible note of Mary Dale.					

Problem VI

Marin Company uses the allowance method in accounting for bad debt losses, and over the past several years it has experienced an average loss equal to one-fourth of 1% of its credit sales. During 2009 the company sold $928,000 of merchandise on credit, including a $98 credit sale to Gus Bell on March 5, 2009. The $98 had not been paid by the year's end.

1. If at the end of 2009 Marin Company, in providing for estimated bad debt losses, assumes history will repeat, it will provide an allowance for 2009 estimated bad debts equal to _____ % of its $928,000 of 2009 charge sales; and the adjusting entry to record the allowance will appear as follows:

DATE	ACCOUNT TITLES AND EXPLANATION	P.R.	DEBIT		CREDIT	
2009						
Dec. 31						
	To record estimated bad debts					

2. The debit of the foregoing entry is to the expense account, _____, which is closed to the _____ account at the end of the accounting period, just as any other expense account is closed.

3. The effect of the foregoing adjusting entry on the 2009 income statement of Marin Company is to cause an estimated amount of bad debts expense to be deducted from the $928,000 of revenue from 2009 charge sales. This complies with the accounting principle of _____
    _____.

Financial Accounting Fundamentals

4. The credit of the foregoing adjusting entry is to the contra account _____. On the December 31, 2009, balance sheet, the balance of this contra account is subtracted from the balance of the _____ account to show the amount that is expected to be realized from the accounts receivable.

5. On March 31, 2010, the Accounts Receivable controlling account and the Allowance for Doubtful Accounts account of Marin Company had the following balances:

Accounts Receivable			Allowance for Doubtful Accounts		
Mar. 31	65,625			Mar. 31	4,475

A balance sheet which was prepared on March 31, 2010, would show that Marin Company expects to collect $ _____ of its accounts receivable.

6. On April 1, 2010, Marin Company decided the $98 account of Gus Bell (sale made on March 5 of the previous year) was uncollectible and wrote it off as a bad debt. Prepare the journal entry and post to the above T-accounts the portions affecting the accounts.

DATE	ACCOUNT TITLES AND EXPLANATION	P.R.	DEBIT	CREDIT
2010				
Apr. 1				
	To write off the account of Gus Bell			

7. If a balance sheet was prepared immediately after the journal entry writing off the uncollectible account of Gus Bell was posted, it would show that Marin Company expected to collect $ _____ of its accounts receivable. Consequently, the write-off _____ (did, did not) affect the net balance sheet amount of accounts receivable. Likewise, the journal entry writing off the account did not record an expense because the expense was anticipated and recorded in the _____ entry made on December 31, 2009 (which corresponds to the year of the sale).

Problem VII

Pell Company sells almost exclusively for cash, but it does make a few small charge sales, and it also occasionally has a small bad debt loss, which it accounts for by the direct write-off method.

1. Give below the entry made by Pell Company on February 5 to write off the $55 uncollectible account of Joan Bond (the goods were sold during the previous period.)

DATE	ACCOUNT TITLES AND EXPLANATION	P.R.	DEBIT	CREDIT
Feb. 5				

2. Writing off the foregoing bad debt directly to the Bad Debts Expense account violates the accounting principle of _____. However, due to the accounting principle _____, the direct write-off is permissible in this case because the company's bad debt losses are very small in relation to its sales.

Problem VIII

A company that ages its accounts receivable and increases its allowance for doubtful accounts to an amount sufficient to provide for estimated bad debts had a $75 debit balance in its Allowance for Doubtful Accounts account on December 31. If, on that date it estimated that $1,800 of its accounts receivable were uncollectible, it should record a year-end adjusting entry crediting $ _____ to its Allowance for Doubtful Accounts account.

Problem IX

Pierce Company allows its customers to use two credit cards: the University National Bank credit card and the Community Credit Card. Using the information given below, prepare the journal entries for Pierce Company to record the following credit card transactions:

a) University National Bank charges a 3% service fee for sales on its credit card. As a commercial customer of the bank, Pierce Company receives immediate credit when it makes its daily deposit of sales receipts.

    May 2   Sold merchandise for $525 to customers who used the University National Bank credit card.

DATE	ACCOUNT TITLES AND EXPLANATION	P.R.	DEBIT	CREDIT

b) Community Credit Card Company charges 4% of sales for use of its card. Pierce Company submits accumulated sales receipts to Community Company and is paid within 30 days.

    May 3   Sold merchandise for $675 to customers using the Community Credit Card. Submitted receipts to Community Company for payment

        30   Received amount due from Community Credit Card Company.

DATE	ACCOUNT TITLES AND EXPLANATION	P.R.	DEBIT	CREDIT

Solutions for Chapter 7

Problem I

1. T
2. T
3. T
4. T
5. F
6. F
7. T
8. F
9. T
10. F
11. T
12. F
13. T
14. T

Problem II

1. A
2. E
3. A
4. C
5. B

Problem III

13	Accounts receivable	2	Maker of a note
1	Accounts receivable turnover	8	Matching principle
12	Aging of accounts receivable	6	Materiality principle
10	Allowance for Doubtful Accounts	11	Maturity date of a note
3	Allowance method	4	Payee of a note
7	Bad debts	16	Principal of a note
5	Direct write-off method	14	Promissory note (or note)
15	Interest	9	Realizable value

Problem IV

Dec. 12	Cash		300	
	Notes Receivable		1,500	
	Accounts Receivable--Guy Hall			1,800
31	Interest Receivable ($1,500 x .12 x 20/360)............................		10	
	Interest Revenue			10
Feb. 9	Cash		1,530	
	Interest Receivable..			10
	Interest Revenue			20
	Notes Receivable			1,500

Problem V

Apr. 30	Accounts Receivable--Mary Dale...		1,224	
	Interest Revenue			24
	Notes Receivable			1,200
Dec. 20	Allowance for Doubtful Accounts......................................		1,224	
	Accounts Receivable--Mary Dale....................................			1,224

Problem VI

1. One fourth of 1%, or .25%

Dec. 31	Bad Debts Expense		2,320	
	Allowance for Doubtful Accounts			2,320

2. Bad Debts Expense, Income Summary

3. matching revenues and expenses

4. Allowance for Doubtful Accounts, Accounts Receivable

5. $61,150

6. Apr. 1   Allowance for Doubtful Accounts   98

         Accounts Receivable—Gus Bell..................................   98

Accounts Receivable				Allowance for Doubtful Accounts		
Mar. 31	65,625				Mar. 31	4,475
		Apr. 1	98	Apr. 1	98	

7. $61,150; did not; adjusting.

Problem VII

1. Feb. 5   Bad Debts Expense...   55
                    Accounts Receivable--Joan Bond   55

2. Matching revenues and expenses; materiality

Problem VIII

$1,875

Problem IX

a) May 2 Cash..   509.25
                Credit Card Expense ($525 × 0.03).........................   15.75
                    Sales   525

b) May 3 Accounts Receivable--Community Company.......................   648.00
                Credit Card Expense ($675 × 0.04).........................   27.00
                    Sales 675.00

        30 Cash..   648.00
                    Accounts Receivable--Community Company................   648.00

CHAPTER 8
ACCOUNTING FOR
LONG-TERM ASSETS

Learning Objective C1:

Describe plant assets and issues in accounting for them.

Plant assets are tangible assets used in the operations of a company and have a useful life of more than one accounting period. Plant assets are set apart from other tangible assets by two important features: use in operations and useful lives longer than one period. The four main accounting issues with plant assets are (1) computing their costs, (2) allocating their costs to the periods they benefit, (3) accounting for subsequent expenditures, and (4) recording their disposal.

Learning Objective C2:

Explain depreciation and the factors affecting its computation.

Depreciation is the process of allocating to expense the cost of a plant asset over the accounting periods that benefit from its use. Depreciation does not measure the decline in a plant asset's market value or its physical deterioration. Three factors determine depreciation: cost, salvage value, and useful life. Salvage value is an estimate of the asset's value at the end of its benefit period. Useful (service) life is the length of time an asset is productively used.

Learning Objective C3:

Explain depreciation for partial years and changes in estimates.

Partial-year depreciation is often required because assets are bought and sold throughout the year. Depreciation is revised when changes in estimates such as salvage value and useful life occur. If the useful life of a plant asset changes, for instance, the remaining cost to be depreciated is spread over the remaining (revised) useful life of the asset.

Learning Objective A1:

Compare and analyze alternative depreciation methods.

The amount of depreciation expense per period is usually different for different methods, yet total depreciation expense over an asset's life is the same for all methods. Each method starts with the same total cost and ends with the same salvage value. The difference is in the pattern of depreciation expense over the asset's life. Common methods are straight-line, double-declining-balance, and units-of-production.

Learning Objective A2:

Compute total asset turnover and apply it to analyze a company's use of assets.

Total asset turnover measures a company's ability to use its assets to generate sales. It is defined as net sales divided by average total assets. While all companies desire a high total asset turnover, it must be interpreted in comparison with that for prior years and its competitors.

Learning Objective P1:

Apply the cost principle to compute the cost of plant assets.

Plant assets are recorded at cost when purchased. Cost includes all normal and reasonable expenditures necessary to get the asset in place and ready for its intended use. The cost of a lump-sum purchase is allocated among its individual assets.

Learning Objective P2:

Compute and record depreciation using the straight-line, units-of-production, and declining-balance methods.

The straight-line method divides cost less salvage value by the asset's useful life to determine depreciation expense per period. The units-of-production method divides cost less salvage value by the estimated number of units the asset will produce over its life to determine depreciation per unit. The declining-balance method multiplies the asset's beginning-of-period book value by a factor that is often double the straight-line rate.

Learning Objective P3:

Distinguish between revenue and capital expenditures, and account for them.

Revenue expenditures expire in the current period and are debited to expense accounts and matched with current revenues. Ordinary repairs are an example of revenue expenditures. Capital expenditures benefit future periods and are debited to asset accounts. Examples of capital expenditures are extraordinary repairs and betterments.

Learning Objective P4:

Account for asset disposal through discarding or selling an asset.

When a plant asset is discarded, sold, or exchanged, its cost and accumulated depreciation are removed from the accounts. Any cash proceeds from discarding or selling an asset are recorded and compared to the asset's book value to determine gain or loss.

Learning Objective P5:

Account for natural resource assets and their depletion.

The cost of a natural resource is recorded in a noncurrent asset account. Depletion of a natural resource is recorded by allocating its cost to depletion expense using the units-of-production method. Depletion is credited to an Accumulated Depletion account.

Learning Objective P6:

Account for intangible assets.

An intangible asset is recorded at the cost incurred to purchase it. The cost of an intangible asset with a definite useful life is allocated to expense using the straight-line method, which is called *amortization*. Goodwill and intangible assets with an indefinite useful life are not amortized—they are annually tested for impairment. Intangible assets include patents, copyrights, leaseholds, goodwill, and trademarks.

Learning Objective P7 (Appendix 8A):

Account for asset exchanges.

For an asset exchange with commercial substance, a gain or loss is recorded based on the difference between the book value of the asset given up and the market value of the asset received. For an asset exchange without commercial substance, no gain or loss is recorded, and the asset received is recorded based on book value of the asset given up.

Section 1—Plant Assets

I.   **Cost Determination**
      Plant assets are tangible assets used in a company's operations that
      have a useful life of more than one accounting period. Consistent
      with *cost principle*, plant assets are recorded at cost when acquired.
      Cost includes all normal and reasonable expenditures necessary to
      get the asset in place and ready for its intended use.

      A. **Land**—has an unlimited life and is not usually used up over time.
          Cost includes:

          1. The total amount paid for the land.

          2. Real estate commissions, title insurance fees, legal fees, and
              any accrued property taxes paid by the purchaser.

          3. Payments for surveying, clearing, grading, and draining, and
              government assessments for public roadways, sewers, and
              sidewalks are included in the cost of land.

          4. Removal of any existing structures (less proceeds from sale
              of salvaged material). These costs are charged to the land
              account. Land is not depreciated.

      B. **Land Improvements**—costs that increase the usefulness of the
          land. Land improvements have limited useful lives and are used
          up.

          1. Examples include parking lot surfaces, driveways, fences,
              and lighting systems.

          2. Costs are charged to a separate Land Improvement account
              so that their costs can be allocated to the periods they
              benefit.

      C. **Buildings**

          1. When purchased, costs usually includes its purchase price,
              brokerage fees, taxes, title fees, attorney costs, and all
              expenditures to make it ready for its intended use including
              any necessary repairs or renovations such as wiring, lighting,
              flooring and wall coverings.

          2. If constructed for own use, cost includes materials and labor
              plus a reasonable amount of indirect overhead costs, such as
              heat, lighting, power, and depreciation on machinery used to
              construct the asset. Cost also includes design fees, building
              permits, and insurance during construction (but not after it is
              placed in use; insurance then becomes an operating expense).

      D. **Machinery and Equipment**
          Costs include all normal and necessary expenditures to purchase
          and prepare them for intended use, including purchase price,
          taxes, transportation charges, insurance while in transit, and the
          installing, assembling and testing of the machinery and
          equipment.

E. **Lump-Sum Purchase**

1. A lump-sum purchase is the purchase of plant assets as a group in a single transaction for a lump-sum price.

2. Individual asset cost is determined by allocating the cost of the purchase among the different types of assets acquired based on their *relative market values.*

II. **Depreciation**—The process of allocating the cost of a plant asset to expense in the accounting periods benefiting from its use.

A. Factors in Computing Depreciation

1. **Cost**—consists of all necessary and reasonable expenditures to acquire the plant asset and to prepare it for its intended use.

2. **Salvage value**—an estimate of the asset's value at the end of its benefit period (also called *residual value* or *scrap value*).

3. **Useful life**—length of time the asset is expected to be productively used in a company's operations (also called *service life*). Factors affecting useful life include:

a. Wear and tear from use in operations.

b. **Inadequacy**—the insufficient capacity of plant assets to meet the company's growing productive demands.

c. **Obsolescence**—refers to a plant asset that is no longer useful in producing goods or services with a competitive advantage because of new inventions and improvements.

B. Depreciation Methods
Depreciation methods are used to allocate a plant asset's cost over the accounting periods in its useful life.

1. Straight-line method—charges the same amount to expense for each period of the asset's useful life; most frequently used method. *Computation:*

a. Cost minus salvage value (equals the *depreciable cost)* divided by the useful life equals annual depreciation expense.

b. Can be expressed as a rate by dividing 100% by the number of periods in the assets' useful life.

2. Units-of-production method—charges a varying amount to expense for each period of an asset's useful life depending on its usage. *Computation:*

a. Cost minus salvage value divided by the total number of units expected to be produced during its useful life equals the depreciation per unit.

b. Depreciation cost per unit times number of units produced in the period equals the period's depreciation expense.

3. Declining-balance method—an **accelerated depreciation method** that yields larger depreciation expense during the early years of an asset's life and less depreciation in the later years. *Computation:*

   a. Multiply the asset's beginning-of-period book value by a multiple of the straight-line rate. (Do not consider salvage value.) **Book value** is computed as the asset's cost less its accumulated depreciation.

   b. A common depreciation rate for the declining-balance method is double the straight-line rate; called the *double-declining-balance method.*

4. Comparing depreciation methods—while the amount of depreciation expense per period differs for different methods, total depreciation expense is the same over a given asset's useful life.

5. Depreciation for tax reporting—differences between financial and tax accounting systems are normal and expected.

   a. Many companies use accelerated depreciation in computing taxable income because it postpones tax payments by charging higher depreciation expense in the early years and lower amounts in the later years.

   b. Federal income tax law rules for depreciating assets are called the **Modified Accelerated Cost Recovery System (MACRS)**.

   c. MACRS is not acceptable for financial reporting because it often allocates costs over an arbitrary period that is less than the asset's useful life and it fails to estimate salvage value.

C. Partial-Year Depreciation
   When an asset is purchased (or disposed of) at a time other than the beginning or end of an accounting period, depreciation is recorded for the part of the year the asset was in use.

D. Changes in Estimates for Depreciation
   Depreciation is based on estimates of salvage value and useful life; later, new information may indicate these estimates are inaccurate.

   1. Use the new estimate to compute depreciation for current and future periods by revising the deprecation expense computation by spreading the cost yet to be depreciated over the remaining useful life.

   2. The revision is referred to as a **change in an accounting estimate** and is reflected in future financial statements; not in prior statements.

Chapter Outline

Notes

E. Reporting Depreciation
1. Both the cost and accumulated depreciation of plant assets are reported on the balance sheet or in its notes.
2. To satisfy the full-disclosure principle, the depreciation method(s) used must be disclosed in notes.
3. Plant assets are reported on the balance sheet at book value; not at market value; emphasis on cost rather than market value is based on the *going concern assumption* unless there is a **permanent** decline in the market value of an asset relative to its book value. In this case, the company must write down the asset to market value.
4. Accumulated Depreciation is a contra asset account with a normal credit balance. It does *not* represent funds accumulated to buy new assets when the currently owned assets are replaced.

III. **Additional Expenditures**
In recording additional expenditures for an assets' operation, maintenance, repair, and improvement, the company must decide whether to capitalize (that is, debit an asset account) or expense them.
A. Types of Additional Expenditures
1. **Revenue expenditures** (also called *income statement expenditures*) are additional costs of plant assets that do not materially increase the asset's life or productive capabilities; they are recorded as expenses and reported on the income statement.
2. **Capital expenditures** (also called *balance sheet expenditures*) are additional costs of plant assets that provide benefits extending beyond the current period; they are debited to asset accounts and reported on the balance sheet.
B. Ordinary Repairs
1. **Ordinary repairs** are expenditures to keep an asset in normal, good operating condition.
2. Ordinary repairs are treated as revenue expenditures; their costs are reported as expenses on the income statement.
C. Betterments and Extraordinary Repairs—accounting for betterments and extraordinary repairs is similar. Both are treated as *capital expenditures*.
1. **Betterments** (Improvements)—are expenditures that make a plant asset more efficient or productive.
2. **Extraordinary Repairs** (Replacements)—are expenditures extending the asset's useful life beyond its original estimate. These are *capital expenditures* because they benefit future periods and their costs are debited to the asset account.

Chapter Outline

Notes

IV. **Disposals of Plant Assets**—Assets may be discarded, sold, or exchanged.

A. Discarding Plant Assets

1. Entry to record disposal of plant assets when *fully depreciated* (when accumulated depreciation is less than the asset's cost): debit Accumulated Depreciation, credit the plant asset account.

2. Entry to record disposal of plant assets when *not fully depreciated* (when accumulated depreciation is less than the asset's cost): first, record depreciation expense through date discarded, then debit Accumulated Depreciation, debit Loss on Disposal (for the remaining book value), credit the plant asset account.

B. Selling Plant Assets
First, record depreciation expense through date sold, then:

1. Entry to record sale at book value: debit cash, debit Accumulated Depreciation, credit the plant asset account.

2. Entry to record sale above book value: debit cash, debit Accumulated Depreciation, credit Gain on Disposal, credit the plant asset account.

3. Entry to record sale below book value: debit cash, debit Loss on Disposal, debit Accumulated Depreciation, credit the plant asset account.

V. **Section 2—Natural Resources**—assets that are physically consumed when used. Examples include timber, mineral deposits, and oil and gas fields. Since they are consumed when used, they are also called *wasting assets*.

A. Cost Determination and Depletion

1. Natural resources are recorded at cost, which includes all expenditures necessary to acquire the resource and prepare it for its intended use.

2. **Depletion** is the process of allocating the cost of a natural resource to the period when it is consumed.

3. Natural resources are reported on the balance sheet at cost less *accumulated depletion*.

4. The depletion expense per period is based on the units extracted; entry to record depletion: debit Depletion Expense, credit Accumulated Depletion.

B. Plant Assets Used in Extracting
When the usefulness of plant assets used in extracting resources is directly related to the depletion of the natural resource, their costs are depreciated using the units-of-production method in proportion to the depletion of the natural resource.

VI.   **Section 3 – Intangible Assets**—nonphysical assets (used in operations) that confer on their owners long-term rights, privileges, or competitive advantages.

  A. Cost Determination and Amortization

  1. An intangible asset is recorded at cost when purchased. Intangibles are then separated into those with limited lives or indefinite lives. For those with a limited life, its cost is systematically allocated to expense over its estimated useful life through a process called **amortization**. If an intangible asset has an **indefinite life**, it should not be amortized.

  2. Amortization is similar to depreciation and depletion, except that only the straight-line method is generally used for amortization.

  3. The effects of amortization are recorded in a contra account called Accumulated Amortization. The gross acquisition cost and accumulated amortization are disclosed in the balance sheet.

  B. Types of Intangibles

  1. **Patent**—an exclusive right granted to its owner to manufacture and sell a patented machine or device, or to use a process, for 20 years.

  2. **Copyright**—the exclusive right given to its owner to publish and sell a musical, literary, or artistic work during the life of the creator plus 70 years.

  3. **Leasehold**—**lessee** is granted the right to use property by the **lessor**, the property's owner.

  4. **Leasehold improvements**—alterations or improvements to leased property, such as partitions, painting, and storefronts.

  5. **Franchises and Licenses**—rights that a company or government grants an entity to deliver a product or service under specified conditions. If for an indefinite period, costs are not amortized.

  6. **Trademarks and Trade Names**—symbols, names, phrases, or jingles identified with a company, product, or service. If the company plans to renew indefinitely its right to the trademark, the cost is not amortized.

  7. **Goodwill**—meaning in accounting: the amount by which the value of a company exceeds the value of its individual assets and liabilities; implies the company as a whole has certain value attributes not measured among its individual assets and liabilities.

  8. **Other Intangibles**-include assets such as *software, noncompete convenants, customer lists,* etc. Record the intangible asset's costs, then determine whether the asset has a limited or indefinite life. If limited, allocate its costs over that period. If indefinite, its costs are not amortized.

VII. Decision Analysis—Total Asset Turnover

A. **Total asset turnover** is a measure of a company's ability to use its assets most efficiently and effectively.

B. Calculated by dividing net sales by average total assets.

C. It is safe to say that all companies desire a high total asset turnover. However, interpreting a company's total asset turnover requires an understanding of the company's operations.

1. Some operations are capital intensive, meaning that a relatively large amount is invested in assets to generate sales, which would suggest a lower total asset turnover.

2. Other operations are labor intensive, meaning that they generate sales more by the efforts of people than the use of assets; a higher total asset turnover would be expected.

VIII. Exchanging Plant Assets (Appendix 8A) Many plant assets are disposed of by exchanging them for newer assets. In a typical exchange, a *trade-in allowance* is received on the old asset and the balance is paid in cash. Accounting for the exchange depends on whether the transaction has *commercial substance*. An exchange has commercial substance if the company's future cash flows change as a result of the transaction. If an asset exchange has commercial substance, a gain or loss is recorded based on the difference between the book value of the asset given up and the market value of the asset received. If an asset exchange lacks commercial substance, no gain or loss is recorded, and the asset received is recorded based on book value of the asset given up.

A. **Exchange with Commercial Substance: A Loss**

When the book value of the assets given up (cash paid plus book value of the old equipment) is more than the market value of the equipment received, a loss is recorded. Entry: debit the new equipment for market value, debit Loss on Exchange of Assets (difference between the book value of the assets given up and the market value of the new asset), debit Accumulated Depreciation for the old equipment, credit Equipment (old) for cost of the old equipment, credit cash for the cash paid.

B. **Exchange with Commercial Substance: A Gain**

When the market value of the equipment received is more than the book value of the assets given up (cash paid plus book value of the old equipment), a gain is recorded. Entry: debit the new equipment for market value, debit Accumulated Depreciation for the old equipment, credit Equipment (old) for cost of the old equipment, credit cash for the cash paid, and credit Gain on Exchange of Assets for the gain (difference between market value of the new asset and the book value of the assets given up).

C. **Exchange without Commercial Substance**

If the transaction lacks commercial substance, any gain or loss which would have been recorded when the transaction had commercial substance is not recorded. The unrecognized gain is subtracted from the new asset's market value to determine its cost basis. The cost basis of the new asset also can be computed by summing the book values of the assets given up.

Problem VII (Appendix 8A)

A machine that cost $45,000 and had been depreciated $20,000 was exchanged for a new machine that had a market value of $55,000. Assuming the balance was paid in cash, prepare the general journal entry to record the transaction under each of the following unrelated assumptions:

1. Cash paid was $28,000, and the transaction had commercial substance.
2. Cash paid was $35,000 and the transaction had commercial substance.
3. Cash paid was $28,000, and the transaction did not have commercial substance.

DATE	ACCOUNT TITLES AND EXPLANATION	P.R.	DEBIT	CREDIT

Problem III

11	Accelerated depreciation method	28	Leasehold
8	Amortization	25	Leasehold improvements
14	Betterments	30	Lessee
10	Book value	33	Lessor
15	Capital expenditures	35	Licenses
16	Change in an accounting estimate	1	Modified Accelerated Cost Recovery System (MACRS)
20	Copyright		
21	Cost	32	Natural resources
7	Declining-balance method	3	Obsolescence
22	Depletion	18	Ordinary repairs
23	Depreciation	27	Patent
19	Extraordinary repairs	29	Plant assets
34	Franchises	17	Revenue expenditures
36	Impairment	2	Salvage value
13	Inadequacy	9	Straight-line depreciation
37	Indefinite useful life	6	Total asset turnover
24	Intangible assets	31	Trademark or trade (brand) names
5	Land improvements	4	Units-of-production depreciation
26	Lease	12	Useful life

Problem IV

1. depreciation; land improvements

2. (a) wear and tear
   (b) inadequacy
   (c) obsolescence

3. straight-line; declining-balance

4. usually much shorter than the estimated service life of an asset

5. ordinary; assets with low costs; extraordinary; betterments

6. the payment of income taxes is deferred

7. they are not being used in the production or sale of other assets or services

8. the accounting periods that benefit from the asset's use; market value; deterioration

9. cost; accumulated depreciation

10. (a) depreciation expense; accumulated depreciation
    (b) asset; accumulated depreciation
    (c) cash received or paid
    (d) gain; loss; book value

Problem V

$7,000 - (\$7,000 \times 2\%) + \$175 + \$575 + \$425 = \$8,035$

Problem VI

1. $(\$8,000 - \$800) \div 8 \times 6/12 = \$450$

2. $[(\$8,000 - \$800) \div 144,000] \times 10,000 = \$500$

3. $(100\%/8) \times 2 = 25\%$ double-declining-balance rate

   $\$8,000 \times 25\% \times 6/12 = \$1,000$

Problem VII

(a)	Machinery...	32,000	
	Accumulated Depreciation Machinery.................................	20,000	
	Cash ($35,000 – $28,000)..		7,000
	Machinery...		45,000
(b)	Machinery...	35,000	
	Accumulated Depreciation Machinery.................................	20,000	
	Loss on Exchange of Machinery.......................................	4,000	
	Cash ($35,000 – $21,000)..		14,000
	Machinery...		45,000
(c)	Machinery...	35,000	
	Accumulated Depreciation Machinery.................................	20,000	
	Gain on Exchange of Machinery...................................		8,000
	Cash ($35,000 – $33,000)..		2,000
	Machinery...		45,000

CHAPTER 9
ACCOUNTING FOR
CURRENT LIABILITIES

Learning Objective C1:

Describe current and long-term liabilities and their characteristics.

Liabilities are probable future payments of assets or services that past transactions or events obligate an entity to make. Current liabilities are due within one year or the operating cycle, whichever is longer. All other liabilities are long term.

Learning Objective C2:

Identify and describe known current liabilities.

Known (determinable) current liabilities are set by agreements or laws and are measurable with little uncertainty. They include accounts payable, sales taxes payable, unearned revenues, notes payable, payroll liabilities, and the current portion of long-term debt.

Learning Objective C3:

Explain how to account for contingent liabilities.

If an uncertain future payment depends on a probable future event and the amount can be reasonably estimated, the payment is recorded as a liability. The uncertain future payment is reported as a contingent liability (in the notes) if (*a*) the future event is reasonably possible but not probable or (*b*) the event is probable but the payment amount cannot be reasonably estimated.

Learning Objective A1:

Compute the times interest earned ratio and use it to analyze liabilities.

Times interest earned is computed by dividing a company's net income before interest expense and income taxes by the amount of interest expense. The times interest earned ratio reflects a company's ability to pay interest obligations.

Learning Objective P1:

Prepare entries to account for short-term notes payable.

Short-term notes payable are current liabilities; most bear interest. When a short-term note's face value equals the amount borrowed, it identifies a rate of interest to be paid at maturity.

Learning Objective P2:

Compute and record *employee* payroll deductions and liabilities.

Employee payroll deductions include FICA taxes, income taxes, and voluntary deductions such as pensions and charities. They make up the difference between gross and net pay.

Learning Objective P3:

Compute and record *employer* payroll expenses and liabilities.

An employer's payroll expenses include employees' gross earnings, any employee benefits, and the payroll taxes levied on the employer. Payroll liabilities include employees' net pay amounts, withholdings from employee wages, any employer-promised benefits, and the employer's payroll taxes.

Learning Objective P4:

Account for estimated liabilities, including warranties and bonuses.

Liabilities for health and pension benefits, warranties, and bonuses are recorded with estimated amounts. These items are recognized as expenses when incurred and matched with revenues generated.

Learning Objective P5 (Appendix 9A):

Identify and describe the details of payroll reports, records and procedures.

Employers report FICA taxes and federal income tax withholdings using Form 941. FUTA taxes are reported on Form 940. Earnings and deductions are reported to each employee and the federal government on Form W-2. An employer's payroll records often include a payroll register for each pay period, payroll checks and statements of earnings, and individual employee earnings reports.

I.   **Characteristics of Liabilities**

A. Defining Liabilities
A liability is a probable future payment of assets or services that a company is presently obligated to make as a result of past transactions or events. Note three crucial factors:

1. Past transaction or event.

2. Present obligation.

3. Future payment of assets or services.

B. Classifying Liabilities

1. **Current liabilities** (also called *short-term liabilities*)—Obligations due within one year or the company's operating cycle, whichever is longer.

2. **Long-term liabilities**—Obligations not expected to be paid within the longer of one year or the company's operating cycle.

C. Uncertainty in Liabilities—answers to the following questions are often decided when a liability is incurred; however, one or more may be uncertain for some liabilities:

1. Whom to pay?

2. When to pay?

3. How much to pay?

II. **Known Liabilities**—Set by agreements, contracts, or laws and are measurable. Examples of these liabilities in the *current* classification include:

A. Accounts Payable
Amounts owed to suppliers for products or services purchased with credit; also known as *trade accounts payable*.

B. Sales Taxes Payable
Amounts the seller has collected as sales taxes from customers when sales occur, which have not yet been remitted to the proper governmental agency.

1. Entry (by seller) to record cash sale subject to sales tax: debit Cash, credit Sales, credit Sales Taxes Payable.

2. Entry (by seller) when sales taxes are remitted: debit Sales Tax Payable, credit Cash.

C. Unearned Revenues

Amounts received in advance from customers for future products or services; also known as *deferred revenues, collections in advance and prepayments*.

1. Entry to record receipt of amounts in advance for future products or services: debit Cash, credit Unearned Revenue.

2. Entry to record revenue for that portion earned: debit Unearned Revenue, credit Revenue.

D. Short-Term Notes Payable

Written promise to pay a specified amount on a definite future date within one year or the company's operating cycle, whichever is longer. Can arise from many transactions; two common examples:

1. Note given to extend credit period; interest-bearing note is substituted for an overdue account payable.

    a. Entry to record partial payment on account and substitution of note payable for overdue amount: debit Accounts Payable, credit Cash, credit Notes Payable.

    b. Entry to record payment when note becomes due: debit Note Payable, debit Interest Expense, credit Cash.

2. Note given to borrow from bank
    Entries (by borrower) to record:

    a. Receipt of cash when note is signed: debit Cash, credit Note Payable.

    b. Payment of principal and interest: debit Note Payable, debit Interest Expense, credit Cash.

    c. Accrual of interest when notes payable are outstanding at the end of a period: debit Interest Expense, credit Interest Payable.

    d. Payment of note when interest has been accrued: debit Interest Expense (amount incurred since accrual date), debit Interest Payable (amount previously accrued), debit Notes Payable, credit Cash (for full amount paid).

E. Payroll Liabilities

An employer incurs several expenses and liabilities from salaries and wages earned, from employee benefits, and from payroll taxes levied on the employer.

1. **Gross pay**—total compensation an employee earns (includes wages, salaries, commissions, bonuses).

2. **Net pay**—gross pay less all deductions; also called *take-home pay*.

3. **Employee Payroll Deductions**—amounts withheld from an employee's gross pay, either required or voluntary; commonly called *withholdings*. The employer withholds payroll deductions from employees' pay and is obligated to remit to the designated organizations.

   a. Employee FICA taxes (*Social Security* and *Medicare taxes*) equal current rate times gross wages *subject to tax*. (For year 2005, Social Security tax is 6.2% of the *first* $90,000 earned by the employee in the calendar year and Medicare tax is 1.45% of *all* amounts earned by the employee).

   b. Employee income tax withholding is determined from tables published by the IRS based on employee's annual earnings rate and the number of *withholding allowances* claimed.

   c. Employee voluntary deductions (charitable contributions, medical insurance premiums, pension contributions, and union dues) are withheld and reported as part of the employer's current liabilities until paid.

4. Illustrative entry (by employer) to accrue payroll expenses and liabilities: debit Salaries Expense, credit FICA-Social Securities Taxes Payable, credit FICA-Medicare Taxes Payable, credit Employee Federal Income Taxes Payable, credit Employee Medical Insurance Payable, credit Employee Union Dues Payable, credit Salaries Payable (for the amount of the net pay).

5. **Employer Payroll Taxes** are recorded as expenses and current liabilities. Employer taxes include:

   a. Employer FICA taxes—employers must pay FICA taxes *equal in amount* to the FICA taxes withheld from their employees.

   b. Federal and state unemployment taxes—Employers must pay a federal unemployment tax on wages and salaries paid to their employees. (For year 2008, employers were required to pay FUTA taxes of as much as 6.2% on the first $7,000 earned by each employee; this tax can be reduced by a credit of up to 5.4% for taxes paid to a state program.) All states place a payroll tax for unemployment insurance on employers; the amounts vary.

   c. Illustrative entry (by employer) to record payroll tax expense and related liabilities: debit Payroll Tax Expense, credit FICA-Social Securities Taxes Payable, credit FICA-Medicare Taxes Payable, credit State Unemployment Taxes Payable, credit Federal Unemployment Taxes Payable.

III. **Estimated Liabilities**—Known obligations of uncertain amounts that can be reasonably estimated. Examples are:

    A. Health and Pension Benefits

        1. Employers often pay all or part of medical, dental, life, and disability insurance, and many employers also contribute to pension plans.

        2. Illustrative entry to record these benefits: debit Employee Benefits Expense, credit Employee Medical Insurance Payable, credit Retirement Program Payable.

    B. Vacation Benefits—Estimated and recorded by the employer during the weeks the employees are working and earning the vacation time.

        1. Many employers offer paid vacations.

        2. Entry to record: debit Vacation Benefits Expense, credit Vacation Benefits Payable. When employees take vacation, employer reduces (debits) the Vacation Benefits Payable and credits Cash.

    C. Bonus Plans

        1. Many companies offer bonuses to employees; many bonuses depend on net income.

        2. The related expense and liability are recorded in a year-end adjusting entry.

    D. Warranty Liabilities

        1. A **warranty** is a seller's obligation to replace or correct a product (or service) that fails to perform as expected within a specified period.

        2. To comply with the *full disclosure* and *matching principles*, the seller reports the expected warranty expense in the period when revenue from the sale of the product or service is reported. The warranty obligation is reported as a liability even though the amount, payee, and date are uncertain. The costs are probably and the amount can be estimated based on past experience.

    E. Multi-Period Estimated Liabilities
       Reported as both current and long-term depending on when payment will be made.

IV.   **Contingent Liabilities**—Potential obligation that depends on a future event arising from past transactions.

    A. Accounting for Contingent Liabilities – depends on the likelihood that a future event will occur and the ability to estimate the future amount owed if this event occurs. Three categories of contingent liabilities:

        1. Future event is probable and the amount can be reasonably estimated. Record as a liability.

        2. Future event is remote. Do not record or disclose in notes.

        3. Future event is reasonably possible. Disclose in notes.

    B. Reasonably Possible Contingent Liabilities – Examples:

        1. Potential legal claims—recorded in the accounts only if payment for damages is probable *and* the amount can be reasonably estimated; if can't be reasonably estimated or is less than probable but reasonably possible, disclose in notes.

        2. Debt guarantees (of a debt owed by another company)—require disclosure if potential liabilities are reasonably possible.

        3. Other contingencies (e.g., environmental damages, possible tax assessments, insurance losses, and government investigations)—require disclosure if potential liabilities are reasonably possible.

        4. Uncertainties that are Not Contingencies – are not contingent liabilities because they are future events *not* arising from past transactions. They are not disclosed.

V.   **Decision Analysis—Times Interest Earned Ratio**

    A. The **times interest earned ratio** is a measure of risk that a business will not earn sufficient income to cover interest.

    B. It is calculated by dividing income before interest expense and income taxes by interest expense.

VI.   **Payroll Reports, Records, and Procedures (Appendix 9A)**

    A. Payroll Reports—employers are required to prepare and submit the following reports:

        1. Reporting FICA and Income Taxes. Employer's Quarterly Federal Tax Return (IRS Form 941)
Filed within one month after the end of each calendar quarter to report FICA and income withholding taxes owed and remitted.

        2. Reporting FUTA and SUTA Taxes. Annual Federal Unemployment Tax Return (IRS Form 940)
Must be mailed on or before January 31 following the end of each tax year to report an employer's FUTA taxes.

3. Reporting Wages and Salaries. Wage and Tax Statement (Form W-2) must be given to employees on or before January 31 following the year covered by the report; employers must give each employee an annual report of the employee's wages subject to FICA and federal income taxes and the amounts of these taxes withheld.

B. Payroll Records

1. Payroll Register
A record for a pay period that shows the pay period dates and the hours worked, gross pay, deductions, and net pay of each employee; contains all the data needed to record payroll (for each pay period) in the General Journal.

2. Payroll Check
Generally accompanied with a detachable *statement of earnings* showing gross pay, deductions, and net pay.

3. Employee's Earnings Report.
A record of an employee's hours worked, gross earnings, deductions, net pay, and certain personal information about the employee; contains the data the employer needs to prepare a Form W-2.

C. Payroll Procedures

1. Computing Federal Income Taxes
Computed using a wage bracket withholding table based on gross pay, number of personal exemptions, the employee's tax status, and pay period.

   a. Withholding allowance—a number that is used to reduce the amount of federal income tax withheld from an employee's pay, and which corresponds to the personal exemptions the employee is allowed to subtract from annual earnings in calculating taxable income.

   b. Form W-4—withholding allowance certificate form. Filed by employee with employer to identify personal exemptions claimed.

2. Payroll Bank Account
A separate **payroll bank account** is used in a company with many employees.

   a. One check for total payroll is drawn on the regular bank account or an *electronic funds transfer* for this amount is executed to provide deposit for the payroll bank account.

   b. Individual payroll checks are drawn on payroll account.

   c. Helps with internal control and reconciling the regular bank account.

3. Who Pays What Payroll Taxes and Benefits—who pays which employee benefits and what portion, is subject to agreements between companies and their workers. Self-employed workers must pay both the employer and employee FICA taxes for social security and Medicare.

VII. **Income Taxes (Appendix 9B)**

A. Income Tax Liabilities

1. Corporations (but not sole proprietorships or partnerships) are subject to income taxes and must estimate their tax liability when preparing financial statements.

2. Entry to record estimated income tax liability: debit Income Taxes Expense, credit Income Taxes Payable.

B. Deferred Income Tax Liabilities

1. Income tax laws and GAAP are different.

2. *Temporary differences* arise when the tax return and the income statement report a revenue or expense in different years. When temporary differences exist, corporations compute income taxes expense on the income reported on the income statement; the result is that the income taxes expense is different from the amount payable to the government; this difference is the **deferred income tax liability.**

3. Entry to record estimated income tax liability when there are temporary differences: debit Income Taxes Expense, credit Income Taxes Payable, credit Deferred Income Tax Liability (for the difference).

4. Temporary differences can also cause corporations to pay income taxes *before* they are reported on the income statement as an expense. The corporation then reports a *Deferred Income Tax Asset* on its balance sheet.

Chapter Nine – Alternate Demonstration Problem #1

On November I, 2009, Orleaon Co. borrowed $200,000 for 90 days at 9% by 7signing a note.

Required:

1. Assume that the face value of the note equals the principal of the loan. Prepare the general journal entries to record issuing the note, accrual of interest at the end of 2009 and the payment of the note at maturity.

2. Assume that the face value of the note ($204,500) includes both the principal of the loan and the interest to be paid at maturity. Prepare the general journal entries to record issuing the note, accrual of interest at the end of 2009 and the payment of the note at maturity.

(If this alternative demonstration problem is not covered in class, see your instructor for the solution.)

Problem I

The following statements are either true or false. Place a (T) in the parentheses before each true statement and an (F) before each false statement.

1. ( ) An example of an estimated liability is a warranty.

2. ( ) Contingent liabilities are generally not recognized on the balance sheet.

3. ( ) A corporation would report a deferred income tax liability when reported income tax expense for the year is greater than the amount of tax actually paid.

4. ( ) Federal unemployment taxes are withheld from employees' wages at the rate of 1.45% on the first $61,200 earned.

5. ( ) Social Security taxes are levied equally on the employee and the employer.

6. ( ) Employee benefit costs represent expenses to the employer in addition to the direct costs of salaries and wages.

7. ( ) Each time a payroll is recorded, a separate journal entry usually is made to record the employer's FICA and state and federal unemployment taxes.

8. ( ) Since federal income taxes withheld from an employee's wages are expenses of the employee, not the employer, they should not be treated as liabilities of the employer.

9. ( ) Since Jon Company has very little employee turnover, the company has received a very favorable merit rating. As a result, Jon Company should expect to pay substantially smaller amounts of FICA taxes than normal.

10. ( ) Select Company's income before interest and taxes is $292,400 and interest expense is $86,000. Select's times interest earned is 3.4 times.

11. ( ) (Appendix 9A) An employer's FICA taxes are reported annually on a Form 940.

12. ( ) (Appendix 9A) If an employer's total FUTA taxes for the year are $100 or less, the amount due may be remitted annually rather than quarterly.

13. ( ) (Appendix 9A) As the number of withholding allowances claimed increases, the amount of income tax to be withheld increases.

14. ( ) (Appendix 9A) A special payroll bank account is used to replenish the regular bank account after all the employees are paid.

Problem II

You are given several words, phrases, or numbers to choose from in completing each of the following statements or in answering the following questions. In each case select the one that best completes the statement or answers the question and place its letter in the answer space provided.

_____ 1. On November 1, 2009, Profitable Company borrowed $50,000 by giving a 90-day, 12% note payable. The company has an annual, calendar-year accounting period and does not make reversing entries. What amount should be debited to Interest Expense on January 30, 2010?

   a. $6,000
   b. $1,500
   c. $1,000
   d. $ 500
   e. $ 0

For the next two questions, use the following information as to earnings and deductions taken from a company's payroll records for the pay period ended November 15:

Employee's Name	Earnings to End of Previous Week	Gross Pay This Week	Federal Income Taxes	Medical Insurance Deducted
Rita Hawn..................................	$25,700	$ 800	$155.00	$ 35.50
Dolores Hopkins........................	930	800	134.00	35.50
Robert Allen	76,100	1,000	193.00	42.00
Calvin Ingram...........................	18,400	740	128.00	42.00
		$3,340	$610.00	$155.00

_____ 2. Employees' FICA taxes are withheld at an assumed rate of 6.2% on the first $90,000 earned for Social Security and 1.45% of all wages earned for Medicare. The journal entry to accrue the payroll should include a:

a. Debit to Accrued Payroll Payable for $3,340.

b. Debit to FICA Taxes Payable for $255.51.

c. Debit to Payroll Taxes Expense for $765.

d. Credit to FICA Taxes Payable for $255.51.

e. Credit to Accrued Payroll Payable for $2,575.

_____ 3. Assume a state unemployment tax rate of 5.4% on the first $7,000 paid each employee and a federal unemployment tax rate of 0.8% on the first $7,000 paid each employee. The journal entry to record the employer's payroll taxes resulting from the payroll should include a debit to Payroll Taxes Expense for:

a. $305.11

b. $277.91

c. $293.23

d. $349.03

e. The entry does not include a debit to Payroll Taxes Expense.

Problem III

Many of the important ideas and concepts that are discussed in Chapter 9 are reflected in the following list of key terms. Test your understanding of these terms by matching the appropriate definitions with the terms. Record the number identifying the most appropriate definition in the blank space next to each term.

_____ Contingent liability	_____ Gross pay
_____ Current liabilities	_____ Known liabilities
_____ Current portion of long-term debt	_____ Long-term liabilities
_____ Deferred income tax liability**	_____ Merit rating
_____ Employee benefits	_____ Net pay
_____ Employee earnings report*	_____ Payroll bank account*
_____ Estimated liability	_____ Payroll deductions
_____ Federal depository bank*	_____ Payroll register*
_____ FICA taxes	_____ Short-term note payable
_____ Form 940*	_____ SUTA
_____ Form 941*	_____ Times interest earned
_____ Form W-2*	_____ Wage bracket withholding table*
_____ Form W-4*	_____ Warranty
_____ FUTA	

Key term discussed in Appendix 9A.
**Key term discussed in Appendix 9B.*

1. Corporation income taxes that are deferred until future years because of temporary differences between GAAP and tax rules.

2. Obligation of an uncertain amount that can be reasonably estimated.

3. Potential liability that depends on a future event arising from a past transaction.

4. Table of the amounts of income tax withheld from employee's wages.

5. A withholding allowance certificate, filed with the employer, identifying the number of withholding allowances claimed.

6. Obligations due within a year or the company's operating cycle, whichever is longer; paid using current assets or by creating other current liabilities.

7. Portion of long-term debt due within one year or the operating cycle, whichever is longer; reported under current liabilities.

8. Annual report by an employer to each employee showing the employee's wages subject to FICA and federal income taxes along with amounts withheld.

9. Taxes assessed on both employers and employees; for Social Security and Medicare programs.

10. Ratio of income before interest expense (and any income taxes) divided by interest expense; reflects risk of interest commitments when income varies.

11. Agreement that obligates the seller to correct or replace a product or service when if fails to perform properly within a specified period.

12. IRS form used to report an employer's federal unemployment taxes (FUTA) on an annual filing basis.

13. Rating assigned to an employer by a state based on the employer's record of employment.

14. Additional compensation paid to or on behalf of employees, such as premiums for medical, dental, life, disability insurance, and contributions to pension plans.

15. Payroll taxes on employers assessed by the federal government to support its unemployment insurance program.

16. State payroll taxes on employers to support its unemployment programs.

17. Total compensation earned by an employee.

18. Current obligation in the form of a written promissory note.

19. Obligations of a company with little uncertainty; set by agreements, contracts or laws; also called *definitely determinable liabilities*.

20. Amounts withheld from an employee's gross pay; also called *withholdings*.

21. Obligations *not* requiring payment within one year or the operating cycle, whichever is longer.

22. Gross pay less all deductions; also called *take-home pay*.

23. Record of an employee's net pay, gross pay, deductions, and year-to-date information.

24. Bank account used solely for paying employees; each pay period an amount equal to the total employees' net pay is deposited in it and the payroll checks are drawn on it.

25. IRS form filed to report FICA taxes owed and remitted.

26. Record for a pay period that shows the pay period dates, regular and overtime hours worked, gross pay, net pay, and deductions.

27. Bank authorized to accept deposits of amounts payable to the federal government.

Problem IV

Complete the following by filling in the blanks.

1. A debt guarantee is an example of a _____ liability.

2. Good employer merit ratings give employers a reduction in their state unemployment tax rates as a reward for _____.

3. The two components of FICA taxes are _____
and _____.

4. Employers pay FICA taxes _____ to those withheld from employees.

5. (Appendix 9A) According to law, a _____
showing wages earned and taxes withheld must be given by the employer to each employee within one month after the year-end.

6. (Appendix 9A) The amount to be withheld from an employee's wages for federal income taxes is determined by (a) _____
and (b)_____.

7. (Appendix 9A) According to the Federal Insurance Contributions Act, an employer must file an Employer's Quarterly Federal Tax Return (Form _____ within one month after the end of each _____.

8. (Appendix 9A) The _____ contains all the data needed to prepare the general journal entry to record payroll.

9. (Appendix 9A) An employee's working time, gross earnings, deductions, and net pay for a full year are summarized in an _____

_____ .

Problem V

Glitz Company estimates that future costs to satisfy its product warranty obligation amount to 3% of sales. In January, the company sold merchandise for $50,000 cash and paid $1,200 to repair products returned for warranty work. Prepare the journal entries related to the product warranty.

DATE	ACCOUNT TITLES AND EXPLANATION	P.R.	DEBIT	CREDIT

Problem VI

The following information as to earnings and deductions for the pay period ended November 15 was taken from a company's payroll records:

Employee's Name	Earnings to End of Previous Week	Gross Pay This Week	Federal Income Taxes	Medical Insurance Deducted
Rita Hawn	$25,700	$ 800	$155.00	$ 35.50
Dolores Hopkins	930	800	134.00	35.50
Robert Allen	89,900	1,000	193.00	42.00
Calvin Ingram	18,400	740	128.00	42.00
		$3,340	$610.00	$155.00

Required:

1. Calculate the employees' FICA taxes withheld assuming a rate of 6.2% on the first $90,000 earned for Social Security and 1.45% of all wages earned for Medicare, and prepare the journal entry to accrue the payroll under the assumption that all of the employees work in the office.

2. Prepare the journal entry to record the employer's payroll taxes resulting from the payroll. Assume a state unemployment tax rate of 2% on the first $7,000 paid each employee and a federal unemployment tax rate of 0.8% on the first $7,000 paid each employee.

DATE	ACCOUNT TITLES AND EXPLANATION	P.R.	DEBIT		CREDIT	

Problem VII (Appendix 9A)

The Payroll Register of Whiteman Sales for the first week of the year follows. The deductions and net pay of the first three employees have been calculated and entered.

1. Use an assumed 8% FICA tax rate (Medicare and Social Security have been combined for this problem) and complete the payroll information opposite the name of the last employee, Fred Clarke. In addition to FICA taxes, Mr. Clarke should have $111 of federal income taxes, $20 of medical insurance, and no union dues withheld from his wages, which are chargeable to office salaries. The overtime premium rate is 50%.

PAYROLL REGISTER

EMPLOYEE'S NAME	CLOCK CARD NUMBER	DAILY TIME							TOTAL HOURS	O.T. HOURS	REG. PAY RATE		REGULAR PAY		O.T. PREMIUM PAY		GROSS PAY		
		M	T	W	T	F	S	S											
Delbert Landau	12	8	8	8	7	4	0	0	35		11	00	385	00			385	00	1
Maria Garza	9	8	8	8	5	4	0	0	35		12	00	396	00			396	00	2
Ralph Webster	15	8	8	7	8	4	0	0	35		13	00	455	00			455	00	3
Fred Clarke	4	8	8	8	8	8	4	0	44	4	14	00							4
																			5

Week ending January 8, 20—

	FICA TAXES		FEDERAL INCOME TAXES		MEDICAL INSURANCE		UNION DUES		TOTAL DEDUC-TIONS		NET PAY		CHECK NUMBER	SALES SALARIES		OFFICE SALARIES		DELIVERY WAGES	
	DEDUCTIONS										PAYMENT			DISTRIBUTION					
1	30	80	65	00	20	00	10	00	125	80	259	20						385	00
2	31	68	63	00	20	00	10	00	124	68	271	32		396	00				
3	36	40	68	00	20	00	10	00	134	40	320	60		455	00				
4																			
5																			

2. Complete the Payroll Register by totaling its columns, and prepare the journal entry to record its information.

DATE	ACCOUNT TITLES AND EXPLANATION	P.R.	DEBIT		CREDIT	

Whiteman Sales uses a special payroll bank account in paying its employees. Each payday, after the general journal entry recording the information of its Payroll Register is posted, a single check for the total of the employees' net pay is drawn and deposited in the payroll bank account. This transfers funds equal to the payroll total from the regular bank account to the payroll bank account. Then special payroll checks are written on the payroll bank account and given to the employees. For the January 8 payroll, four payroll checks beginning with payroll Check No. 102 were drawn and delivered to the employees. Record this information in the Payroll Register.

3. Prepare the journal entry to record the transfer of cash to the payroll bank account for the January 8 payroll.

DATE	ACCOUNT TITLES AND EXPLANATION	P.R.	DEBIT		CREDIT	

4. Prepare the journal entry to record the payroll taxes levied on Whiteman Sales as a result of the payroll entered in its January 8 Payroll Register. The company has a merit rating that reduces its state employment tax rate to 1% of the first $7,000 paid each employee. (Assume the federal unemployment tax rate is 0.8%.)

DATE	ACCOUNT TITLES AND EXPLANATION	P.R.	DEBIT			CREDIT		

Solutions for Chapter 9

Problem I

1. T
2. T
3. T
4. F
5. T
6. T
7. T
8. F
9. F
10. T
11. F
12. T
13. F
14. F

Problem II

1. D
2. D
3. A

Problem III

3	Contingent liability		17	Gross pay
6	Current liabilities		19	Known liabilities
7	Current portion of long-term debt		21	Long-term liabilities
1	Deferred income tax liability**		13	Merit rating
14	Employee benefits		22	Net pay
23	Employee earnings report*		24	Payroll bank account*
2	Estimated liability		20	Payroll deductions
27	Federal depository bank*		26	Payroll register*
9	FICA taxes		18	Short-term note payable
12	Form 940*		16	SUTA
25	Form 941*		10	Times interest earned
8	Form W-2*		4	Wage bracket withholding table*
5	From W-4*		11	Warranty
15	FUTA			

Key term discussed in Appendix 9A.
**Key term discussed in Appendix 9B.*

Problem IV

1. contingent
2. providing stable employment for employees
3. Social Security taxes; Medicare taxes
4. Equal
5. Form W-2 (Wage and Tax Statement)
6. (a) the amount of his or her wages; (b) the number of his or her withholding allowances
7. 941; calendar quarter
8. Payroll Register
9. Employee's Individual Earnings Record

Problem V

Jan. __	Warranty Expense ($50,000 × 0.03)	1,500.00	
	Estimated Warranty Liability		1,500.00
__	Estimated Warranty Liability	1,200.00	
	Cash		1,200.00

Problem VI

Nov. 15	Office Salaries Expense..	3,340.00	
	FICA Taxes Payable...		199.71
	Employees' Federal Income Taxes Payable......................		610.00
	Employees' Hospital Insurance Payable		155.00
	Accrued Payroll Payable		2,375.29

$($800 + $800 + $100 + $740) \times .062 = 151.28
$$3,340 \times .0145 = $48.43$$
$$151.28 + $48.43 = $199.71$$

15	Payroll Taxes Expense	222.11	
	FICA Taxes Payable...		199.71
	State Unemployment Taxes Payable		16.00
	Federal Unemployment Taxes Payable		6.40

$$800 \times 0.02 = $16$$
$$800 \times 0.008 = $6.40$$

Problem VII (Appendix 9A)

1.

EMPLOYEE'S NAME	CLOCK CARD NUMBER	DAILY TIME M	T	W	T	F	S	S	TOTAL HOURS	O.T. HOURS	REG. PAY RATE		REGULAR PAY		O.T. PREMIUM PAY		GROSS PAY		
Delbert Landau	12	8	8	8	7	4	0	0	35		11	00	385	00			385	00	1
Maria Garza	9	8	8	8	5	4	0	0	35		12	00	396	00			396	00	2
Ralph Webster	15	8	8	7	8	4	0	0	35		13	00	455	00			455	00	3
Fred Clarke	4	8	8	8	8	8	4	0	44	4	14	00	560	00	84	00	644	00	4
													1,796	00	84	00	1,880	00	5

Week ending January 8, 20--

	FICA TAXES		FEDERAL INCOME TAXES		HOSPITAL INSURANCE		UNION DUES		TOTAL DEDUC-TIONS		NET PAY		CHECK NUMBER	SALES SALARIES		OFFICE SALARIES		DELIVERY WAGES	
1	30	80	65	00	20	00	10	00	125	80	259	20	102					385	00
2	31	68	63	00	20	00	10	00	124	68	271	32	103	396	00				
3	36	40	68	00	20	00	10	00	134	40	320	60	104	455	00				
4	51	52	111	00	20	00			182	52	461	48	105			644	00		
5	150	40	307	00	80	00	30	00	567	40	1,312	60		851	00	644	00	385	00

2. Jan. 8 Sales Salaries Expense 851.00
            Office Salaries Expense 644.00
            Delivery Wages Expense 385.00
                FICA Taxes Payable.. 150.40
                Employees' Federal Income Taxes Payable...................... 307.00
                Employees' Medical Insurance Payable.......................... 80.00
                Employees' Union Dues Payable 30.00
                Accrued Payroll Payable 1,312.60

3. Jan. 8 Accrued Payroll Payable 1,312.60
                Cash.. 1,312.60

4. Jan. 8 Payroll Taxes Expense 184.24
                FICA Taxes Payable.. 150.40
                State Unemployment Taxes Payable 18.80
                Federal Unemployment Taxes Payable 15.04

CHAPTER 10
ACCOUNTING FOR
LONG-TERM LIABILITIES

Learning Objective C1:

Explain the types and payment patterns of notes.

Notes repaid over a period of time are called *installment notes* and usually follow one of two payment patterns: (1) decreasing payments of interest plus equal amounts of principal or (2) equal total payments. Mortgage notes also are common.

Learning Objective C2 (Appendix 10A):

Explain and compute the present value of an amount(s) to be paid at a future date(s).

The basic concept of present value is that an amount of cash to be paid or received in the future is worth less than the same amount of cash to be paid or received today. Another important present value concept is that interest is compounded, meaning interest is added to the balance and used to determine interest for succeeding periods. An annuity is a series of equal payments occurring at equal time intervals. An annuity's present value can be computed using the present value table for an annuity (or a calculator).

Learning Objective C3 (Appendix 10C):

Describe the accrual of bond interest when bond payments do not align with accounting periods.

Issuers and buyers of debt record the interest accrued when issue dates or accounting periods do not coincide with debt payment dates.

Learning Objective C4 (Appendix 10D):

Describe the accounting for leases and pensions.

A lease is a rental agreement between the lessor and the lessee. When the lessor retains the risks and rewards of asset ownership (an *operating lease*), the lessee debits Rent Expense and credits Cash for its lease payments. When the lessor substantially transfers the risks and rewards of asset ownership to the lessee (a *capital lease*), the lessee capitalizes the leased asset and records a lease liability. Pension agreements can result in either pension assets or pension liabilities.

Learning Objective A1:

Compare bond financing with stock financing.

Bond financing is used to fund business activities. Advantages of bond financing versus stock include (1) no effect on owner control, (2) tax savings, and (3) increased earnings due to financial leverage. Disadvantages include (1) interest and principal payments and (2) amplification of poor performance.

Learning Objective A2:

Assess debt features and their implications.

Certain bonds are secured by the issuer's assets; other bonds, called *debentures,* are unsecured. Serial bonds mature at different points in time; term bonds mature at one time. Registered bonds have each bondholder's name recorded by the issuer; bearer bonds are payable to the holder. Convertible bonds are exchangeable for shares of the issuer's stock. Callable bonds can be retired by the issuer at a set price. Debt features alter the risk of loss for creditors.

Learning Objective A3:

Compute the debt-to-equity ratio and explain its use.

Both creditors and equity holders are concerned about the relation between the amount of liabilities and the amount of equity. A company's financing structure is at less risk when the debt-to-equity ratio is lower, as liabilities must be paid and usually with periodic interest.

Learning Objective P1:

Prepare entries to record bond issuance and bond interest expense.

When bonds are issued at par, Cash is debited and Bonds Payable is credited for the bonds' par value. At bond interest payment dates (usually semiannual), Bond Interest Expense is debited and Cash credited; the latter for an amount equal to the bond par value multiplied by the bond contract rate.

Learning Objective P2:

Compute and record amortization of bond discount.

Bonds are issued at a discount when the contract rate is less than the market rate, making the issue (selling) price less than par. When this occurs, the issuer records a credit to Bonds Payable (at par) and debits both Discount on Bonds Payable and Cash. The amount of bond interest expense assigned to each period is computed using either the straight-line or effective interest method.

Learning Objective P3:

Compute and record amortization of bond premium.

Bonds are issued at a premium when the contract rate is higher than the market rate, making the issue (selling) price greater than par. When this occurs, the issuer records a debit to Cash and credits both Premium on Bonds Payable and Bonds Payable (at par). The amount of bond interest expense assigned to each period is computed using either the straight-line or effective interest method. The Premium on Bonds Payable is allocated to reduce bond interest expense over the life of the bonds.

Learning Objective P4:

Record the retirement of bonds.

Bonds are retired at maturity with a debit to Bonds Payable and a credit to Cash at par value. The issuer can retire the bonds early by exercising a call option or purchasing them in the market. Bondholders can also retire bonds early by exercising a conversion feature on convertible bonds. The issuer recognizes a gain or loss for the difference between the amount paid and the bond carrying value.

Learning Objective P5:

Prepare entries to account for notes.

Interest is allocated to each period in a note's life by multiplying its beginning-period carrying value by its market rate at issuance. If a note is repaid with equal payments, the payment amount is computed by dividing the borrowed amount by the present value of an annuity factor (taken from a present value table) using the market rate and the number of payments.

I.   **Basics of Bonds**

Projects that demand large amounts of money often are funded from bond issuances.

A. Bond Financing

1. A **bond** is its issuer's written promise to pay an amount identified as the par value of the bond with interest.

    a. Most bonds require the issuer to make periodic interest payments.

    b. The **par value of a bond**, also called the *face amount* or *face value*, is paid at a specified future date known as the *maturity date*.

2. Advantages of bonds

    a. *Bonds do not affect owner control.*

    b. *Interest on bonds is tax deductible.*

    c. *Bonds can increase return on equity.* A company that earns a higher return with borrowed funds than it pays in interest on those funds increases its return on equity. This process is called *financial leverage* or *trading on the equity.*

3. Disadvantages of bonds

    a. *Bonds can decrease return on equity.* A company that earns a lower return with borrowed funds than it pays in interest on those funds decreases its return on equity.

    b. *Bonds require payment of both periodic interest and par value at maturity.* Equity financing, by contrast, does not require any payments because cash withdrawals (dividends) are paid at the discretion of the owner (board).

B. Bond Trading

1. Bonds can be traded on exchanges including both the New York Stock Exchange and the American Stock Exchange.

2. A bond *issue* consists of a large number of bonds (denominations of $1,000 or $5,000, etc.) that are sold to many different lenders.

3. Market value (price) is expressed as a percentage of par (face) value. Examples: bonds issued at 103 ½ means that they are sold for 103.5% of their par value. Bonds issued at 95 means that they are sold for 95% of their par value.

C. Bond-Issuing Procedures

Governed by state and federal laws. Bond issuers also insure they do not violate any existing contractual agreements.

1. **Bond indenture** is the contract between the bond issuer and the bondholders; it identifies the obligations and rights of each party. A bondholder may also receive a **bond certificate** that includes specifics such as the issuer's name, the par value, the contract interest rate, and the maturity date.

2. Issuing corporation normally sells its bonds to an investment firm (the *underwriter*), which resells the bonds to the public.

3. A *trustee* (usually a bank or trust company) monitors the issuer to ensure it complies with the obligations in the indenture.

II. Bond Issuances

A. Issuing Bonds at Par—bonds are sold for face amount. Entries are:

1. Issue date: debit Cash, credit Bonds Payable (face amount).

2. Interest date: debit Interest Expense, credit Cash (face times bond interest rate times interest period).

3. Maturity date: debit Bonds Payable, credit Cash (face amount).

B. Bond Discount or Premium—bonds are sold for an amount different than the face amount.

1. **Contract rate**—(also called *coupon rate, stated rate,* or *nominal rate*) annual interest rate *paid* by the issuer of bonds (applied to par value).

2. **Market rate**—annual rate borrowers are willing to pay and lenders are willing to accept for a particular bond and its risk level.

3. When contract rate and market rate are equal, bonds sell at par value; when contract rate is above market rate, bonds sell at a *premium* (above par); when the contract rate is below market rate, bonds sell at a *discount* (below par).

C. Issuing Bonds at a Discount—sell bonds for *less* than par value.

1. The **discount on bonds payable** is the difference between the par (face) value of a bond and its lower issuance price.

2. Entry to record issuance at a discount: debit Cash (issue price), debit Discount on Bonds Payable (amount of discount), credit Bonds Payable (par value).

3. Discount on Bonds Payable is a contra liability account; it is *deducted* from par value to yield the **carrying (book) value** of the bonds payable.

4. Amortizing a Bond Discount

a. Total bond interest expense is the *sum* of the interest payments and bond discount (or can be computed by comparing total amount borrowed to total amount repaid over life).

b. Discount must be systematically reduced (*amortized*) over the life of the bond to report periodic interest expense incurred.

c. Requires crediting Discount on Bonds Payable when bond interest expense is recorded (payment and/or accruals) and increasing Interest Expense by the amortized amount.

d. Amortizing the discount increases book value; at maturity, the unamortized discount equals zero and the carrying value equals par value.

5. Straight-line method—allocates an equal portion of the total discount to bond interest expense in each of the six-month interest periods.

D. Issuing Bonds at a Premium—sell bonds for *more* than par value.

1. The **premium on bonds payable** is the difference between the par value of a bond and its higher issuance price.

2. Entry to record issuance at a premium: debit Cash (issue price), credit Premium on Bonds Payable (amount of premium), credit Bonds Payable (par value).

3. Premium on Bonds Payable is an adjunct liability account; it is added to par value to yield the carrying (or book) value of the bonds payable.

4. Amortizing a Bond Premium

   a. Total bond interest expense incurred is the interest payments *less* the bond premium.

   b. Premiums must be systematically reduced (*amortized*) over the life of the bond to report periodic interest expense incurred.

   c. Requires debiting Premium on Bonds Payable when bond interest expense is recorded (payment and/or accruals) and decreasing Interest Expense by the amortized amount.

   d. Amortizing the premium decreases book value; at maturity, book value = face value.

5. Straight-line method allocates an equal portion of the total premium to bond interest expense in each of the six-month interest periods.

E. Bond Pricing

The price of a bond is the present value of the bond's future cash flows discounted at the current market rate. Present value tables can be used to compute price, which is the *combination of* the:

1. Present Value of a Discount Bond. Present value of the maturity payment is found by using single payment table, the market rate, and number of periods until maturity.

2. Present Value of a Premium Bond. Present value of the semiannual interest payments is found by using annuity table, the market rate, and number of periods until maturity.

3. Present values found in present value tables in Appendix B at the end of this book.

III. **Bond Retirement**

A. Bond Retirement at Maturity

1. Carrying value at maturity will always equal par value.

2. Entry to record bond retirement at maturity: debit Bonds Payable, credit Cash.

    B. Bond Retirement Before Maturity

        1. Two common approaches to retire bonds before maturity:

            a. Exercise a call option—pay par value plus a call premium.

            b. Purchase them on the open market.

        2. Difference between the purchase price and the bonds' carrying value is recorded as a gain (or loss) on retirement of bonds.

    C. Bond Retirement by Conversion
Convertible bondholders have the right to convert their bonds to stock. If converted, the carrying value of bonds is transferred to equity accounts and no gain or loss is recorded.

IV.   Long-Term Notes Payable

Notes are issued to obtain assets, such as cash. Notes are typically transacted with a single lender, such as a bank.

    A. Installment Notes—obligations requiring a series of periodic payments to the lender.

        1. Entry to record issuance of an installment note for cash: debit Cash, credit to Notes Payable.

        2. Payments include interest expense accruing to the date of the payment plus a portion of the amount borrowed (*principal*).

            a. Equal total payments consist of changing amounts of interest and principal.

            b. Entry to record installment payment: debit Interest Expense (issue rate times the declining carrying value of note), debit Notes Payable (for difference between the equal payment and the interest expense), credit Cash for the amount of the equal payment.

    B. Mortgage Notes and Bonds
A **mortgage** is a legal agreement that helps protect a lender if a borrower fails to make required payments. A *mortgage contract* describes the mortgage terms.

        1. Accounting for mortgage notes and bonds—same as accounting for unsecured notes and bonds.

        2. Mortgage agreements must be disclosed in financial statements.

V.   Decision Analysis—Debt Features and the Debt-to-Equity Ratio

Collateral Agreements—reduce the risk of loss for both bonds and notes; unsecured bonds and notes are riskier because the issuer's obligation to pay interest and principal has the same priority as all other unsecured liabilities in the event of bankruptcy.

    A. Features of Bonds and Notes

        1. Secured or Unsecured

            a. **Secured bonds** and notes have specific assets of the issuer pledged (or *mortgaged*) as collateral.

          b. Unsecured bonds and notes also called *debentures*, are backed by the issuer's general credit standing. Unsecured debt is riskier than secured debt.

    2. Term or Serial

          a. **Term bonds** and notes are scheduled for maturity on one specified date.

          b. **Serial bonds** and notes mature at more than one date (often in series) and are usually repaid over a number of periods.

    3. Registered or Bearer

          a. **Registered bonds** are issued in the names and addresses of their holders. Bond payments are sent directly to registered holders.

          b. **Bearer bonds**, also called *unregistered* bonds, are made payable to whoever holds them (the bearer). Many bearer bonds are also **coupon bonds**; which are interest coupons that are attached to the bonds.

    4. Convertible and/or Callable

          a. **Convertible bonds** and notes can be exchanged for a fixed number of shares of the issuing company's common stock.

          b. **Callable bonds** and notes have an option exercisable by the issuer to retire them at a stated dollar amount before maturity.

B. Debt-to-Equity Ratio

    1. Knowing the level of debt helps in assessing the risk of a company's financing structure.

    2. A company financed mainly with debt is riskier than a company financed mainly with equity because liabilities must be repaid.

    3. Debt-to-equity ratio measures the risk of a company's financing structure.

    4. Debt-to-equity ratio is computed by dividing total liabilities by total equity.

VI. **Present Values of Bonds and Notes (Appendix 10A)**

A. Present Value Concepts

    1. Cash paid (or received) in the future has less value now than the same amount of cash paid (or received) today.

    2. An amount borrowed equals the present value of the future payment.

    3. *Compounded interest* means that interest during a second period is based on the total of the amount borrowed plus the interest accrued from the first period.

    4. Present Value tables can be used to determine the present value of future cash payments of a single amount or an annuity.

B. Present Value Tables (Complete tables in Appendix B)

1. Present values can be computed using a formula or a table.

2. Present value of $1 table is used to compute present value of a single payment.

3. Present value of an annuity of $1 table is used to compute present value of a series of equal payments (annuity).

C. Applying a Present Value Table (Complete tables in Appendix B)

1. Determine the column with the interest rate.

2. Determine the row with the periods hence.

3. The column and row will intersect at the factor number.

4. To convert the single payment to its present value, multiply this amount by the factor.

D. Present Value of an Annuity (Complete tables in Appendix B)

1. Determine the column with the interest rate.

2. Determine the row with the number of periods.

3. The column and row will intersect at the factor number.

4. To convert the annuity to its present value, multiply the annuity amount by the factor.

E. Compounding Periods Shorter than a Year

1. Interest rates are generally stated as annual rates.

2. They can be allocated to shorter periods of time.

VII. **Effective Interest Amortization (Appendix 10B)**

A. Effective Interest Amortization of a Discount Bond

1. The straight-line method yields changes in the bonds' carrying value while the amount for bond interest expense remains constant.

2. The **effective interest method** allocates total bond interest expense over the bonds' life in a way that yields a constant rate of interest.

3. The key difference between the two methods lies in computing bond interest expense. Instead of assigning an equal amount of bond interest expense in each period, the effective interest method assigns a bond interest expense amount that increases over the life of a discount bond.

4. Both methods allocate the same amount of bond interest expense to the bonds' life, but in different patterns.

5. Except for differences in amounts, journal entries recording the expense and updating the Discount on Bonds Payable account balance are the same under both methods.

B. Effective Interest Amortization of a Premium Bond

1. As noted above, the **effective interest method** allocates total bond interest expense over the bonds' life in a way that yields a constant rate of interest.

2. Except for differences in amounts between the two methods (that is, the straight-line and effective interest methods), journal entries recording the expense and updating the Premium on Bonds Payable account are the same under both methods.

VIII. **Issuing Bonds Between Interest Dates (Appendix 10C)**

A. Procedure used to simplify recordkeeping:

1. Buyers pay the purchase price plus any interest accrued since the prior interest payment date.

2. This accrued interest is repaid to these buyers on the next interest date.

3. Entry to record issuance of bonds between interest dates: debit Cash, credit Interest Payable (for any interest accrued since the prior interest payment date), credit Bonds Payable.

4. Entry to record first semiannual interest payment for bonds issued between interest dates: debit Interest Payable (for amount accrued in entry above), debit Interest Expense (for interest accrued since issuance date), credit Cash.

B. Accruing Bond Interest Expense

1. Necessary when bond's interest period does not coincide with issuer's accounting period.

2. Adjusting entry is necessary to record bond interest expense accrued since the most recent interest payment and requires amortization of the premium or discount for this period.

3. Affects the subsequent interest payment date entry.

VIV. **Leases and Pensions (Appendix 10D)**

A. Lease Liabilities

A **lease** is a contractual agreement between a *lessor* (asset owner) and a *lessee* (asset renter or tenant) that grants the lessee the right to use the asset for a period of time in return for cash (rent) payments.

1. **Operating leases** are short-term (or cancelable) leases in which the lessor retains the risks and rewards of ownership.

a. Lessee records lease payments as expenses.

b. Lessor records lease payments as revenues.

2. **Capital leases** are long-term (or noncancelable) leases in which the lessor transfers substantially all risks and rewards of ownership to the lessee. The lease must meet *any one of the four* following criteria:

a. Transfer title of leased asset to lessee.

b. Contain a bargain purchase option.

c. Have lease term of 75% or more of leased asset's useful life.

       d. Have present value of leased payments of 90% or more of leased asset's market value.

         Capital leases are recorded as assets and liabilities. The asset is depreciated. At each lease payment date, the liability is amortized to record interest expense incurred.

  B. Pension Liabilities

    A pension plan is a contractual agreement between an employer and its employees for the employer to provided benefits (payments) to employees after they have retired.

    1. Employer records their payment into pension plan as a debit to Pension Expense and a credit to Cash.

    2. Based on contracted benefits, pension plans can be overfunded (resulting in plan assets) or underfunded (resulting in plan liabilities).

Chapter Ten – Alternate Demonstration Problem #1
(Appendix 10B)

ABC Company issued $200,000 face value bonds on January 1, 2009, with semiannual interest payments to be made on June 30 and December 31 at a contract rate of 10%. The bonds were scheduled to mature five years after they were issued. ABC Company uses the effective interest method of amortization.

On January 1, 2012, three years after the bonds were issued, the company repurchased 40% of the outstanding bonds for $79,000.

Required:

Part A

1. Assume that the bonds were issued when the market rate of interest was 9%. Prepare a schedule showing the bond interest expense and amounts of amortization for the life of the bonds.

2. Prepare the journal entry to record the bond issuance.

3. Prepare journal entries for the first two interest payments.

4. Prepare the journal entry to recognize the partial repurchase of the bonds.

Part B

Redo Part A under the assumption that the market rate on the bonds when issued was 16%.

(If this alternative demonstration problem is not covered in class, see your instructor for the solution.)

Problem I

The following statements are either true or false. Place a (T) in the parentheses before each true statement and an (F) before each false statement.

1. ( ) Interest expense on installment notes is calculated each period as the interest rate multiplied by the beginning-of-period principal balance.

2. ( ) Bondholders do not share in either management or earnings of the issuing corporation.

3. ( ) Bondholders are creditors of the issuing corporation.

4. ( ) If bonds are sold at par value, the entry to record the sale has a debit to Cash and a credit to Bonds Payable.

5. ( ) Investors will be willing to pay more than par (buy at a premium) for bonds when the market rate of interest is higher than the contract rate of interest.

6. ( ) To determine the price of bonds, the present value of the future cash flows is calculated by discounting the amounts to be received in the future at the contract rate of interest.

7. ( ) If the market rate of interest is 12%, it is 4% semiannually.

8. ( ) The straight-line method of amortizing bond premium allocates an equal portion of the premium to each interest period.

9. ( ) When the straight-line method is used to amortize bond premium or bond discount, interest expense as a percentage of carrying amount is the same each period the bonds are outstanding.

10. ( ) Callable bonds are bonds that can be redeemed at the option of the investor.

11. ( ) The debt-to-equity ratio is computed by dividing total liabilities by total equity.

12. ( ) The carrying amount of a payable decreases each year by the amount of discount amortized that year.

13. ( ) The process of allocating the interest on a noninterest-bearing note payable is called amortizing the discount.

14. ( ) (Appendix 10A) The concept of present value is based on the idea that the right to receive $1 a year from now is worth more than $1 today.

15. ( ) (Appendix 10A) Receiving $500 on June 30 and $500 on December 31 has the same present value as receiving $1,000 on December 31.

16. ( ) (Appendix 10A) If a note requires quarterly payments and the borrower could obtain a 12% annual rate of interest in borrowing money, a 3% quarterly interest rate should be used to determine the present value of the note.

17. ( ) (Appendix 10B) To calculate the amount of interest expense each period using the effective interest method, the beginning of-period carrying amount of the bonds must be multiplied by the market rate of interest at the time the bonds were issued.

18. ( ) (Appendix 10D) In a capital lease the lessor retains substantially all the risks and rewards of ownership.

19. ( ) (Appendix 10D) Based on contracted benefits, an overfunded pension plan will result in plan assets.

20. ( ) (Appendix 10D) Operating leases are generally short-term and cancelable.

Problem II

You are given several words, phrases, or numbers to choose from in completing each of the following statements or in answering the following questions. In each case select the one that best completes the statement or answers the question and place its letter in the answer space provided.

_____ 1. On December 31, the interest payment date, the carrying value of Taylor Company's issued bonds is $106,000. The bonds have a par value of $100,000. On January 1, Taylor buys and retires the outstanding bonds. The market price on this date is 103.5. The entry to retire the bonds includes a:

    a. $6,000 credit to Premium on Bonds Payable.

    b. $3,500 debit to Loss on Retirement of Bonds.

    c. $3,500 credit to Gain on Retirement of Bonds.

    d. $2,500 credit to Gain on Retirement of Bonds.

    e. $100,000 credit to Cash.

_____ 2. Commonly used payment patterns on installment notes include:

    a. Installment payments consisting of equal amounts of interest and equal amounts of principal.

    b. Installment payments of accrued interest plus equal amounts of principal.

    c. Installment payments that are equal in total amount and consist of changing amounts of interest and principal.

    d. A and C

    e. B and C

_____ 3. Unsecured bonds that are supported by only the general credit standing of the issuer are called:

    a. Callable bonds

    b. Sinking fund bonds

    c. Serial bonds

    d. Coupon bonds

    e. Debentures

_____ 4. (Appendix 10A) Indigo, Inc., is offered a contract whereby it will be paid $15,000 every six months for the next five years. The first payment will be received six months from today. What will the company be willing to pay for this contract if it expects a 16% annual return on the investment? [Use the appropriate present value table in the Appendix B.]

    a. $ 10,209.00

    b. $ 6,948.00

    c. $100,651.50

    d. $ 59,890.50

    e. Cannot be determined from information provided.

_____ 5. (Appendix 10A) On June 30, 20X9, the DEF Corporation sold bonds with a face value of $100,000. The contract rate of bond interest was 9% with interest payments on December 31 and June 30. The bonds mature in 10 years. When the bonds were sold, the market rate of bond interest was 12%. How much money did the DEF Corporation receive when it sold the bonds? (Use the present value tables in Appendix B and round amounts to the nearest whole dollar.)

   a. $119,252

   b. $110,042

   c. $100,000

   d. $ 82,795

   e. $ 83,052

_____ 6. (Appendix 10B) How is the interest expense for each period calculated when the effective interest method is used to amortize bond discount?

   a. The par value of the bonds is multiplied by the contract rate of bond interest.

   b. The par value of the bonds is multiplied by the market rate of bond interest which applied to the bonds at the time the bonds were issued.

   c. The beginning balance of the bond liability is multiplied by the market rate of bond interest which applied to the bonds at the time the bonds were issued.

   d. The beginning balance of the bond liability is multiplied by the contract rate of bond interest.

   e. The total amount of discount at the time of issue is divided by the number of periods to maturity and added to the cash payment of interest.

_____ 7. (Appendix 10B) On June 30, 20×9, the DEF Corporation sold bonds with a face value of $100,000. The contract rate of bond interest was 9% with interest payments on December 31 and June 30. The bonds mature in 10 years. When the bonds were sold, the market rate of bond interest was 12% and they were issued for $82,795. What is the entry to record the payment of interest on December 31, 20×9? DEF uses the effective interest method of amortizing bond discount or premium.

   a. Interest Expense.. 4,500.00
       Cash...   4,500.00
   b. Interest Expense.. 4,968.00
       Cash...   4,500.00
       Discount on Bonds Payable................................   468.00
   c. Interest Expense.. 6,000.00
       Cash...   6,000.00
   d. Interest Expense.. 4,500.00
       Premium on Bonds Payable............................... 1,500.00
       Cash...   6,000.00
   e. Interest Expense.. 4,500.00
       Cash...   4,230.00
       Discount on Bonds Payable................................   270.00

Problem III

Many of the important ideas and concepts discussed in Chapter 10 are reflected in the following list of key terms. Test your understanding of these terms by matching the appropriate definitions with the terms. Record the number identifying the most appropriate definition in the blank space next to each term.

_____ Annuity
_____ Bearer bonds
_____ Bond
_____ Bond certificate
_____ Bond indenture
_____ Callable bonds
_____ Capital leases**
_____ Carrying value of bonds
_____ Contract rate
_____ Convertible bonds
_____ Coupon bonds
_____ Debt-to-equity ratio
_____ Discount on bonds payable
_____ Effective interest method*
_____ Installment note

_____ Lease**
_____ Market rate
_____ Mortgage
_____ Off-balance-sheet financing**
_____ Operating leases**
_____ Par value of a bond
_____ Pension plan**
_____ Premium on bonds payable
_____ Registered bonds
_____ Secured bonds
_____ Serial bonds
_____ Sinking fund bonds
_____ Straight-line method
_____ Term bonds
_____ Unsecured bonds

*   Key term discussed in Appendix 10B.
** Key term discussed in Appendix 10D.

1. Contract between the bond issuer and the bondholders; identifies the parties' rights and obligations.

2. Difference between a bond's par value and its lower issue price or carrying value; occurs when the contract rate is less than the market rate.

3. Interest rate borrowers are willing to pay and lenders are willing to accept for a specific debt agreement at its risk level.

4. Allocates interest expense over the bond life to yield a constant rate of interest; interest expense for a period is found by multiplying the balance of the liability at the beginning of the period by the bond market rate at issuance; also called _interest method_.

5. Bonds that bondholders can exchanged for a set number of the issuer's shares.

6. Bonds made payable to whoever holds them (the _bearer_); also called _unregistered bonds_.

7. Net amount at which bonds are reported on the balance sheet; equals the par value of the bonds less any unamortized discount or plus any unamortized premium; also called _carrying amount_.

8. Legal agreement that protects a lender by giving the lender the right to be paid from the cash proceeds from the sale of the borrower's assets identified in the mortgage.

9. Difference between bond's par value and its higher issue price or carrying value; occurs when the contract rate is higher than the market rate.

10. Bonds that require the issuer to make deposits to a separate account; bondholders are repaid at maturity from that account.

11. Bonds consisting of separate amounts that mature at different dates.

12. Bonds with interest coupons attached to their certificates; bondholders detach coupons when they mature and present them to a bank or broker for collection.

13. Bonds that give the issuer an option to retire them at a stated amount prior to maturity.

14. Interest rate specified in a bond indenture; multiplied by the bonds' par value to determine the interest paid each period; also called *coupon rate*, *stated rate*, or *nominal rate*.

15. Amount the bond issuer agrees to pay at maturity and the amount on which interest payments are based; also called *face amount* or *face value*.

16. Series of equal payments at equal intervals.

17. Measures the risk of a company's financing structure.

18. Method allocating an equal amount of interest expense to each period in the life of bonds.

19. Liability requiring a series of periodic payments to the lender.

20. Bonds owned by investors whose names and addresses are recorded by the issuer; interest payments are made to the registered owners.

21. Written promise to pay the bond's par (or face) value and interest at a stated contract rate; often issued in denominations of $1,000.

22. Bonds backed only by the issuer's credit standing; almost always riskier than secured bonds; also called *debentures*.

23. Bonds scheduled for payment (mature) at a single specified date.

24. Bonds that have specific assets of the issuer pledged as collateral.

25. Document containing bond specifics such as the issuer's name, bond par value, contract interest rate, and maturity date.

26. Contractual agreement between *lessor* and *lessee* that grants a lessee the right to use an asset for a period of time in return for cash payments.

27. Short-term (or cancelable) leases in which lessor retains risks and rewards of ownership.

28. Acquisition of assets by agreeing to liabilities not reported on the balance sheet.

29. Contractual agreement between an employer and its employees to provide benefits to employees after they retire.

30. Long-term leases in which the lessor transfers substantially all risk and rewards of ownership to the lessee.

Problem IV

Complete the following by filling in the blanks.

1. Two important rights given to the owner of a bond are:

   a. _____
      _____, and

   b. _____
      _____.

2. Often a corporation cannot obtain debt financing without providing security to the creditors by the issuance of a _____.

3. The rate of interest a corporation agrees to pay on a bond issue is called the _____ rate. This rate is applied to the _____ value of the bonds to determine the amount of interest that must be paid.

4. If a corporation offers to sell a bond issue when the contract rate of interest is below the market rate, the bonds will sell at a _____ and if it offers to sell bonds when the contract rate is above the market rate, the bonds will sell at a _____.

5. A $1,000 bond with a contract rate of bond interest of 9% would provide semiannual interest payments of $_____.

6. Bonds that may be redeemed at the issuing company's option are known as _____ bonds.

7. (Appendix 10C) When a corporation sells bonds between interest dates, it collects accrued interest from the purchasers. On the interest payment date, the accrued interest is _____ to the purchaser.

8. The accounting procedure for allocating a discount to each period in the life of a bond is called
   _____.

9. The terms of installment notes payable require one of two payment plans:

   a. _____
      _____, or

   b. _____
      _____.

10. When the issuing company retires bonds, it recognizes a gain or loss for the difference between the
    _____ and the retirement price.

11. (Appendix 10D) Capital leases must meet one of the following four criteria:
    a. _____
    b. _____
    c. _____
    d. _____

Problem V

(Appendix 10C) On December 15, 2009, Candida Corporation deposited a bond indenture with the trustee of its bondholders authorizing it to issue $1,000,000 of 10.2%, 20-year bonds dated January 1, 2010, and upon which interest is payable each June 30 and December 31. The bonds were issued at par plus accrued interest on February 1, 2010.

1. Prepare the 2009 journal entries for this bond issue.

DATE	ACCOUNT TITLES AND EXPLANATION	P.R.	DEBIT		CREDIT	
2009 Feb 1						
	Sold $1,000,000 of 10.2%, 20-year bonds at par plus					
	one month's accrued interest.					
June 30						
	Paid the semiannual interest on the bonds.					
Dec. 31						
	Paid the semiannual interest on the bonds.					

2. Post to the T-account below the portions of the above entries that affect bond interest expense and then complete the statement that follows.

Bond Interest Expense

Candida Corporation's 2009 income statement should show $_____ of bond interest expense and its 2010 income statement should show $_____ of bond interest expense.

Problem VI

On January 1, 2009, a day on which the market rate of interest for Bullock Company's bonds was 10%, Bullock Company sold bonds having a $100,000 par value, a five-year life, and on which interest was to be paid semiannually at a 9% annual rate. The bonds were issued for $96,138.

1. The buyer of these bonds received two rights:
   (a) the right to receive $_____ in interest at the end of each six-month interest period throughout the five-year life of the bond issue, and
   (b) the right to receive $_____ at the end of the bond issue's life.

2. Bullock Corporation's journal entry to record the sale of the bonds would be as follows:

DATE	ACCOUNT TITLES AND EXPLANATION	P.R.	DEBIT		CREDIT	
2009 Jan. 1						
	Sold bonds at a discount					

3. At the end of the first semiannual interest period Bullock Corporation calculated the number of dollars of interest to be paid to bondholders as follows:

   $ _____ × _____ % = $ _____

4. (Appendix 10B) Using the effective interest method, the company then calculated the amount of interest expense to be recorded at the end of the first semiannual interest period as follows:

   $ _____ × _____ % = $ _____

5. (Appendix 10B) Next, the company determined the amount of discount to be amortized with this calculation:

   $ _____ − $ _____ = $ _____

6. (Appendix 10B) After making these calculations, Bullock Corporation would record the interest paid its bondholders and the discount amortized with the following journal entry:

DATE	ACCOUNT TITLES AND EXPLANATION	P.R.	DEBIT		CREDIT	
2009 June 30						
	Paid the semiannual interest on the bonds and					
	amortized a portion of the discount					

7. (Appendix 10A) To prove that the issue price equaled the present value of the rights received, the buyer of the bonds should discount the rights at the _____ % (semiannual) market rate for bond interest prevailing on the day of the purchase.

8. (Appendix 10A) The calculations for determining the present value of the bond buyer's two rights, using the tables in Appendix B in the text are:

   Present value of $100,000 to be received _____ periods hence,
   discounted at _____ % per period ($100,000 × _____) $ _____
   Present value of $ _____ to be received periodically
   for _____ periods, discounted at _____ %
   ($ _____ × _____) ....   _____
   Price to pay for the bonds .... $ _____

Problem VII

On December 31, 2009, HX Company borrowed $60,000 by signing a 14% installment note that is to be repaid with six annual payments, the first of which is due on December 31, 2010.

a. Prepare the journal entry to record the borrowing of the money.

DATE	ACCOUNT TITLES AND EXPLANATION	P.R.	DEBIT	CREDIT

b. Assume that the payments are to consist of accrued interest plus equal amounts of principal. Prepare the journal entries to record the first and second installment payments.

DATE	ACCOUNT TITLES AND EXPLANATION	P.R.	DEBIT	CREDIT

c. Contrary to the assumption in (b) above, assume now that the note requires each installment payment to be $15,464. Prepare journal entries to record the first and second installment payments. (Round all amounts to the nearest whole dollar.)

DATE	ACCOUNT TITLES AND EXPLANATION	P.R.	DEBIT	CREDIT

Problem VIII (Appendix 10A)

1. Use the present value tables in the text (Appendix B) to calculate the following present values:
    a. $1 to be received 9 years hence, at 10%. $_____
    b. $2,000 to be received 6 years hence, at 8%. $_____
    c. $1 to be received at the end of each year for 10 years, at 4%. _____
    d. $1,000 to be received at the end of each year for 7 years, at 6%. _____
2. When the rate of interest on an investment is 8% compounded annually, the present value of $1,000 to be received three years hence is the amount of money that must be invested today that together with the 8% compound interest earned on the investment will equal $_____ at end of three years. The amount is $1,000 × _____ = $_____.
3. If the interest rate is changed from 8% to 5%, will the present value of $1 to be received in one year be increased or decreased? _____

Solutions for Chapter 10

Problem I

1. T
2. T
3. T
4. T
5. F
6. F
7. F
8. T
9. F
10. F
11. T
12. F
13. T
14. F
15. F
16. T
17. T
18. F
19. T
20. T

Problem II

1. D
2. E
3. E
4. C
5. D
6. C
7. B

Problem III

16	Annuity	3	Market rate
6	Bearer bonds	8	Mortgage
21	Bond	28	Off-balance-sheet financing**
25	Bond certificate	27	Operating leases**
1	Bond indenture	15	Par value of a bond
13	Callable bonds	29	Pension plan**
30	Capital leases**	17	Pledged assets to secured liabilities
7	Carrying value of bonds	9	Premium on bonds payable
14	Contract rate	20	Registered bonds
5	Convertible bonds	24	Secured bonds
12	Coupon bonds	11	Serial bonds
17	Debt-to-equity ratio	10	Sinking fund bonds
2	Discount on bonds payable	18	Straight-line method
4	Effective interest method*	23	Term bonds
19	Installment note	22	Unsecured bonds
26	Lease**		

* Key term discussed in Appendix 10B.
** Key term discussed in Appendix 10D.

Problem IV

1. a. the right to receive periodic interest payments, and
   b. the right to receive the face amount of the bond when it matures
2. mortgage
3. contract; par
4. discount; premium
5. $45
6. callable
7. refunded
8. amortizing the bond discount
9. a. payments of accrued interest plus equal amounts of principal, or
   b. payments that are equal in total amount, consisting of changing amounts of interest and principal
10. carrying value of the bonds
11. a. Transfer title of leased asset to lessee.
    b. Contain a bargain purchase option.
    c. Have lease term of 75% or more of leased asset's useful life.
    d. Have present value of leased payments of 90% or more of leased asset's market value

Problem V

1. Feb. 1   Cash.. 1,008,500.00

            Bond Interest Payable 8,500.00
            Bonds Payable...   1,000,000.00
            ($1,000,000 × 0.102)/12 = $8,500

    June 30   Bond Interest Payable 8,500.00
              Bond Interest Expense   42,500.00
              Cash...   51,000.00
              ($1,000,000 × 0.102)/2 = $51,000

    Dec. 31   Bond Interest Expense...   51,000.00
              Cash...   51,000.00

2.

	Bond Interest Expense
June 30	42,500.00
Dec. 31	51,000.00

$93,500; $102,000

Problem VI

1. (a) $4,500, (b) $100,000
2. Jan. 1   Cash..   96,138.00

             Discount on Bonds Payable 3,862.00
             Bonds Payable..   100,000.00
3. $100,000 × 0.045 = $4,500
4. $96,138 × 0.05 = $4,807 (rounded to the nearest whole dollar)
5. $4,807 − $4,500 = $307
6. June 30   Bond Interest Expense..   4,807.00

              Discount on Bonds Payable...............................   307.00
              Cash...   4,500.00
7. 5
8. Present value of $100,000 to be received 10 periods hence, discounted at 5%
    per period ($100,000 × 0.6139) $61,390
    Present value of $4,500 to be received periodically for 10 periods, discounted
    at 5% ($4,500 × 7.7217)..   34,748
    Price to pay for the bonds (rounded to the nearest whole dollar) $96,138

Problem VII

a. 2009
    Dec. 31   Cash 60,000.00

              Notes Payable 60,000.00
b. 2010
    Dec. 31   Interest Expense ($60,000 × 0.14)..............................   8,400.00
              Notes Payable 10,000.00
              Cash 18,400.00

```
        2011
        Dec. 31   Interest Expense ($60,000 - $10,000) × 0.14) ............   7,000.00
                  Notes Payable ..............................................................  10,000.00
                        Cash ..................................................................................                   17,000.00
  c.    2010
        Dec. 31   Interest Expense ($60,000 × 0.14) ...........................   8,400.00
                  Notes Payable ..............................................................   7,064.00
                        Cash ..................................................................................                   15,464.00
        2011
        Dec. 31   Interest Expense ($60,000 − $7,064) × 0.14 ..............   7,411.00
                  Notes Payable ..............................................................   8,053.00
                        Cash ..................................................................................                   15,464.00
```

Problem VIII

1.   a. $0.4241
      b. $2,000 × 0.6302 = $1,260.40
      c. $8.1109
      d. $1,000 × 5.5824 = $5,582.40

2. $1,000, $1,000 × 0.7938 = $793.80

3.   increased

CHAPTER 11
ACCOUNTING FOR EQUITY

Learning Objective C1:

Identify characteristics of corporations and their organization.

Corporations are legal entities whose stockholders are not liable for its debts. Stock is easily transferred, and the life of a corporation does not end with the incapacity of a stockholder. A corporation acts through its agents, who are its officers and managers. Corporations are regulated and subject to income taxes.

Learning Objective C2:

Describe the components of stockholders' equity.

Authorized stock is the stock that a corporation's charter authorizes it to sell. Issued stock is the portion of authorized shares sold. Par value stock is a value per share assigned by the charter. No-par value stock is stock *not* assigned a value per share by the charter. Stated value stock is no-par stock to which the directors assign a value per share. Stockholders' equity is made up of (1) contributed capital and (2) retained earnings. Paid-in capital consists of funds raised by stock issuances. Retained earnings consists of cumulative net income (losses) not distributed.

Learning Objective C3:

Explain characteristics of common and preferred stock.

Preferred stock has a priority (or senior status) relative to common stock in one or more areas, usually (1) dividends and (2) assets in case of liquidation. Preferred stock usually does not carry voting rights and can be convertible or callable. Convertibility permits the holder to convert preferred to common. Callability permits the issuer to buy back preferred stock under specified conditions.

Learning Objective C4:

Explain the items reported in retained earnings.

Many companies face statutory and contractual restrictions on retained earnings. Corporations can voluntarily appropriate retained earnings to inform others about their disposition. Prior period adjustments are corrections of errors in prior financial statements.

Learning Objective A1:

Compute earnings per share and describe its use.

A company with a simple capital structure computes basic EPS by dividing net income less any preferred dividends by the weighted-average number of outstanding common shares. A company with a complex capital structure must usually report both basic and diluted EPS.

Learning Objective A2:

Compute price-earnings ratio and describe its use in analysis.

A common stock's price-earnings (PE) ratio is computed by dividing the stock's market value (price) per share by its EPS. A stock's PE is based on expectations that can prove to be better or worse than eventual performance.

Learning Objective A3:

Compute dividend yield and explain its use in analysis.

Dividend yield is the ratio of a stock's annual cash dividends per share to its market value (price) per share. Dividend yield can be compared with the yield of other companies to determine whether the stock is expected to be an income or growth stock.

Learning Objective A4:

Compute book value and explain its use in analysis.

Book value per common share is equity applicable to common shares divided by the number of outstanding common shares. Book value per preferred share is equity applicable to preferred shares divided by the number of outstanding preferred shares.

Learning Objective P1:

Record the issuance of corporate stock.

When stock is issued, its par or stated value is credited to the stock account and any excess is credited to a separate contributed capital account. If a stock has neither par nor stated value, the entire proceeds are credited to the stock account. Stockholders must contribute assets equal to minimum legal capital or be potentially liable for the deficiency.

Learning Objective P2:

Record transactions involving cash dividends.

Preferred stockholders usually hold the right to dividend distributions before common stockholders. When preferred stock is cumulative and in arrears, the amount in arrears must be distributed to preferred before any dividends are distributed to common.

Learning Objective P3:

Account for stock dividends and stock splits.

Neither a stock dividend nor a stock split alters the value of the company. However, the value of each share is less due to the distribution of additional shares. The distribution of additional shares is according to individual stockholders' ownership percent. Small stock dividends (<=25%) are recorded by capitalizing retained earnings equal to the market value of distributed shares. Large stock dividends (>25%) are recorded by capitalizing retained earnings equal to the par or stated value of distributed shares. Stock splits do not yield journal entries but do yield changes in the description of stock.

Learning Objective P4:

Distribute dividends between common stock and preferred stock.

Cash dividends involve three events. On the date of declaration, the directors bind the company to pay the dividend. A dividend declaration reduces retained earnings and creates a current liability. On the date of record, recipients of the dividend are identified. On the date of payment, cash is paid to stockholders and the current liability is removed.

Learning Objective P5:

Record purchases and sales of treasury stock and the retirement of stock.

When a corporation purchases its own previously issued stock, it debits the cost of these shares to Treasury Stock. Treasury stock is subtracted from equity in the balance sheet. If treasury stock is reissued, any proceeds in excess of cost are credited to Paid-in Capital, Treasury Stock. If the proceeds are less than cost, they are debited to Paid-in Capital, Treasury Stock to the extent a credit balance exists. Any remaining amount is debited to Retained Earnings. When stock is retired, all accounts related to the stock are removed.

Chapter Outline

Notes

I. **Corporate Form of Organization**—An entity created by law that is separate from its owners. Owners are called *stockholders*. A *publicly held* corporation offers its stock for public sale (organized stock market) whereas a *privately held* corporation does not.

  A. Characteristics of **Corporations**

    Advantages of Corporate Characteristics:

    1. **Separate legal entity**—a corporation, through its agents (officers and managers), conducts business affairs with the same rights, duties, and responsibilities of a person.

    2. **Limited liability of stockholders**—generally limited to investment. Stockholders are not liable for corporate acts or corporate debt.

    3. **Transferable ownership rights**—through stock sale has no effect on the corporation.

    4. **Continuous life**—perpetual life as long as it continues to be successful.

    5. **Lack of mutual agency for stockholders**—stockholders do not have the power to bind the corporation to contracts.

    6. **Ease of capital accumulation**—enables a corporation to accumulate large amounts of capital from the combined investments of many stockholders.

    Disadvantages of Corporate Characteristics:

    7. **Governmental regulation**—must meet requirements of a state's incorporation laws.

    8. **Corporate taxation**—corporate income is taxed; and when income is distributed to shareholders as dividends, it is taxed a second time as personal income (*double taxation*).

  B. Corporate Organization and Management

    1. Incorporation—a charter application must be filed with the state. Upon payment of fees and issuance of the charter, the corporation is formed.

    2. **Organizational Expenses** are the costs to organize a corporation and include legal fees, promoters' fees, and amounts paid to obtain a charter; these costs are expensed as incurred because it is difficult to determine the amount and timing of future benefits.

    3. Management of a Corporation

      a. Stockholders have ultimate control through vote to elect board of directors.

      b. Board of directors has final managing authority, but it usually limits its actions to establishing broad policy.

      c. Day-to-day direction of corporate business is delegated to executive officers appointed by the board.

C. Stockholders of Corporations
   1. Rights of stockholders
      Specific rights are granted by the charter and *general* rights by state laws. Common stockholders rights include right to:
      a. Vote at stockholders' meeting.
      b. Sell or otherwise dispose of their stock.
      c. Purchase their proportional share of any common stock later issued; this **preemptive right** protects stockholders' proportionate interest in the corporation.
      d. Share with other common stockholders in any dividends.
      e. Share equally in any assets remaining after creditors and preferred stockholders are paid when, and if the corporation is liquidated.
      f. Receive timely financial reports.
   2. Stock Certificates and Transfer—a stock certificate is sometimes received as proof of share ownership.
   3. Registrar and Transfer Agents—if stock is traded on a major exchange, the corporation must have:
      a. *Registrar* who keeps stockholder records and prepares official lists of stockholders for stockholders' meetings and dividend payments.
      b. *Transfer agent* who assists purchases and sales of shares by receiving and issuing certificates as necessary.

D. Basics of Capital Stock
   Capital stock refers to any shares issued to obtain capital (owner financing).
   1. **Authorized stock**—the total amount of stock that charter authorizes for sale.
      a. *Outstanding stock* refers to issued stock held by stockholders.
      b. No formal journal entry is required for stock authorization; the number of shares authorized is disclosed in the financial statements.
   2. Selling (Issuing) Stock—can be sold directly or indirectly to stockholders
      a. To sell *directly*, the corporation advertises its stock issuance to potential buyers.
      b. To sell *indirectly*, a corporation pays a brokerage house (investment banker) to issue its stock.
      c. A brokerage house may *underwrite* issuance (buy the stock from the corporation and take all gains or losses from its resale).

3. Market Value of Stock—**market value per share** is the price at which a stock is bought or sold.

   a. Influenced by expected future earnings, dividends, growth, and other company and economic events.

   b. Current market value of previously issued shares does not impact that corporation's stockholders' equity accounts.

4. Classes of Stock

   a. Common—stock is called **common stock** when all classes have the same rights and privileges.

   b. Additional classes—corporation is sometimes authorized to issue more than one class of stock.

5. **Par Value Stock**—assigned a value per share by the corporation in its charter. No minimum legal capital.

   a. Printed on the stock certificate.

   b. Establishes the **minimum legal capital** which is the least amount that the buyers of stock must contribute to the corporation or be subject to paying at a future date. Creditor's claims are limited to the corporation's assets and any minimum legal capital.

6. **No-Par Value Stock**—*not* assigned a value per share by the corporate charter.

7. **Stated Value Stock**—no-par stock that is assigned a "stated" value per share by the directors; becomes the minimum legal capital per share.

8. Stockholders' Equity—has two parts

   a. **Paid-in** (or contributed) **capital**—the total amount of cash and other assets received by the corporation from its stockholders in exchange for stock.

   b. **Retained earnings**—the cumulative net income (and loss) retained by a corporation.

II. **Common Stock**—Issuance of stock affects only paid-in capital accounts, not retained earnings accounts.

Note: When the corporation issues par value stock, it can only credit the stock account for the par value of shares issued.

A. Issuing Par Value Stock

   1. Issuing Par Value Stock at Par—debit Cash, credit Common Stock (both for the amount received which is the total *par value* of the shares issued).

  2. Issuing Par Value Stock at a Premium

    a. A **premium on stock** is an amount paid in excess of par by the purchasers of newly issued stock.

    b. Entry to record issuance of par value stock at a premium: debit Cash (for amount received or issue price), credit Common Stock (for par value), credit Paid-in capital in Excess of Par Value, Common Stock (for the amount of the premium).

  3. Issuing Par Value Stock at a Discount

    a. A **discount on stock** occurs when stock corporation sells its stock for less than its par (or stated) value.

    b. Entry to record issuance of par value stock at a discount: debit Cash (for amount received or issue price), debit Discount on Common Stock, a contra to the common stock account (for the amount of the discount), credit Common Stock (for par value).

    c. Issuance of par value stock at a discount is prohibited in most states since investment is below the minimum legal capital. When allowed, the purchasers usually become contingently liable to the corporation's creditors for the amount of the discount.

 B. Issuing No-Par Value Stock

  1. When no-par stock is issued and is not assigned a stated value, the entire amount received becomes legal capital and is recorded as Common Stock.

  2. Entry to record issuance of no-par value stock: debit Cash, credit Common Stock (for the entire proceeds).

 C. Issuing Stated Value Stock

  1. Stated value becomes legal capital and is credited to a stated value stock account. If stock is issued at an amount in excess of stated value, this excess is credited to Paid-in Capital in Excess of Stated Value, Common Stock.

  2. Entry to record issuance of no-par value stock: debit Cash, credit Common Stock, credit Contributed Capital in Excess of Stated Value, Common Stock (for the excess).

    D. Issuing Stock for Noncash Assets

        1. Issuing par value stock for other assets
Entry to record: debit the accounts relating to the asset(s) received (at market value(s) as of the date of the transaction), credit Common Stock, credit Paid-in Capital in Excess of Par Value, Common Stock (for the amount of the premium, if any).

        2. Issuing par value stock for organizational expenses
Entry to record: debit Organization Expenses, credit Common Stock , credit Paid-in Capital in Excess of Par Value, Common Stock (for the amount of the premium, if any).

III.   **Dividends**

    A. Cash Dividends
Many corporations pay cash dividends to their stockholders at regular dates. Cash dividends reduce, in equal amounts, both cash and the retained earnings component of stockholders' equity.

        1. Accounting for Cash Dividends
Generally a cash dividend requires:

            a. Retained earnings (requirement of many states).

            b. Sufficient cash.

            c. Decision by the board of directors.

        2. Dividend dates

            a. **Date of Declaration**—date the directors vote to declare and pay a dividend (legal liability created). Journal entry required.

            b. **Date of Record**—date specified for identifying stockholders (owners on this date) who will receive the dividend. No journal entry required.

            c. **Date of Payment**—date stockholders receive payment. Journal entry required.

        3. Cash Dividend Entries

            a. Entry at declaration date: debit Retained Earnings, credit Dividends Payable.

            b. Entry at distribution date: debit Dividends Payable, credit Cash

        4. Deficits and Cash Dividends
A corporation with a debit (abnormal) balance in its Retained Earnings account has a **retained earnings deficit**.

            a. Arises when cumulative losses and/or dividends are greater than total earnings from current and prior years; reported as a deduction on the balance sheet.

b. Most states prohibit a corporation with a deficit from paying cash dividends.

c. Some states allow a **liquidating cash dividend** where capital contributed by stockholders is returned to the investors.

B. Stock Dividends

A **stock dividend** is a distribution of additional shares of the corporation's own stock to its stockholders without receipt of any payment in return.

1. Reasons for Stock Dividends

    a. Keep the market price of stock affordable.

    b. Provide evidence of management's confidence that the company is doing well.

2. Accounting for Stock Dividends—A stock dividend affects the components of equity by transferring part of retained earnings to contributed capital accounts.

    a. A **small stock dividend** is a distribution of 25% or less of the previously outstanding shares.

        i. The market value of the shares to be distributed is capitalized.

        ii. Entry to record a small stock dividend upon declaration: debit Retained Earnings (for the current market value of the stock to be distributed), credit Common Stock Dividend Distributable (for the par value of the stock to be distributed), credit Paid-in Capital in Excess of Par Value, Common Stock (for the excess).

        iii. Entry to record a small stock dividend at date of payment: debit Common Stock Dividend Distributable, credit Common Stock.

    b. A **large stock dividend** is a distribution of more than 25% of the shares outstanding before the dividend.

        i. Only the legally required minimum amount (par or stated value of shares) must be capitalized.

        ii. Entry to record a large stock dividend upon declaration: debit Retained Earnings, credit Common Stock Dividend Distributable (for the par value of the stock to be distributed).

        iii. Entry to record a large stock dividend at date of payment: debit Common Stock Dividend Distributable, credit Common Stock.

    C. Stock Splits

A **stock split** is the distribution of additional shares of stock to stockholders according to their percent ownership. The corporation "calls in" the outstanding shares of stock and issues more than one share in exchange for each old share. A stock split reduces the par or stated value per share.

      1. No journal entry is made - only a memorandum entry is required.

      2. Total par value of outstanding shares does not change; retained earnings is not capitalized.

IV. **Preferred Stock**—Has special rights that give it priority over common stock in one or more areas such as preference for receiving dividends and for the distribution of assets if the corporation is liquidated. Usually does not have right to vote.

    A. Issuance of Preferred Stock

Usually has a par value; can be sold at a price different from par.

      1. Separate capital accounts are used to record preferred stock.

      2. Preferred Stock account is used to record the par value of shares issued; Paid-in Capital in Excess of Par Value, Preferred Stock is used to record any value received above the par value.

      3. Entry to record issuance of preferred stock: debit Cash, credit Preferred Stock account (for the par value of shares issued), credit Paid-in Capital in Excess of Par Value, Preferred Stock (for the value received above the par value).

    B. Dividend Preference of Preferred Stock

Preferred stockholders are allocated their dividends before any dividends are allocated to common stockholders.

      1. Cumulative or Noncumulative Dividend

        a. **Cumulative preferred stock** has a right to be paid both current and all prior periods' unpaid dividends before any dividend is paid to common stockholders. Unpaid dividends are referred to as **dividends in arrears**.

        b. **Noncumulative preferred stock** confers no right to prior periods' unpaid dividends if they were not declared in those prior periods.

        c. *Full-disclosure principle* requires that the amount of preferred dividends in arrears be reported as of the balance sheet date, normally in a note to the financial statements.

      2. Participating or Nonparticipating Dividend

        a. **Nonparticipating preferred stock**—dividends are limited each year to a maximum amount determined by applying either the stated percentage or the stated specific dollar amount per share to the par value.

        b. **Participating preferred stock**—allows its owners the right to share with common stockholders in any dividends paid in excess of the stated percentage or dollar amount.

    C. Convertible Preferred Stock

      1. **Convertible preferred stock** gives holders the option of exchanging their preferred shares into common shares at a specified rate.

      2. If a company's common stock increases in value, the convertible preferred stockholders can share in this success by converting their stock into more valuable common stock.

    D. Callable Preferred Stock

      1. **Callable preferred stock** gives the issuing corporation the right to purchase (retire) this stock from its holders at specified future prices and dates.

      2. Amount paid to call and retire a preferred share is its **call price**, or *redemption value*, and is set when the stock is issued.

      3. Any dividends in arrears must also be paid when stock is called.

    E. Reasons for Issuing Preferred Stock

      1. Raise capital without sacrificing control of the corporation.

      2. Boost the return earned by common stockholders; called **financial leverage** or *trading on equity*.

V. **Treasury Stock**—A corporation acquires its own shares for several reasons such as to acquire another company, to avoid a hostile takeover, or to use for employee compensation. A corporation's treasury stock does not receive any cash or stock dividends, nor do they allow the corporation voting rights.

    A. Purchasing Treasury Stock—reduces the corporation's assets and stockholders' equity by equal amounts.

      1. Debit Treasury Stock (contra equity) and credit Cash for full cost (reduces total assets and total equity).

      2. Treasury Stock is a contra equity account; the equity reduction is reported by deducting the cost of treasury stock in the equity section of the balance sheet.

      3. The resulting restriction on retained earnings must be disclosed.

    B. Reissuing Treasury Stock

        1. Selling treasury stock at cost: debit Cash, credit Treasury Stock, Common.

        2. Selling treasury stock above cost: debit Cash, credit Treasury Stock, Common, credit Paid-in Capital, Treasury Stock (for the amount received in excess of cost).

        3. Selling treasury stock below cost: entry depends on whether the Paid-in Capital, Treasury Stock account has a balance.

           i. If the Paid-in Capital, Treasury Stock account has no balance, the excess of cost over sales price is debited to Retained Earnings.

           ii. If the Paid-in Capital, Treasury Stock account has a balance, then it is debited for the excess of the cost over the sales price, not to exceed the balance in the account.

    C. Retiring Stock—Retiring stock reduces the number of shares issued and results in a reduction in assets and equity equal to the amount paid for the retired stock.

        1. When stock is purchased for retirement, all paid-in capital amounts that relate to the retired shares are removed from the accounts.

        2. Any excess of original issuance price over cost from the transaction should be credited to Paid-in Capital from Retirement of Stock.

        3. Any excess of cost over original issuance price from the transaction should be debited to Retained Earnings.

VI. Reporting of Equity

    A. **Statement of Retained Earnings** – generally consist of a company's cumulative net income less any net losses and dividends declared since its inception.

        1. Restricted and Appropriations

           a. **Restricted retained earnings**—Amount of retained earnings that are not available for dividends and refers to both statutory and contractual restrictions.

           b. **Appropriated retained earnings**—amount that the corporation *voluntarily restricts* from retained earnings which are available for dividends.

        2. **Prior Period Adjustments -** corrections of material errors made in prior periods.

           a. Include arithmetic mistakes, using unacceptable accounting principles, and ignoring relevant facts.

           b. Reported in *statement of retained earnings* as corrections to the beginning retained earnings balance.

3. **Changes in Accounting Estimates -** Adjustments to previously made assumptions.

   a. No adjustment is made for prior periods.

   b. Revised estimate is applied in calculating the appropriate revenue or expense of the current and future periods.

B. Statement of Stockholders' Equity – lists the beginning and ending balances of each equity account and describes the changes that occurred during the period.

   1. Provided by most companies rather than a separate statement of retained earnings.

   2. Statement of changes in stockholders' equity includes changes in retained earnings.

C. Reporting Stock Options

   1. **Stock options** are rights to purchase common stock at a fixed price over a specified period of time.

   2. Stock options are said to motivate managers and employees to focus on company performance, take a long-run perspective, and remain with the company.

VII. **Decision Analysis—Earnings per Share, Price-Earnings Ratio, Dividend Yield, and Book Value per Share**

A. Earnings per Share (EPS)—reported in final section of income statement. **Earnings per share** is the amount of income earned by each share of outstanding common stock (one of the most widely cited items of accounting information).

   1. **Basic earnings per share** is calculated as net income – preferred dividends (the numerator) divided by the weighted-average common shares outstanding.

      a. If preferred stock is *non*cumulative, the income available to common stockholders (the numerator) is the current period net income less any preferred dividends *declared* in that same period.

      b. If preferred stock is *cumulative*, the income available (numerator) is the current period net income less the preferred dividends, whether declared or not.

B. Price-Earnings Ratio (PE ratio)

   1. The **price earnings ratio** is used to gain understanding of the market's expected earnings for the stockholders.

   2. It is calculated as market value per share divided by earnings per share.

   3. It can be based on current or *expected* EPS.

C. Dividend Yield

1. The **dividend yield** shows the annual amount of cash dividends distributed to common shares relative to their market value.

2. It is used to determine whether a company's stock is an income stock (pays large and regular dividends) or a growth stock (pays little or no cash dividends).

3. It is calculated as annual cash dividends per share divided by market value per share.

D. Book Value per Share

1. **Book value per common share**

    a. If only one class outstanding, equals total stockholders' equity divided by the number of common shares outstanding.

    b. If two classes of stock outstanding, equals stockholders' equity applicable to common shares (total stockholders' equity less *equity applicable to preferred stock*—see section below) divided by the number of common shares outstanding.

2. **Book value per preferred share**

    a. The stockholders' *equity applicable to preferred* shares equals the preferred share's call price (or par value if the preferred is not callable) plus any cumulative dividends in arrears. The remaining stockholders' equity is the portion applicable to common shares.

    b. Book value per preferred share equals *equity applicable to preferred* shares divided by number of preferred shares outstanding.

Chapter Eleven – Alternate Demonstration Problem #1

Uzi Company received a charter granting the right to issue 200,000 shares of $1 par value common stock and 10,000 shares of 8% cumulative and nonparticipating, $50 par value preferred stock that is callable at $80 per share. Selected transactions are presented below.

2009
Feb. 19 Issued 45,000 shares of common stock at par for cash.

22 Gave the corporation's promoters 30,000 shares of common stock for their services in getting the corporation organized. The directors valued the services at $50,000.

Mar 30 Exchanged 100,000 shares of common stock for the following assets at fair market values: land, $25,000; building, $100,000; and machinery, $125,000.

Dec. 31 Closed the Income Summary account. A $25,000 loss was incurred.

2010
Jan. 12 Issued 1,000 shares of preferred stock at $75 per share.

Dec. 15 The board of directors declared an 8% dividend on preferred shares and $0.10 per share on outstanding common shares, payable on January 31 to the January 17 stockholders of record.

31 Closed the Income Summary and Dividend Declared accounts. A $69,000 net income was earned.

2011
Jan. 31 Paid the previously declared dividends.

Required:

1. Prepare general journal entries to record the selected transactions.
2. Prepare a stockholders' equity section as of the close of business on December 31, 2010.
3. Determine the book value per preferred share and per common stock as of December 31, 2010.

(If this alternative demonstration problem is not covered in class, see your instructor for the solution.)

Problem I

The following statements are either true or false. Place a (T) in the parentheses before each true statement and an (F) before each false statement.

1. ( ) Par value has nothing to do with a stock's worth.

2. ( ) Final authority in the management of corporation affairs rests with its board of directors.

3. ( ) The life of a corporation may be unlimited.

4. ( ) To transfer and sell his or her interest in a corporation, a stockholder must secure permission from the corporation's secretary.

5. ( ) The chief executive officer of a corporation is usually elected by the stockholders at one of their annual meetings.

6. ( ) The president of a corporation is responsible to its board of directors for management of the corporation's affairs.

7. ( ) A discount on stock is the difference between market value and the amount at which stock is issued when the stock is issued at a price below its par value.

8. ( ) A small stock dividend should be recorded by capitalizing retained earnings equal to the book value of the stock to be distributed.

9. ( ) In most states, a corporation must have current net income in order to pay a cash dividend.

10. ( ) Since a stock dividend is payable in stock rather than in assets, it is not a liability of its issuing corporation.

11. ( ) A stock split has no effect on total stockholders' equity, the equities of the individual stockholders, or on the balances of any of the contributed or retained capital accounts.

12. ( ) Dividend yield is an estimate of how much one share of stock will yield in cash dividends per year.

13. ( ) A company with common stock having a market value of $45 per share and earnings of $5 per share has a price-earnings ratio of 9.

14. ( ) A cash dividend reduces a corporation's cash and its stockholders' equity, but a stock dividend does not affect either cash or total stockholders' equity.

15. ( ) For companies with simple capital structures, earnings per share is calculated by dividing net income minus preferred dividends, if any, by the weighted-average number of common shares outstanding.

16. ( ) Hadley Corporation stock has a current market value of $16 and is expected to pay cash dividends of $1.20 during the next year. The expected dividend yield of Hadley stock is 7.5%.

Problem II

You are given several words, phrases, or numbers to choose from in completing each of the following statements or in answering the following questions. In each case select the one that best completes the statement or answers the question and place its letter in the answer space provided.

_____ 1. The difference between the par value of stock and its issue price when it is issued at a price above par value is the:

      a. Paid-in capital.

      b. Stock dividend.

      c. Minimum legal capital.

      d. Premium on stock.

      e. Discount on stock.

_____ 2. Vector Corporation has outstanding 3,000 shares of $100 par value, 7% cumulative and nonparticipating preferred stock and 10,000 shares of $10 par value common stock. Dividends have not been paid on the preferred stock for the current and one prior year. The corporation has recently prospered, and the board of directors has voted to pay out $49,000 of the corporation's retained earnings in dividends. If the $49,000 is paid out, how much should the preferred and common stockholders receive per share?

      a. $14.00 per share preferred, $0.70 per share common.

      b. $ 7.00 per share preferred, $2.80 per share common.

      c. $12.25 per share preferred, $1.23 per share common.

      d. $ 1.14 per share preferred, $4.56 per share common.

      e. $16.33 per share preferred, $ -0- per share common.

_____ 3. Vector Corporation has outstanding 3,000 shares of $100 par value, 7% noncumulative and nonparticipating preferred stock and 10,000 shares of $10 par value common stock. Dividends have not been paid on the preferred stock for the current and one prior year. The corporation has recently prospered, and the board of directors has voted to pay out $49,000 of the corporation's retained earnings in dividends. If the $49,000 is paid out, how much should the preferred and common stockholders receive per share?

      a. $ 1.14 per share preferred, $4.56 per share common.

      b. $9.33 per share preferred, $2.10 per share common.

      c. $ 7.00 per share preferred, $2.80 per share common.

      d. $14.00 per share preferred, $0.70 per share common.

      e. $12.25 per share preferred, $0.23 per share common.

_____ 4. Participating preferred stock is:

      a. Preferred stock that can be exchanged for shares of the issuing corporation's common stock at the option of the preferred stockholder.

      b. Preferred stock on which undeclared dividends accumulate annually until they are paid.

      c. Preferred stock on which the right to receive dividends is forfeited for any year that the dividends are not declared.

d. Preferred stock that the issuing corporation, at its option, may retire by paying a specified amount to the preferred stockholders plus any dividends in arrears.

e. Preferred stock that gives its owners the right to share in dividends in excess of the stated percentage or amount.

_____ 5. Stated value of stock is:

a. One share's portion of the issuing corporation's net assets as recorded in the corporation's accounts.

b. An arbitrary amount assigned to stock by the corporation's board of directors which is credited to the stock account when the stock is issued.

c. The difference between the par value of stock and its issue price when it is issued at a price below or above par value.

d. The market value of the stock on the date of issuance.

e. The price at which a share of stock can be bought or sold.

_____ 6. Bartlett Company had 20,000 shares of common stock outstanding at the beginning of 2010. On April 1, the company sold 20,000 additional shares of its common stock, and on November 1 the company declared a 2-for-1 stock split. For the purpose of determining earnings per share, calculate the weighted-average number of common shares outstanding during the year.

a. 60,000.00
b. 80,000.00
c. 70,000.00
d. 41,666.66
e. 83,333.33

_____ 7. Poseidon Corporation issued $10 par value common stock for $15, with the premium being credited to Paid-in Capital in Excess of Par Value; Common Stock. Later, 500 shares of this stock was repurchased and retired at a cost of $17. The entry to record the retirement is as follows:

a.	Common Stock	5,000	
	Paid-in Capital in Excess of Par Value, Common Stock	2,500	
	Retained Earnings	1,000	
	Cash		8,500
b.	Common Stock	5,000	
	Paid-in Capital in Excess of Par Value, Common Stock	2,500	
	Paid-in Capital from the Retirement of Common Stock	1,000	
	Cash		8,500
c.	Common Stock	5,000	
	Paid-in Capital in Excess of Par Value, Common Stock	3,500	
	Cash		6,500
d.	Common Stock	5,000	
	Paid-in Capital in Excess of Par Value, Common Stock	2,500	
	Cash		6,500
	Paid-in Capital from the Retirement of Common Stock		1.000
e.	Treasury Stock	8,500	
	Cash		8,500

8. The statement of stockholders' equity is:

   a. A financial statement that discloses the inflows and outflows of cash during the period.

   b. A financial report showing the assets, liabilities, and equity of an enterprise on a specific date.

   c. A financial statement showing revenues earned by a business, the expenses incurred in earning the revenues, and the resulting net income or net loss.

   d. A financial statement that lists the beginning and ending balances of each equity account and describes all the changes that occurred during the year.

   e. None of the above.

9. On December 15, RTA Corporation declares a $.75 per share cash dividend on its 4,000 outstanding shares. Payment date is January 15. On December 15, RTA should make the following entry related to the cash dividend:

a.	Cash Dividends Declared	3,000	
	Retained Earnings		3,000
b.	Common Dividend Payable	3,000	
	Cash Dividends Declared		3,000
c.	Retained Earnings	3,000	
	Cash Dividends Declared		3,000
d.	Retained Earnings	3,000	
	Common Dividend Payable		3,000
e.	No entry should be made on December 15 related to the cash dividend.		

Problem III

Many of the important ideas and concepts discussed in Chapter 11 are reflected in the following list of key terms. Test your understanding of these terms by matching the appropriate definitions with the terms. Record the number identifying the most appropriate definition in the blank space next to each term.

_____ Appropriated retained earnings	_____ Noncumulative preferred stock
_____ Authorized stock	_____ Nonparticipating preferred stock
_____ Basic earnings per share	_____ No-par value stock
_____ Book value per common share	_____ Organization expenses
_____ Book value per preferred share	_____ Paid-in capital
_____ Callable preferred stock	_____ Paid-in capital in excess of par
_____ Call price	_____ Participating preferred stock
_____ Capital stock	_____ Par value
_____ Changes in accounting estimates	_____ Par value stock
_____ Common stock	_____ Preemptive right
_____ Complex capital structure	_____ Preferred stock
_____ Convertible preferred stock	_____ Premium on stock
_____ Corporation	_____ Price-earnings (PE) ratio
_____ Cumulative preferred stock	_____ Prior period adjustment
_____ Date of declaration	_____ Proxy
_____ Date of payment	_____ Restricted retained earnings
_____ Date of record	_____ Retained earnings
_____ Diluted earnings per share	_____ Retained earnings deficit

_____ Dilutive securities   _____ Reverse stock split

_____ Discount on stock   _____ Simple capital structure

_____ Dividend in arrears   _____ Small stock dividend

_____ Dividend yield   _____ Stated value of stock

_____ Earnings per share   _____ Statement of stockholders' equity

_____ Financial leverage   _____ Stock dividend

_____ Large stock dividend   _____ Stockholders' equity

_____ Liquidating cash dividend   _____ Stock options

_____ Market value per share   _____ Stock split

_____ Minimum legal capital   _____ Treasury stock

1. Total amount of cash and other assets received from stockholders in exchange for stock.

2. Unpaid dividend on cumulative preferred stock; must be paid before any regular dividends on preferred stock and before any dividends on common stock.

3. Preferred stock on which the right to receive dividends is lost for any period when dividends are not declared.

4. Total amount of stock that a corporation's charter authorizes it to sell.

5. Preferred stock that the issuing corporation, at its option, may retire by paying the call price plus any dividends in arrears.

6. Preferred stock on which undeclared dividends accumulate until paid; common stockholders cannot receive dividends until cumulative dividends are paid.

7. Earning a higher return on equity by paying dividends on preferred stock or interest on debt at a rate lower than the return earned with the assets from issuing preferred stock or debt.

8. Stock dividend that is more than 25% of the previously outstanding shares.

9. Ratio of a company's market value per share to its earnings per share.

10. Occurs when a corporation calls in its stock and replaces each share with less than one new share; increases both the market value per share and any par or stated value per share.

11. Equity applicable to preferred shares (equals its call price [or par value if not callable] plus any cumulative dividends in arrears) divided by the number of preferred shares outstanding.

12. Amount that must be paid to call and retire a preferred share.

13. Amount of assets defined by law that stockholders must invest (potentially) and leave invested in a corporation; usually defined as par value of the stock; intended to protect creditors.

14. Corporation's own stock that it reacquired and still holds.

15. Price at which stock is bought or sold.

16. Capital structure that consists of only common stock and non-convertible preferred stock; consists of no dilutive securities.

17. Preferred stock on which dividends are limited to a maximum amount each year.

18. Stock dividend that is 25% or less of a corporation's previously outstanding shares.

19. Cumulative income less cumulative losses and dividends.

20. A corporation's basic stock; usually carries voting rights for controlling the corporation.

21. Debit (abnormal) balance in Retained Earnings; occurs when cumulative losses and dividends exceed cumulative income.

22. Rights to purchase common stock at a fixed price over a specified period of time.

23. Financial statement that lists the beginning and ending balances of each equity account and describes all changes in those accounts.

24. Retained earnings not available for dividends because of legal or contractual limitations.

25. Corporation's distribution of its own stock to its stockholders without the receipt of any payment.

26. Correction of an error in a prior year that is reported in the statement of retained earnings (or statement of changes in stockholders' equity) net of any income tax effects.

27. Difference between the par value of stock and its issue price when issued at a price below par value.

28. Preferred stock with an option to exchange it for common stock at a specified rate.

29. Stock class that has not been assigned a par value by the corporate charter.

30. Distribution of assets that returns part of the original investment to the stockholders; charged to contributed capital accounts.

31. Legal document giving a stockholder's agent the power to exercise the stockholder's voting rights.

32. Retained earnings reported separately as a way of informing stockholders of funding needs.

33. Date the directors vote to pay a dividend.

34. Ratio of the annual amount of cash dividends distributed to common shareholders relative to the common stock's market value (price).

35. Class of stock assigned a par value by the corporate charter.

36. Recorded amount of equity applicable to common shares divided by the number of common shares outstanding.

37. Date specified by the directors for identifying stockholders to receive dividends.

38. Amount of income earned by each share of a company's outstanding common stock; also called *net income per share*.

39. Stock with a priority status over common stockholders in one or more ways, such as paying of dividends or distributing assets.

40. Preferred stock that shares with common stockholders any dividends paid in excess of the percent stated on preferred stock.

41. Occurs when a corporation calls in its stock and replaces each share with more than one new share; decreases both the market value per share and the par or stated value per share.

42. No-par stock assigned a stated value per share; this amount is recorded in the stock account when the stock is issued.

43. Occurs when a corporation sells its stock for more than par value.

44. Revisions to previous estimates of future events and outcomes; accounted for in current and future periods.

45. Earnings per share calculation that requires dilutive securities be added to the denominator of the basic EPS calculation.

46. Stockholders' right to maintain their proportionate interest in a corporation with any additional shares issued.

47. Corporation's equity; also called *shareholders' equity* or *corporate capital*.

48. Value assigned a share of stock by the corporate charter when the stock is authorized.

49. Securities having the potential to increase common shares outstanding; examples are options, rights, convertible bonds and convertible preferred stock.

50. Net income less preferred dividends divided by the weighted-average common shares outstanding.

51. Capital structure that includes outstanding rights or options to purchase common stock, or securities that are convertible into common stock.

52. Date the corporation makes the dividend payment.

53. Costs such as legal fees and promoter fees to bring an entity into existence.

54. General term referring to a corporation's stock used in obtaining capital (owner financing).

55. Entity created by law and separate from its owners.

56. Account credited for the difference between the par value of stock and its issue price when issued at a price above par.

Problem IV

Complete the following by filling in the blanks.

1. Laws establishing minimum legal capital requirements were written to protect _____ with the protection resulting from making illegal the payment of any dividends that reduce stockholders' equity below _____.

2. When stock is issued at a price above its par value, the difference between par and the price at which the stock is issued is called a _____.

3. Advantages claimed for no-par stock are: (a) It may be issued at any price without _____, (b) Uninformed persons buying such stock are not misled as to the stock's worth by a _____ printed on the certificates.

4. Laws setting minimum legal capital requirements normally require stockholders to invest, in a corporation, assets equal in value to minimum legal capital or be contingently liable to _____ for the deficiency.

5. A preferred stock is so called because of the preferences granted its owners. The two most common preferences are a preference as to _____, and a preference _____.

6. In many jurisdictions when a corporation issues par value stock, it establishes for itself a _____ equal to the par value of the issued stock.

7. In addition to its separate legal existence, other characteristics of a corporation as a form of business organization are _____.

8. A corporation is said to be a separate legal entity; this phrase means that in a legal sense a corporation is _____.

9. When a corporation purchases treasury stock, a portion of its retained earnings equal to the cost of the treasury stock becomes _____ and unavailable for _____.

10. If treasury stock is reissued at a price above cost, the amount received in excess of cost is credited to _____. If treasury stock is sold below cost the difference between cost and the sale price is debited to either _____ or _____.

11. A stock dividend enables a corporation to give its shareholders some evidence of their interest in its retained earnings without reducing the corporation's _____.

12. Issued stock that has been reacquired by the issuing corporation is called _____.

13. If the book value of a share of common stock before the declaration and distribution of a 20% stock dividend was $90, the declaration and distribution of the dividend changed the book value to $_____.

14. If a corporation has sufficient cash to pay a dividend, it must also have sufficient _____ before it pays that dividend.

15. A small stock dividend contains a number of shares amounting to _____% or less of the previously outstanding shares.

16. Changes in accounting estimates _____ (are, are not) prior period adjustments.

17. Earnings per share calculated as if all dilutive securities had already been converted are called _____.

Problem V

The stockholders' equity section from Sonar Corporation's balance sheet shows the following:

Capital Stock And Retained Earnings

Preferred stock, $100 par value, 8% cumulative and nonparticipating, issued and outstanding 2,000 shares	$200,000	
Common stock, $10 par value, issued and outstanding 25,000 shares.......	250,000	
Total contributed capital..		$450,000
Retained earnings		230,000
Total stockholders' equity..		$680,000

1. If there are no dividends in arrears, the book value per share of the corporation's preferred stock is $_____ and the book value per share of its common stock is $_____.

2. If a total of two years' dividends are in arrears on the preferred stock, the book value per share of the preferred stock is $_____, and the book value per share of the common stock is $_____.

Problem VI

On August 10 Mainline Corporation purchased for cash 2,000 shares of its own $25 par value common stock at $27 per share. On October 3 it sold 1,000 of the shares at $30 per share. Prepare the journal entries below to record the purchase and sale of the stock.

DATE	ACCOUNT TITLES AND EXPLANATION	P.R.	DEBIT		CREDIT	
Aug. 10						
	Purchased 2,000 shares of treasury stock.					
Oct. 3						
	Sold 1,000 shares of treasury stock.					

Problem VII

The May 31 balance sheet of Eastwood Corporation carried the following stockholders' equity section:

Stockholders' Equity

Common stock, $10 par value, 25,000 shares authorized, 20,000 shares issued $200,000
Retained earnings 44,000
Total stockholders' equity $244,000

On the balance sheet date, with the common stock selling at $12 per share, the corporation's board of directors voted a 2,000-share stock dividend distributable on June 30 to the June 20 stockholders of record.

Required:

1. Prepare the journal entries to record the declaration and distribution of the dividend.

DATE	ACCOUNT TITLES AND EXPLANATION	P.R.	DEBIT		CREDIT	

2. Harold Jax owned 2,000 shares of the corporation's common stock before the declaration and distribution of the stock dividend; as a result, his portion of the dividend was _____ shares. The total book value of Jax's 2,000 shares before the dividend was $_____, the total book value of his shares after the dividend was $_____; consequently, Jax gained $_____ in the book value of his interest in the corporation.

Problem VIII

Retained earnings and shares issued and outstanding for Endel, Incorporated, are as follows:

	Retained Earnings	Shares Issued and Outstanding
December 31, 2010	$475,000	35,000
December 31, 2011	$447,000	38,500

On April 3, 2011, the board of directors declared a $0.775 per share dividend on the outstanding stock. On August 7, while the stock was selling for $17.50 per share, the corporation declared a 10% stock dividend on the outstanding shares to be issued on November 7.

Under the assumption that there were no transactions affecting retained earnings other than the ones given, determine the 2011 net income of Endel, Incorporated.

Solutions for Chapter 11

Problem I

1. T
2. T
3. T
4. F
5. F
6. T
7. F
8. F
9. F
10. T
11. T
12. F
13. T
14. T
15. T
16. T

Problem II

1. D
2. A
3. C
4. E
5. B
6. D
7. A
8. D
9. D

Problem III

32	Appropriated retained earnings		3	Noncumulative preferred stock
4	Authorized stock		17	Nonparticipating preferred stock
50	Basic earnings per share		29	No-par value stock
36	Book value per common share		53	Organization expenses
11	Book value per preferred share		1	Paid-in capital
5	Callable preferred stock		56	Paid-in capital in excess of par
12	Call price		40	Participating preferred stock
54	Capital stock		48	Par value
44	Changes in accounting estimates		35	Par value stock
20	Common stock		46	Preemptive right
51	Complex capital structure		39	Preferred stock
28	Convertible preferred stock		43	Premium on stock

55	Corporation	9	Price-earnings (PE) ratio
6	Cumulative preferred stock	26	Prior period adjustment
33	Date of declaration	31	Proxy
52	Date of payment	24	Restricted retained earnings
37	Date of record	19	Retained earnings
45	Diluted earnings per share	21	Retained earnings deficit
49	Dilutive securities	10	Reverse stock split
27	Discount on stock	16	Simple capital structure
2	Dividend in arrears	18	Small stock dividend
34	Dividend yield	42	Stated value of stock
38	Earnings per share	23	Statement of stockholders' equity
7	Financial leverage	25	Stock dividend
8	Large stock dividend	47	Stockholders' equity
30	Liquidating cash dividend	22	Stock options
15	Market value per share	41	Stock split
13	Minimum legal capital	14	Treasury stock

Problem IV

1. corporation creditors, minimum legal capital

2. premium

3. (a) discount liability, (b) par value

4. corporation creditors

5. the payment of dividends, in the distribution of assets if the corporation is liquidated

6. minimum legal capital

7. lack of stockholder liability, ease of transferring ownership rights, continuity of life, stockholders are not agents, ease of capital assembly, increased governmental regulation, and double taxation

8. an individual body, separate and distinct from its stockholders

9. restricted, dividends

10. Paid-in Capital, Treasury Stock; Paid-in capital, Treasury Stock; Retained Earnings

11. cash or other assets

12. treasury stock

13. $75

14. retained earnings

15. 25

16. are not

17. diluted earnings per share

Problem V

1. $100; $19.20
2. $116; $17.92

Problem VI

Aug. 10	Treasury Stock, Common	54,000	
	Cash		54,000
Oct. 3	Cash	30,000	
	Treasury Stock, Common		27,000
	Paid-in Capital, Treasury Stock		3,000

Problem VII

1.

May 31	Retained Earnings	24,000	
	Common Stock Dividend Distributable		20,000
	Paid-in Capital in Excess of Par Value, Common Stock		4,000
June 30	Common Stock Distributable	20,000	
	Common Stock		20,000

2. 200; $24,400; $24,400; $0

Problem VIII

Retained earnings as of December 31, 2010		$475,000
Reductions in retained earnings due to transactions:		
Dividends declared:		
April 3, on 35,000 shares	$27,125	
Retained earnings capitalized in stock dividend	61,250	
Total reductions		88,375
Retained earnings balance before transfer of net income from Income Summary account		$386,625
Retained earnings, December 31, 2011, after transfer of net income from Income Summary account		$447,000
Deduct retained earnings balance before transfer of net income from Income Summary account		386,625
Net income		$ 60,375

CHAPTER 12
ACCOUNTING FOR CASH FLOWS

Learning Objective C1:

Explain the purpose and importance of cash flow information.

The main purpose of the statement of cash flows is to report the major cash receipts and cash payments for a period. This includes identifying cash flows as relating to either operating, investing, or financing activities. Most business decisions involve evaluating activities that provide or use cash.

Learning Objective C2:

Distinguish between operating, investing, and financing activities.

Operating activities include the transactions and events that determine net income. Investing activities include transactions and events that mainly affect long-term assets. Financing activities include transactions and events that mainly affect long-term liabilities and equity.

Learning Objective C3:

Identify and disclose noncash investing and financing activities.

Noncash investing and financing activities must be disclosed in either a note or in a separate schedule to the statement of cash flows. Examples are the retirement of debt by issuing equity and the exchange of a note payable for plant assets.

Learning Objective C4:

Describe the format of the statement of cash flows.

The statement of cash flows separates cash receipts and payments into operating, investing, or financing activities.

Learning Objective A1:

Analyze the statement of cash flows.

To understand and predict cash flows, users stress identification of the sources and uses of cash flows by operating, investing, and financing activities. Emphasis is on operating cash flows since they derive from continuing operations.

Learning Objective A2:

Compute and apply the cash flow on total assets ratio.

The cash flow on total assets ratio is defined as operating cash flows divided by average total assets. Analysis of current and past values for this ratio can reflect a company's ability to yield regular and positive cash flows. It is also viewed as a measure of earnings quality.

©The McGraw-Hill Companies, Inc., 2009

Learning Objective P1:

Prepare a statement of cash flows.

Preparation of a statement of cash flows involves five steps: (1) Compute the net increase or decrease in cash, (2) compute net cash provided (used) by operating activities (using either the direct or indirect method), (3) compute net cash provided (used) by investing activities, (4) compute net cash provided (used) by financing activities, and (5) report the beginning and ending cash balance and prove that it is explained by net cash flows. Noncash investing and financing activities are also disclosed.

Learning Objective P2:

Compute cash flows from operating activities using the indirect method.

The indirect method for reporting net cash provided (used) by operating activities starts with net income and then adjusts it for three items: (1) changes in noncash current assets and current liabilities related to operating activities, (2) revenues and expenses not providing (using) cash, and (3) gains and losses from investing and financing activities.

Learning Objective P3:

Determine cash flows from both investing and financing activities.

Cash flows from both investing and financing activities are determined by identifying the cash flow effects of transactions and events affecting each balance sheet account related to these activities. All cash flows from these activities are identified when we can explain changes in these accounts from the beginning to the end of the period.

Learning Objective P4 (Appendix 12A):

Illustrate use of a spreadsheet to prepare a statement of cash flows.

A spreadsheet is a useful tool in preparing a statement of cash flows. Six steps (described in the appendix) are applied when using the spreadsheet to prepare a statement of cash flows.

Learning Objective P5 (Appendix 12B):

Compute cash flows from operating activities using the direct method.

The direct method for reporting net cash provided (used) by operating activities lists major classes of operating cash inflows less cash outflows to yield net cash inflow or outflow from operations.

I.   Basics of Cash Flow Reporting

  A. Purpose of the **Statement of Cash Flows**
      To report cash receipts (inflows) and cash payments (outflows)
      during a period. This report classifies cash flows into operating,
      investing, and financing activities. It answers important
      questions such as:

      1. How does a company obtain its cash?

      2. Where does a company spend its cash?

      3. What is the change in the cash balance?

  B. Importance of Cash Flows
      Information about cash flows, and its sources and uses, can
      influence decision makers in important ways. This information
      helps users decide whether a company can pay its debts and
      other obligations, and its ability to take advantage of new
      business opportunities.

  C. Measurement of Cash Flows
      The phrase, *cash flows* refers to *both* cash and cash equivalents.
      A *cash equivalent* must satisfy two criteria:

      1. Be readily convertible to a known amount of cash.

      2. Be sufficiently close to its maturity date so its market value
          is unaffected by interest rate changes.

  D. Classification of Cash Flows
      Cash receipts and cash payments are classified and reported in
      one of three categories:

      1. **Operating activities** include transactions and events that
          determine net income (with some exceptions such as unusual
          gains and losses). Specific examples:

          a. Cash inflows from cash sales, collections on credit sales,
              receipts of dividends and interest, sale of trading
              securities, and settlements of lawsuits.

          b. Cash outflows for payments to suppliers for goods and
              services, employees for wages, lenders for interest,
              government for taxes, charities, and purchase of trading
              securities.

      2. **Investing activities** include transactions and events that
          affect long-term assets. Specific examples:

          a. Cash inflows from selling long-term assets, selling
              short-term investments other than cash equivalents, and
              collecting money the company has loaned to others.

          b. Cash outflows from purchasing long-term assets,
              purchasing short-term investments other than cash
              equivalents, and lending money to others.

   3. **Financing activities** include transactions and events that
      affect long-term liabilities and equity:
      a. Cash inflows from issuing debt and obtaining cash from
         owners.
      b. Cash outflows from repaying amounts borrowed and
         distributing cash to owners.
E. Noncash Investing and Financing Activities
   Noncash investing and financing activities do not affect cash
   receipts or payments; however, they are disclosed at the bottom
   of the statement of cash flows or in a note to the statement
   because of their importance and the *full disclosure* principle.
F. Format of the Statement of Cash Flows
   1. Lists cash flows by categories (operating, financing and
      investing) and identifies the net cash inflow or outflow in
      each category.
   2. Combines the net cash flow in each of the three categories
      and identifies the net change (increase or decrease) in cash
      for the period.
   3. Combines the net change in cash with the beginning cash to
      prove the ending cash.
   4. Contains a separate schedule at bottom (or notes) to report
      the noncash financing and investing activities.
G. Preparing the Statement of Cash Flows
   1. Five steps:
      a. Compute the net increase or decrease in cash.
      b. Compute net cash provided (used) by operating activities
         (using either the direct or indirect method).
      c. Compute net cash provided (used) by investing
         activities.
      d. Compute net cash provided (used) by financing
         activities.
      e. Compute net cash flows by combining the net cash
         provided (used) by operating, investing, and financing
         activities and then *prove it* by adding it to the beginning
         cash to show that it equals the ending cash.
   2. Alternative approaches to preparing the statement:
      a. Analyzing the cash account.
      b. Analyzing noncash accounts.
   3. Information to Prepare the Statement
      a. Comparative balance sheets.
      b. The current income statement.
      c. Other information—generally derived from analyzing
         noncash balance sheet accounts.

Chapter Outline

II.   **Cash Flows from Operating** – cash flows from operating activities are reported in one of two ways—the direct method or the indirect method. Amount is *identical* under both methods.

   A. Indirect and Direct Methods of Reporting

      1. The **direct method** separately lists each major item of operating cash receipts and each major item of operating cash payments. (See illustration in Exhibit 12.7.)

      2. The **indirect method** reports net income and then adjusts it for items necessary to obtain net cash provided (used) by operating activities. Reports the necessary adjustments to reconcile net income to net cash provided (used) by operating activities. (See illustration in Exhibit 12.9). This method is the most widely used.

   B. Application of the Indirect Method of Reporting

      a. *Add*, as adjustments to net income: noncash expenses (e.g., depreciation), decreases in current assets, increases in current liabilities, and losses.

      b. *Subtract*, as adjustments to net income: increases in current assets, decreases in current liabilities, and gains.

      c. Does *not* report individual items of cash inflows and cash outflows from operating activities.

      d. Exhibit 12-12 summarizes the adjustments for the indirect method.

III.   **Cash Flows from Investing**
Three-stage process is used to determine cash provided (used) by investing activities: (1) Identify changes in investing-related accounts, (2) explain these changes using reconstruction method, and (3) report their cash flow effects.

   A. Analysis of Noncurrent Assets

      1. Plant Asset Transactions: determine changes in all noncurrent asset accounts (plant assets, intangible assets, investments)

      2. Analyze changes in these accounts using available information to determine their effect, if any, on cash.

   B. Analysis of Other Assets

      1. Certain other asset transactions such as those involving current notes receivable and investments in debt and equity securities (excluding trading) are considered investing activities.

      2. Analyze using same process used for noncurrent asset accounts.

Chapter Outline

Notes

IV. Cash Flows from Financing

Three-stage process is used to determine cash provided (used) by investing activities: (1) Identify changes in financing-related accounts, (2) explain these changes using reconstruction method, and (3) report their cash flow effects.

A. Analysis of Noncurrent Liabilities

1. Determine changes in noncurrent liability accounts (e.g., long-term debt, notes payable, bonds payable).

2. Analyze changes in these accounts using available information to determine their effect, if any, on cash.

B. Analysis of Equity

1. Common Stock Transactions: determine changes in equity accounts (e.g., owner's capital, all stock accounts, and retained earnings).

2. Retained Earnings Transactions: analyze changes in these accounts using available information to determine their effect, if any, on cash.

C. Proving Cash Balances – the last step in preparing the statement is to report the beginning and ending cash balances and prove that the *net change in cash* is explained by operating, investing, and financing cash flows.

V. Decision Analysis—Cash Flow Analysis

A. Analyzing Cash Sources and Uses

1. Managers stress understanding and predicting cash flows for business decisions.

2. Creditor and investor decisions are also based on a company's cash flow evaluations.

3. Operating cash flows are generally considered to be most significant because they represent results of ongoing operations.

B. Cash Flow on Total Assets

1. The **cash flow on total assets** ratio is similar to return on total assets except the return is analyzed based on operating cash flows rather than net income.

2. Calculated by dividing cash flow from operations by average total assets.

VI. **Spreadsheet Preparation of the Statement of Cash Flows (Appendix 12A)**
A spreadsheet approach may be used to organize and analyze the information to prepare a statement of cash flows by the indirect method, including the supplemental disclosures of noncash investing and financing activities.

  A. The spreadsheet has four columns containing dollar amounts.

    1. Columns one and four contain the beginning and ending balances of each balance sheet account.

    2. Columns two and three are for reconciling the changes in each balance sheet account.

  B. Separate sections on the working paper present (a) balance sheet items with debit balances; (b) balance sheet items with credit balances; (c) cash flows from operating activities, starting with net income; (d) cash flows from investing activities; (e) cash flows from financing activities; and (f) noncash investing and financing activities.

  C. Information for sections (c) – (f) is developed in four steps in the Analysis of Changes columns:

    1. By adjusting net income for the changes in all noncash current asset and current liability account balances. This reconciles the changes in these accounts.

    2. By eliminating from net income the effects of all noncash revenues and expenses. This begins the reconciliation of noncurrent assets.

    3. By eliminating from net income any gains or losses from investing and financing activities. This involves the reconciliation of noncurrent assets and noncurrent liabilities and perhaps the recording of disclosures.

    4. By entering any remaining items, such as dividend payments, which are necessary to reconcile the changes in all balance sheet accounts.

VII. **Direct Method of Reporting Operating Cash Flows (Appendix 12B)**
The direct method adjusts accrual-based income statement items to the cash basis. Usual approach is to adjust income statement accounts related to operating activities for changes in their related balance sheet accounts. Separately list each major item or class of operating cash receipts and cash payments.

  A. Operating Cash Receipts—include cash received from sales, rent, interest, and dividends.

  B. Operating Cash Payments—include cash paid suppliers, for wages and other operating expense, interest, and income taxes.

    C. Summary of Adjustments for the Direct Method
        Exhibit 12B.6 summarizes the common adjustments for the items making up net income to arrive at net cash provided (used) by operating activities under the direct method.

    D. Direct Method Format of Operating Activities

        1. Major items of cash inflows and cash outflows are listed separately in the operating activities section.

        2. The items to be listed are determined by adjusting individual accrual basis income statement items to cash basis items. This is done by determining the impact from changes in their related balance sheet accounts.

        3. The operating cash outflows are subtracted from the operating cash inflows to determine the net cash provided (used) by operating activities.

        4. This is the method recommended (but not required) by the FASB.

        5. When the direct method is used, the FASB requires a reconciliation of net income to net cash provided (used) by operating activities. This is operating cash flows computed using the indirect method.

CLASSIFYING ACTIVITIES IN THE STATEMENT OF CASH FLOWS

OPERATING ACTIVITIES

Cash inflows from
- Sale of goods or services
- Interest
- Dividends
- Sale of trading securities
- Other operating receipts

Cash outflows to
- Suppliers of goods and services
- Salaries and wages
- Government for taxes
- Lenders for interest
- Purchase trading securities
- Others for expenses

INVESTING ACTIVITIES

Cash inflows from
- Sale of property plant, and equipment
- Sale of debt or equity securities of other entities
- Collection of principal on loans to other entities
- Selling (discounting) of loans

Cash outflows to
- Purchase property, plant, and equipment
- Purchase debt or equity securities of other entities
- Make loans to another entity

FINANCING ACTIVITIES

Cash inflows from
- Sale of capital stock (or owner investment)
- Issuance of debt (bonds and notes)
- Issuing short-term liabilities

Cash outflows to
- Shareholders as dividends (or owner's withdrawal)
- Repay debts
- Purchase treasury stock

NONCASH INVESTING AND FINANCING ACTIVITIES
- Retirement of debt by issuing stock
- Conversion of preferred stock to common stock
- Purchase of a long-term asset by issuing a note payable
- Leasing of assets classified as a capital lease

STEPS TO DETERMINE INFORMATION
STATEMENT OF CASH FLOWS

1. Find <u>change</u> in Cash—This is the target number.

2. Find cash flow from operations
   (Using direct or indirect method)

3. Find Cash Flow from   A. Financing <u>and</u>
                                 B. Investing

   Procedure:

   In real life: Using data from comparative balance sheets, trace changes through ledgers and journals probably using a worksheet to organize, analyze, and prove data disclosed.

   In the classroom: Determine the changes in noncurrent accounts and notes from comparative balance sheets. Use the relevant data the text provides that comes from the ledgers and the journals to systematically analyze the data using chart and/or reconstructing journal entries.

4. Combine cash flows from all three activities (from 2 and 3) to find net cash flow and prove change in cash. (Target number determined in Step 1).

Note: Once the above information has been gathered, the statement can be prepared following the required format. If the direct method was used, GAAP requires a reconciliation of net income to cash provided from operations.

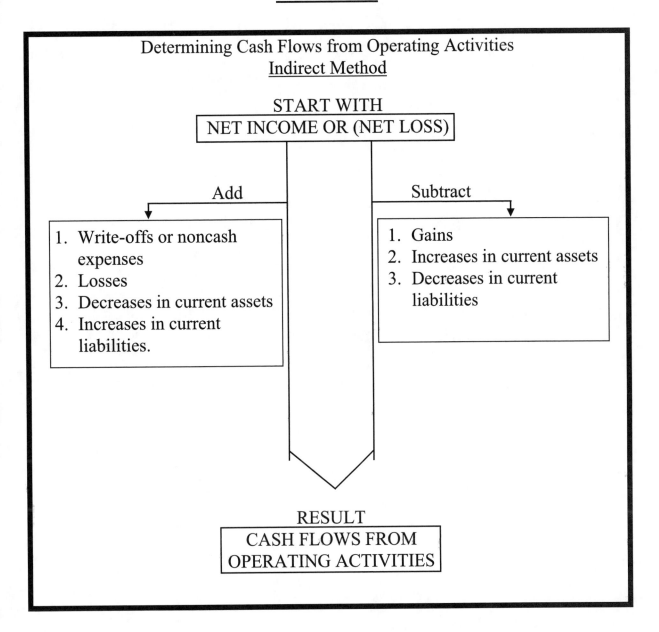

Determining Cash Flows from Operating Activities
Indirect Method

START WITH
NET INCOME OR (NET LOSS)

Add

1. Write-offs or noncash expenses
2. Losses
3. Decreases in current assets
4. Increases in current liabilities.

Subtract

1. Gains
2. Increases in current assets
3. Decreases in current liabilities

RESULT
CASH FLOWS FROM
OPERATING ACTIVITIES

Determining Cash Flows from Operating Activities
Direct Method (Appendix 12B)
(Need income statement and balance sheet data)

1. Cash = Sales
   Receipts
   from Customers*

   ⌐ + Decrease in
       Accounts
       Receivable
       or
   └ – Increase in
       Accounts
       Receivable

2. Cash = Cost of
   Payments   Goods Sold
   to Suppliers

   ⌐ + Increase in
       Inventory
       or
   └ – Decrease in
       Inventory

   ⌐ + Decrease in
       Accounts
       Payable
       or
   └ – Increase in
       Accounts
       Payable

3. Cash = Operating
   Payments   Expenses
   for
   Operating**
   Expenses

   ⌐ + Increase in
       Prepaid
       Expenses
       or
   └ – Decrease in
       Prepaid
       Expenses

   ⌐ + Decrease in
       Accrued
       Liabilities
       or
   └ – Increase in
       Accrued
       Liabilities

   ⌐ – Depreciation
       and Other
       Noncash
   └   Expenses

4. Cash = Income
   Payments   Taxes
   for   Expense
   Income
   Taxes

   ⌐ + Decrease in
       Income
       Taxes
       Payable
       or
   └ – Increase in
       Income
       Taxes
       Payable

5. Cash = Interest
   Payments   Expense
   for
   Interest

   ⌐ + Decreases in
       Interest Payable
   └ – Increase in
       Interest Payable

*use similar computations for
CR from Interest
CR from Dividends

**Wage expense would be
taken out if CP for wages was
to be reported separately.
The related prepaids and
payables would be considered
in the computation.

The Carpet Company's 2010 and 2009 balance sheets:

	December 31	
	2010	2009
Debits		
Cash	$10,500	$ 4,000
Accounts receivable	8,000	9,000
Merchandise inventory	21,000	18,000
Equipment	18,000	15,000
Totals	$57,500	$46,000
Credits		
Accumulated depreciation, equipment	$ 4,000	$ 3,000
Accounts payable	7,000	5,000
Taxes payable	1,000	2,000
Dividends payable	1,500	0
Common stock, $10 pay value	27,000	25,000
Contributed capital in excess of par, common stock	6,000	5,000
Retained earnings	11,000	6,000
Totals	$57,500	$46,000

The Carpet Company's income statement:

For the Year Ended December 31, 2010

Sales		$61,000
Cost of goods sold	$40,000	
Wages and other operating expenses	6,300	
Income taxes expense	4,200	
Depreciation expense	1,500	52,000
Net income		$ 9,000

Additional information includes the following:

a. Equipment costing $3,500 was purchased during the year.

b. Fully depreciated equipment that cost $500 was discarded and its cost and accumulated depreciation were removed from the accounts.

c. Two hundred shares of stock were sold and issued at $15 per share.

d. The company declared $4,000 of cash dividends and paid $2,500.

Required:

Prepare the statement of cash flows for the year ended December 31, 2010 using the:

1. Indirect method.

2. Direct method (Appendix 12B).

(If this alternative demonstration problem is not covered in class, see your instructor for the solution.)

Problem I

The following statements are either true or false. Place a (T) in the parentheses before each true statement and an (F) before each false statement.

1. ( ) The FASB encourages companies to use the direct method of presenting cash flows from operating activities.

2. ( ) A statement of cash flows should explain the differences between the beginning and ending balances of cash and cash equivalents.

3. ( ) Cash outflows to purchase items classified as cash equivalents are not shown on a statement of cash flows.

4. ( ) A payment by a company in the form of a loan is an example of a financing activity.

5. ( ) The Cash account provides all of the information necessary to prepare a statement of cash flows.

6. ( ) If a company purchases all merchandise for cash and the ending balance of Merchandise Inventory is unchanged from the beginning balance, then cost of goods sold equals the total cash payments for merchandise.

Problem II

You are given several words, phrases, or numbers to choose from in completing each of the following statements or in answering the following questions. In each case select the one that best completes the statement or answers the question and place its letter in the answer space provided.

_____ 1. Bat Company purchased a plant asset that cost $30,000 by paying $5,000 in cash and paying for the balance owed on a Note Payable. What would be reported on the statement of cash flows?

     a. Cash outflow from investing activities: $5,000.

     b. Cash inflow from financing activities: $25,000.

     c. Cash outflow from investing activities: $30,000.

     d. The transaction would only be reported on the schedule of noncash investing and financing activities.

     e. Both a and b.

_____ 2. (Appendix 12B) If a company purchases merchandise on account and there are some changes in the Merchandise Inventory balance during a period, what calculations are necessary to calculate cash payments for merchandise?

     a. Purchases + Decrease (– Increase) in Merchandise Inventory.

     b. Cost of Goods Sold + Increase (–Decrease) in Merchandise Inventory.

     c. Purchases + Decrease (–Increase) in Accounts Payable.

     d. Both a and b.

     e. Both b and c.

_____ 3. (Appendix 12B) Given the following T-account (partially completed), determine the cash payment for interest.

Interest Payable	
12/31/09 Bal.	12,000
Interest expense	8,000
12/31/09 Bal.	13,000

a. $ 7,000.

b. $ 4,000.

c. $ 8,000.

d. $12,000.

e. $20,000.

Problem III

Many of the important ideas and concepts discussed in Chapter 12 are reflected in the following list of key terms. Test your understanding of these terms by matching the appropriate definitions with the terms. Record the number identifying the most appropriate definition in the blank space next to each term.

_____ Cash flow on total assets   _____ Investing activities

_____ Direct method   _____ Operating activities

_____ Financing activities   _____ Statement of cash flows

_____ Indirect method

1. Transactions with owners or creditors that include obtaining cash from issuing debt, repaying amounts borrowed, and obtaining cash from or distributing cash to owners.

2. Activities that involve the production or purchase of merchandise and the sale of goods and services to customers, including expenditures related to administering the business.

3. Presentation of the net cash from operating activities that lists major operating cash receipts, less the major operating cash payments.

4. Financial statement that reports cash inflows and outflows for an accounting period and classifies them as operating, investing, or financing activities.

5. Presentation that reports net income and then adjusts it by adding and subtracting items necessary to yield net cash from operating activities.

6. Transactions that involve purchasing and selling long-term assets, including making and collecting notes receivable and investments in other than cash equivalents.

7. Ratio of operating cash flows to average total assets; not affected by income recognition and measurement rules, reflects earnings quality.

Problem IV

Opposite each transaction, place an "X" in the box below the caption that best describes its disclosure category on a statement of cash flows or supplemental schedule in the case of noncash investing and financing activities.

Transaction	Operating Activity	Investing Activity	Financing Activity	Noncash Investing & Financing Activity
1. Paid wages and salaries.				
2. Cash sale of used equipment.				
3. Received a cash dividend.				
4. Issued a long-term bond payable for cash.				
5. Cash sale of merchandise.				
6. Purchased land in exchange for common stock.				
7. Paid a cash dividend.				
8. Paid interest expense.				
9. Purchased stock in another company for cash.				
10. Repaid a six-month note payable.				

Problem V (Appendix 12B)

Analyze the information presented in each question below and determine the missing amounts.

1. Accounts receivable decreased from $25,000 at the beginning of the period to $18,000 at the end of the period. Sales revenue was $280,000. Assume all sales were on account. There were no uncollectible accounts written off during the period. How much cash was collected from customers during the period? $_____

2. Merchandise inventory increased from $90,000 at the beginning of the period to $100,000 at the end of the period. Cost of goods sold was $160,000. How much merchandise inventory was purchased during the period? $_____

3. The accounts payable balance decreased during the period from $30,000 to $26,000. Disregard your answer to question 2 and assume purchases of merchandise during the period totaled $120,000. Assume all purchases were on account. How much cash was paid to merchandise suppliers during the period? $_____

4. The balance of accumulated depreciation increased during the period from $200,000 to $220,000. Also, machinery originally costing $10,000 with accumulated depreciation of $8,000 was sold during the period. What was the amount of the period's depreciation expense? $_____

5. Refer back to question 1. Instead of assuming all sales revenues of $280,000 were on account, assume cash sales totaled $100,000 and credit sales totaled $180,000. How much cash was collected from customers during the period? $_____

Problem VI

Iker Company's 2010 and 2009 balance sheets are presented below along with its 2010 income statement.

IKER COMPANY
Balance Sheet
December 31, 2010, and 2009
Assets

	2010		2009	
Cash..		$ 8,000		$ 5,000
Accounts receivable		15,000		12,000
Merchandise inventory.................................		30,000		33,000
Equipment	$40,000		$38,000	
Less accumulated depreciation.....................	16,000	24,000	18,000	20,000
Total assets		$77,000		$70,000

Liabilities and Stockholders' Equity

	2010	2009
Accounts payable	$21,000	$17,000
Accrued liabilities...	4,000	5,000
Common stock, $5 par value.........................	35,000	30,000
Retained earnings	17,000	18,000
Total liabilities and stockholders' equity	$77,000	$70,000

IKER COMPANY
Income Statement
For Year Ended December 31, 2010

Sales...		$80,000
Cost of goods sold..		30,000
Gross profit on sales.......................................		50,000
Operating expenses...	$20,000	
Depreciation expense	10,000	
Loss from sale of plant assets........................	5,000	35,000
Net income		$15,000

Additional information about the company's activities in 2010:

1. Sold used equipment costing $20,000 with accumulated depreciation of $12,000 for $3,000 cash.

2. Purchased equipment costing $22,000 by paying $17,000 cash and issuing 1,000 shares of common stock.

3. Paid cash dividends of $16,000.

Required:

Note: If you are responsible for Appendix 12A, complete part (a) and then (b). If you are not responsible for the appendix, skip part (a) and complete only part (b).

a. A partially completed spreadsheet for Iker Company's statement of cash flows (assuming the indirect method is used) for the year ended December 31, 2010 appears below. Complete the spreadsheet.

b. Prepare the Iker Company's statement of cash flows for the year ended December 31, 2010 using the indirect method.

a.

IKER COMPANY
Spreadsheet for Statement of Cash Flows (Indirect Method)
For Year Ended December 31, 2010

	December 31, 2009	Analysis of Changes		December 31, 2010
		Debit	Credit	
Balance sheet—Debits:				
Cash	5,000			8,000
Accounts receivable	12,000			15,000
Merchandise inventory	33,000			30,000
Equipment	38,000			40,000
	88,000			93,000
Balance sheet—Credits:				
Accumulated depreciation	18,000			16,000
Accounts payable	17,000			21,000
Accrued liabilities	5,000			4,000
Common stock, $5 par value	30,000			35,000
Retained earnings	18,000			17,000
	88,000			93,000
Statement of Cash Flows				

b.

IKER COMPANY		
Statement of Cash Flows		
For Year Ended December 31, 2010		

Solutions for Chapter 12

Problem I

1. T
2. T
3. T
4. T
5. F
6. T

Problem II

1. A
2. C
3. A

Problem III

7	Cash flow on total assets	6	Investing activities
3	Direct method	2	Operating activities
1	Financing activities	4	Statement of cash flows
5	Indirect method		

Problem IV

	Transaction	*Classification*
1.	Paid wages and salaries.	Operating activity
2.	Cash sale of used equipment.	Investing activity
3.	Received a cash dividend.	Operating activity
4.	Issued a long-term bond payable for cash.	Financing activity
5.	Cash sale of merchandise.	Operating activity
6.	Purchased land in exchange for common stock.	Noncash investing and financing activity
7.	Paid a cash dividend.	Financing activity
8.	Paid interest expense.	Operating activity
9.	Purchased stock in another company for cash.	Investing activity
10.	Repaid a six-month note payable.	Financing activity

Problem V (Appendix 12B)

1. Cash collections from customers $280,000 + $25,000 − $18,000 = $287,000
2. Merchandise purchases $160,000 + $100,000 − $90,000 = $170,000
3. Cash payments for merchandise $120,000 + $30,000 − $26,000 = $124,000
4. Depreciation expense $220,000 − $200,000 + $8,000 = $28,000
5. Cash collections from customers $100,000 + $180,000 + $25,000 − $18,000 = $287,000

Problem VI

a.

IKER COMPANY
Spreadsheet for Statement of Cash Flows (Indirect Method)
For Year Ended December 31, 2010

	December 31, 2009	Analysis of Changes		December 31, 2010
		Debit	Credit	
Balance sheet—Debits:				
Cash	5,000			8,000
Accounts receivable	12,000	3,000 (b)		15,000
Merchandise inventory	33,000		3,000 (c)	30,000
Equipment	38,000	22,000 (h)	20,000 (g)	40,000
	88,000			93,000
Balance sheet—Credits:				
Accumulated depreciation	18,000	12,000 (g)	10,000 (f)	16,000
Accounts payable	17,000		4,000 (d)	21,000
Accrued liabilities	5,000	1,000 (e)		4,000
Common stock, $5 par value	30,000		5,000 (h)	35,000
Retained earnings	18,000	16,000 (i)	15,000 (f)	17,000
	88,000			93,000
Statement of Cash Flows				
Operating activities:				
Net Income		15,000 (a)		
Increase in accounts receivable			3,000 (b)	
Decrease in merchandise inventory		3,000 (c)		
Increase in accounts payable		4,000 (d)		
Decrease in accrued liabilities			1,000 (e)	
Depreciation expense		10,000 (f)		
Loss on sale of equipment		5,000 (g)		
Investing activities				
Proceeds from sale of equipment		3,000 (g)		
Payment for purchase of equipment			17,000 (h)	
Financing activities				
Payment of cash dividends			16,000 (i)	
Noncash investing and financing activities				
Issued stock to purchase equipment		5,000 (h)	5,000 (h)	
		99,000	99,000	

b.

IKER COMPANY
Statement of Cash Flows
For Year Ended December 31, 2010

Cash flows from operating activities		
Net income...	$ 15,000	
Adjustments to reconcile net income to net cash provided by operating activities		
Increase in accounts receivable......................................	(3,000)	
Decrease in merchandise inventory	3,000	
Increase in accounts payable...	4,000	
Decrease in accrued liabilities...	(1,000)	
Depreciation expense	10,000	
Loss on sale of equipment...	5,000	
Net cash provided by operating activities........................		$ 33,000
Cash flows from investing activities		
Cash received from sale of equipment.............................	3,000	
Cash paid for purchase of equipment	(17,000)	
Net cash used in investing activities..............................		(14,000)
Cash flows from financing activities		
Cash paid for dividends...	(16,000)	
Net cash used in financing activities		(16,000)
Net increase in cash		3,000
Cash balance at beginning of 2010.....................................		5,000
Cash balance at end of 2010		$ 8,000

CHAPTER 13
INTERPRETING
FINANCIAL STATEMENTS

Learning Objective C1:

Explain the purpose of analysis.

The purpose of financial statement analysis is to help users make better business decisions. Internal users want information to improve company efficiency and effectiveness in providing products or services. External users want information to make better and more informed decisions in pursuing their goals. The common goals of all users are to evaluate a company's (1) past and current performance, (2) current financial position, and (3) future performance and risk.

Learning Objective C2:

Identify the building blocks of analysis.

Financial statement analysis focuses on four "building blocks" of analysis: (1) liquidity and efficiency—ability to meet short-term obligations and efficiently generate revenues; (2) solvency—ability to generate future revenues and meet long-term obligations; (3) profitability—ability to provide financial rewards sufficient to attract and retain financing; and (4) market prospects—ability to generate positive market expectations.

Learning Objective C3:

Describe standards for comparisons in analysis.

Standards for comparisons include (1) intracompany—prior performance and relations between financial items for the company under analysis; (2) competitor—one or more direct competitors of the company; (3) industry—industry statistics; and (4) guidelines (rules-of-thumb)—general standards developed from past experiences and personal judgments.

Learning Objective C4:

Identify the tools of analysis.

The three most common tools of financial statement analysis are: (1) horizontal analysis—comparing a company's financial condition and performance across time; (2) vertical analysis—comparing a company's financial condition and performance to a base amount such as revenues or total assets; and (3) ratio analysis—using and quantifying key relations among financial statement items.

Learning Objective A1:

Summarize and report results of analysis.

A financial statement analysis report is often organized around the building blocks of analysis. A good report separates interpretations and conclusions of analysis from the information underlying them. An analysis report often consists of six sections: (1) executive summary; (2) analysis overview; (3) evidential matter; (4) assumptions; (5) key factors; and (6) inferences.

Learning Objective A2: (Appendix 13A)

Explain the form and assess the content of a complete income statement.

An income statement has four *potential* sections: (1) continuing operations, (2) discontinued segments, (3) extraordinary items, and (4) earnings per share.

Learning Objective P1:

Explain and apply methods of horizontal analysis.

Horizontal analysis is a tool to evaluate changes in data across time. Two important tools of horizontal analysis are comparative statements and trend analysis. Comparative statements show amounts for two or more successive periods, often with changes disclosed in both absolute and percent terms. Trend analysis is used to reveal important changes occurring from one period to the next.

Learning Objective P2:

Describe and apply methods of vertical analysis.

Vertical analysis is a tool to evaluate each financial statement item or group of items in terms of a base amount. Two tools of vertical analysis are common-size statements and graphical analyses. Each item in common-size statements is expressed as a percent of a base amount. For the balance sheet, the base amount is usually total assets, and for the income statement, it is usually sales.

Learning Objective P3:

Define and apply ratio analysis.

Ratio analysis provides clues to and symptoms of underlying conditions. Ratios, properly interpreted, identify areas requiring further investigation. A ratio expresses a mathematical relation between two quantities such as a percent, rate, or proportion. Ratios can be organized into the building blocks of analysis: (1) liquidity and efficiency, (2) solvency, (3) profitability, and (4) market prospects.

Chapter Outline

I. **Basics of Analysis**—Transforming data into useful information for decision making.

A. Purpose of Analysis
To help users (both internal and external) make better business decisions.

1. Internal users (managers, officers, internal auditors, consultants, budget officers, and market researchers) make the strategic and operating decisions of a company.

2. External users (shareholders, lenders, directors, customers, suppliers, regulators, lawyers, brokers, and the press) rely on financial statement analysis to make decisions in pursuing their own goals.

3. The common goal of all users is to evaluate:

a. Past and current performance.

b. Current financial position.

c. Future performance and risk.

B. Building Blocks of Analysis
The four areas of inquiry or building blocks are:

1. Liquidity and efficiency—ability to meet short-term obligations and to efficiently generate revenues.

2. Solvency—ability to generate future revenues and meet long-term obligations.

3. Profitability—ability to provide financial rewards sufficient to attract and retain financing.

4. Market Prospects—ability to generate positive market expectations.

C. Information for Analysis

1. Most users rely on **general purpose financial statements** that include:

a. Income statement

b. Balance sheet

c. Statement of changes in stockholders' equity (or statement of retained earnings)

d. Statement of cash flows

e. Notes related to the statements

2. **Financial reporting**—is the communicataion of financial information useful for making investment, credit, and other business decisions. Includes information from SCE 10-K or other filings, press releases, shareholders' meetings, forecasts, management letters, auditor's reports, and Webcasts.

D. Standards for Comparisons
    Used to determine if analysis measures suggest good, bad, or average performance. Standards can include the following types of comparisons:

1. *Intracompany*—based on prior performance and relationships between its financial items.

2. *Competitor*—compared to one or more direct competitors (often best).

3. *Industry*—published industry statistics (available from services like Dun & Bradstreet, Standard and Poor's, and Moody's).

4. *Guidelines (rules-of-thumb)*—general standards developed from past experiences.

E. Tools of Analysis – includes horizontal, vertical and ratio analysis.

II. **Horizontal Analysis**—Tool to evaluate changes in financial statement data *across time*. This analysis utilizes:

A. Comparative Statements—reports financial amounts for more than one period placed side by side in columns on a single statement.

1. Computation of Dollar Changes and Percentage Changes—usually shown in line items.

    a. Dollar change = Analysis period amount minus Base period amount.

    b   Percent change = Analysis period amount minus Base period amount divided by Base period amount times 100.

    Notes:
    (1)   When a negative amount appears in the base period and a positive amount in the analysis period (or vice versa)— a meaningful percentage change cannot be computed.
    (2)   When there is no value in the base period—percentage change is not computable.
    (3)   When an item has a value in the base period and zero in the next period—the decrease is 100 percent.

2. Comparative balance sheets

    a. Consist of balance sheet amounts from two or more balance sheet dates arranged side by side.

    b. Usefulness is improved by showing each item's dollar change and percent change to highlight large changes.

3. Comparative income statements

    a. Amounts for two or more period are placed side by side.

    b. Additional columns are included for dollar and percent changes.

    B. Trend Analysis—used to reveal patterns in data across successive periods. Involves computing trend percents (or *index number*) as follows:

        1. Select a *base period* and assign each item in the base period a weight of 100%.

        2. Express financial numbers as a percent of their base period number.

        3. Trend percent equals analysis period amount divided by base period amount times 100.

III.   **Vertical Analysis**—Comparing financial condition and performance to a *base amount*. The analysis tools include:

    A. **Common-Size Statements**—reveal changes in the relative importance of each financial statement item. All amounts are redefined in terms *of common-size percents*.

        1. Common-size percentage equals analysis amount divided by base amounts multiplied by 100.

        2. Common-size balance sheets—base amount is usually total assets.

        3. Common-size income statements—base amount is usually revenues.

    B. Common-Size Graphics
Graphical analysis (e.g., pie charts and bar charts) of common-size statements that visually highlight comparison information.

IV.   **Ratio Analysis**—Using key relationships among financial statement items. Ratios organized into the four (items A through D below) building blocks of analysis:

    A. Liquidity and Efficiency

        1. *Liquidity* refers to the availability of resources to meet short-term cash requirement.

        2. *Efficiency* refers to how productive a company is in using its assets. Efficiency is usually measured relative to how much revenue is generated for a certain level of assets.

        3. Ratios in this block:

            a. Working capital—the excess of current assets over current liabilities.

            b. Current ratio—current assets divided by current liabilities; describes a company's ability to pay its short-term obligations.

            c. Acid-test ratio—similar to current ratio but focuses on quick assets (i.e., cash, short-term investments and current receivables) rather than current assets. Calculated as quick assets divided by current liabilities.

      d. Accounts receivable turnover—net sales or credit sales divided by average accounts receivable; a measure of how long it takes a company to collect its accounts.

      e. Inventory turnover—cost of goods sold divided by average inventory; the number of times a company's average inventory is sold during an accounting period.

      f. Days' sales uncollected—accounts receivable divided by net credit sales multiplied by 365 days; measures how frequently a company collects its accounts receivable.

      g. Days' sales in inventory—ending inventory divided by cost of goods sold multiplied by 365; measures how many days it will take to convert the inventory on hand at the end of the period into accounts receivable or cash.

      h. Total asset turnover—net sales divided by average total assets; describes the ability to use assets to generate sales.

B. Solvency

    1. *Solvency* refers to a company's long-run financial viability and its ability to cover long-term obligations. *Capital structure* is one of the most important components of solvency analysis.

    2. *Capital structure* refers to a company's sources of financing.

    3. Ratios in this block:

      a. Debt ratio—total liabilities divided by total assets.

      b. Equity ratio—total stockholders' equity divided by total assets.

        Note: A company is considered less risky if its capital structure (equity and long-term debt) is composed more of equity.

      c. Debt-to-Equity Ratio – total liabilities divided by total equity; measure of solvency. A larger debt-to-equity ratio implies greater risk.

      d. Times interest earned—income before interest expense and income taxes divided by interest expense; reflects the risk of loan repayments with interest to creditors.

C. Profitability

    1. *Profitability* refers to a company's ability to generate an adequate return on invested capital.

    2. *Return* is judged by assessing earnings relative to the level and sources of financing.

                                          Financial Accounting Fundamentals

   3. Ratios in this block:
       a. Profit margin—net income divided by net sales; describes
           the ability to earn net income from sales.
       b. Return on total assets—net income divided by average total
           assets; a summary measure of operating efficiency;
           comprises profit margin (net income divided by net sales)
           and total asset turnover (net sales divided by average total
           assets).
       c. Return on common stockholders' equity—net income less
           preferred dividends divided by average common
           stockholders' equity; measures the success of a company in
           earning net income for its owners.

   D. Market Prospects
       1. Market measures are useful for analyzing corporations with
           publicly traded stock.
       2. Market measures use stock price in their computation.
       3. Ratios in this block:
           a. Price-earnings ratio—market price per common stock
               divided by earnings per share; used to evaluate the
               profitability of alternative common stock investments.
           b. Dividend yield—annual cash dividends paid per share of
               stock divided by market price per share; used to compare
               the dividend-paying performance of different investment
               alternatives.

   E. Summary of Ratios
       Exhibit 13.16 sets forth the names of each of the common ratios by
       category, and includes the formula and a description of what is
       measured by each ratio.

V. **Decision Analysis—Analysis Reporting**
    Goal of financial statement analysis report is to reduce uncertainty
    through rigorous and sound evaluation. A good analysis report usually
    consists of six sections:
       1. Executive summary.
       2. Analysis overview.
       3. Evidential matter.
       4. Assumptions.
       5. Key factors.
       6. Inferences.

VI. **Sustainable Income – Appendix 13A**
     When a company's activities involve income-related events that are not
     part of its normal, continuing operations, it often separates the income
     statement into different sections as follows:

Chapter Outline

A. Continuing Operations
Reports the revenues, expenses, and income generated by the company's continuing operations.

B. Discontinued Segments

1. A **business segment** is a part of a company's operations that serves a particular line of business or class of customers.

2. A company's gain or loss from selling or closing down a segment is separately reported as follows:

   a. Income from operating the discontinued segment for the current period prior to its disposal.

   b. The gain or loss from disposing of the segment's net assets.

C. Extraordinary Items

1. **Extraordinary gains and losses** are those that are *both unusual* and *infrequent*.

   a. An **unusual gain or loss** is abnormal or otherwise unrelated to the company's regular activities and environment.

   b. An **infrequent gain or loss** is not expected to recur given the company's operating environment.

2. Reporting extraordinary items in a separate category helps users predict future performance, absent the effects of the extraordinary items.

3. Items that are either unusual or infrequent, but *not* both, are reported in the income statement but after the normal revenues and expenses.

D. Earnings per Share (EPS)— is the amount of income earned by each share of outstanding common stock and is reported in the final section of income statement. One of the most widely cited items of accounting information.

E. Changes in Accounting Principles

1. The *consistency principle* requires a company apply the same accounting principles across periods (examples in this context: (include inventory or depreciation methods). Changes in accounting principles are acceptable if justified as improvements in financial reporting.

2. Cumulative effect of the change on prior periods' incomes should be reported on the income statement (net of taxes) below extraordinary items.

3. A footnote should describe and justify the change and report what income would have been under the old method.

F. Comprehensive Income is net income plus certain gains and losses that bypass the income statement. The change in equity for the period, excluding investments from and distributions to its stockholders.

Following are data from the statements of two companies selling similar products:

Current Year-End Balance Sheets

	Sled Company	Zip Company
Cash	$ 11,900	$ 20,000
Notes receivable	7,700	3,200
Accounts receivable, net	42,000	64,000
Inventory..	58,800	87,680
Prepaid expenses	1,680	3,520
Plant and equipment, net...............................	232,120	274,400
Total assets	$354,200	$452,800
Current liabilities	$ 56,000	$ 80,800
Mortgage payable	70,000	80,000
Common stock, $10 par value	140,000	160,000
Retained earnings..	88,200	132,000
Total liabilities and stockholders' equity	$354,200	$452,800

Beginning-of-Year Data

	Sled Company	Zip Company
Inventory..	$ 53,200	$ 85,120
Total assets	345,800	443,200
Stockholders' equity	217,000	285,120

Data from the Current Year's Income Statement

	Sled Company	Zip Company
Sales...	$672,000	$880,000
Cost of goods sold	528,080	699,840
Interest expense	4,200	5,600
Net income	23,373	28,896

Required:

1. Calculate current ratios, acid-test ratios, inventory turnovers, and days' sales uncollected for the two companies. Then state which company you think is the better short-term credit risk and why.
2. Calculate return on total assets employed and return on stockholders' equity. Then, under the assumption that each company's stock can be purchased at book value, state which company's stock you think is the better investment and why.

(If this alternative demonstration problem is not covered in class, see your instructor for the solution.)

Problem I

The following statements are ether true or false. Place a (T) in the parentheses before each true statement and an (F) before each false statement.

1. ( ) A current ratio of 2 to 1 always indicates that a company can easily meet it's current debts.

2. ( ) Accounts receivable turnover of 6.4 times in 2009 and 8.2 times in 2008 indicates that a company is collecting its accounts receivable more rapidly in 2009 than in 2008.

3. ( ) If accounts receivable is $150,000, and net credit sales is $1,000,000, days' sales uncollected is 15.

4. ( ) On a common-size income statement, the amount of net sales is assigned a value of 100%.

5. ( ) To calculate inventory turnover, cost of goods sold is divided by gross sales.

6. ( ) The ratios and turnovers of a selected group of competitive companies normally are the best bases of comparison for analyzing financial statements.

7. ( ) Return on total assets summarizes the two components of operating efficiency—profit margin and total asset turnover.

8. ( ) Current ratio, acid-test ratio, accounts receivable turnover, and inventory turnover are tools for evaluating short-term liquidity.

9. ( ) The cumulative effect on prior years' incomes of a change in accounting principle is reported on the statement of retained earnings. (Appendix 13A).

Problem II

You are given several words, phrases, or numbers to choose from in completing each of the following statements or in answering the following questions. In each case select the one that best completes the statement or answers the question and place its letter in the answer space provided.

_____1. To analyze long-term risk and capital structure, the following ratios and statistics for analysis would be used:

    a. Debt ratio.
    b. Equity ratio.
    c. Times fixed interest charges earned.
    d. Pledged assets to secured liabilities.
    e. All of the above.

_____2. During 2008, a company's sales were $360,000. In 2009 they were $334,800 and in 2010 they were $374,400. Express the sales in trend percentages, using 2008 as the base year.

    a. 2008—96%;   2009—89%; 2010—100%,
    b. 2008—100%; 2009—108%; 2010—96%.
    c. 2008—100%; 2009—100%; 2010—100%.
    d. 2008—104%; 2009—112%; 2010—100%.
    e. 2008—100%; 2009—93%;   2010—104%.

_____ 3. Information from the 2008 income statement of Becker Company follows:

Sales	$320,000
Gross profit on sales	138,000
Operating income	32,000
Income before taxes	22,000
Net income	16,800

If the company's 2008, accounts receivable were $23,200 and $28,000 at January 1 and December 31, 2008, respectively, what was the company's accounts receivable turnover?

a. 7.1 times.
b. 5.4 times.
c. 12.5 times.
d. 3.9 times.
e. 10.1 times.

_____ 4. Use the following information from the 2008 income statement of Sumner Company to calculate the company's inventory turnover:

Sales	$300,000
Cost of goods sold:	
Inventory, January 1, 2008	28,480
Purchases, net	171,040
Goods available for sale	199,520
Inventory, December 31, 2008	19,520
Cost of goods sold	180,000
Gross profit on sales	120,000
Operating expenses	34,000
Income from operations	$ 86,000

a. 7.5 times.
b. 9.2 times.
c. 12.5 times.
d. 8.3 times.
e. 17.9 times.

_____ 5. The Keyes Company had the following comparative income statements for 2009 and 2008:

	2009	2008
Net sales	$630,000	$552,000
Cost of goods sold	428,400	389,160
Gross profit from sales	201,600	162,840
Operating expenses	97,500	78,600
Net income	$104,100	$ 84,240

What are the cost of goods sold in common-size percentages for 2009 and 2008?

a. 110.1% in 2009; 100.0% in 2008.
b. 24.3% in 2009; 21.6% in 2008.
c. 41.2% in 2009; 46.2% in 2008.
d. 68.0% in 2009; 70.5% in 2008.
e. 147.0% in 2009; 141.8% in 2008.

_____ **6.** Captan, Inc., has a depreciable asset that cost $500,000 (no salvage value) and has decided to switch from straight-line depreciation to declining-balance depreciation at twice the straight-line rate. The company depreciated the asset for 1 year based on straight-line depreciation and a 5-year life. The company is subject to a 30% income tax rate. Calculate the amount of depreciation expense to be reported in the current year (year 2).

    a. $200,000.

    b $100,000.

    c. $120,000.

    d. $180,000.

    e. $20,000.

Problem III

Many of the important ideas and concepts discussed in Chapter 13 are reflected in the following list of key terms. Test your understanding of these terms by matching the appropriate definitions with the terms. Record the number identifying the most appropriate definition in the blank space next to each term.

_____ Business segment

_____ Common-size financial statement

_____ Comparative financial statement

_____ Efficiency

_____ Equity ratio

_____ Extraordinary gains and losses

_____ Financial reporting

_____ Financial statement analysis

_____ General-purpose financial statements

_____ Horizontal analysis

_____ Infrequent gain or loss

_____ Liquidity

_____ Market prospects

_____ Profitability

_____ Ratio analysis

_____ Solvency

_____ Unusual gain or loss

_____ Vertical analysis

_____ Working capital

1. Process of communicating information relevant to investors, creditors, and others in making investment, credit, and other decisions.

2. Statements published periodically for use by a variety of interested parties; includes the income statement, balance sheet, statement of changes in equity (or statement of retained earnings), statement of cash flows, and notes to these statements.

3. Statement with data for two or more successive periods placed in side-by-side columns, often with changes shown in dollar amounts and percents.

4. Current assets minus current liabilities.

5. Statement that expresses each amount as a percentage of a base amount. In the balance sheet, total assets are usually the base amount and is expressed as 100%. In the income statement, net sales are usually the base.

6. Portion of total assets provided by equity, calculated as total equity divided by total assets.

7. Evaluation of each financial statement item or group of items in terms of a specific base amount.

8. Availability of resources to meet short-term cash requirements.

9. Company's productivity in using its assets; usually measured relative to how much revenue a certain level of assets generates.

10. Company's long-run financial viability and its ability to cover long-term obligations.

11. Application of analytical tools to general-purpose financial statements and related data for making business decisions.

12. Company's ability to generate an adequate return on invested capital.

13. Comparison of a company's financial condition and performance across time.

14. Expectations (both good and bad) about a company's future performance as assessed by users and other interested parties.

15. Determination of key relationships between financial statement items.

16. Gain or loss that is abnormal or unrelated to the ordinary activities and environment.

17. Gains or losses reported separately from continuing operations because they are both unusual and infrequent.

18. Part of operations that serves a line of business or class of customers and that has assets, liabilities, and operating results distinguishable from other parts.

19. Gain or loss is not expected to recur, given the operating environment of the business.

Problem IV

The sales, cost of goods sold, and gross profits from sales of the Laker Company for a five-year period are shown below:

	2006	2007	2008	2009	2010
Sales	$350,000	$385,000	$413,000	$455,000	$497,000
Cost of goods sold	250,000	280,000	305,000	345,000	375,000
Gross profit	100,000	105,000	108,000	110,000	122,000

Laker Company's sales are expressed in trend percentages below. Express its cost of goods sold and gross profit in trend percentages in the spaces provided.

	2006	2007	2008	2009	2010
Sales	100	110	118	130	142
Cost of goods sold					
Gross profit					

Comment on the situation shown by the data: _____

_____

_____

_____

_____

Problem V

Complete the following by filling in the blanks.

1. When calculating accounts receivable turnover, the preferable sales number to use is _____ (cash, credit, total) sales.

2. The acid-test ratio is calculated by dividing _____ by _____.

3. Inventory turnover is calculated by dividing _____ by _____.

4. A slower turnover of inventory _____ (will, will not) tend to increase working capital requirements.

5. The current ratio is calculated by dividing _____ by _____. It is an indication of a company's _____ to meet its current obligations.

6. Return on total assets is calculated by dividing _____ by the amount of _____.

7. Times fixed interest charges earned is calculated by dividing income before deducting _____ and _____ by the amount of _____.

8. Days' sales uncollected is calculated by dividing _____ by _____ and multiplying the resulting quotient by _____. Days' sales uncollected is an indication of _____.

9. The price-earnings ratio for a company's common stock is calculated by dividing the _____ per share of the common stock by _____.

10. Return on common stockholders' equity is calculated by dividing _____ _____ by _____ stockholders' equity.

11. Compared to companies with an average growth rate, companies in a growth industry would be expected to have a _____ (higher, lower) price-earnings ratio.

12. Days' stock on hand is calculated by dividing _____ by _____ and multiplying by 365.

13. The results of discontinued segments are separated from the results of other activities on the income statement in order to _____.

Problem VI

Following are the condensed income statements of two companies of unequal size. Common-size percents are often used in comparing the statements of companies of unequal size. The income statement amounts of Company A have already been expressed in common-size percents in the condensed income statements presented below. Express the income statement amounts of Company Z in common-size percents in the spaces provided.

COMPANIES A AND Z

Income Statements

For Year Ended December 31, 20—

	Dollar Amounts		Common-Size Percentages	
	Company A	Company Z	Company A	Company Z
Sales...	$325,000	$265,000	100.0	_____
Cost of goods sold	204,750	164,300	63.0	_____
Gross profit on sales	120,250	100,700	37.0	_____
Selling expenses	61,750	49,025	19.0	_____
Administrative expenses.................	42,250	34,450	13.0	_____
Total operating expenses	104,000	83,475	32.0	_____
Net income	$ 16,250	$ 17,225	5.0	_____

Based on a review of the income statement amounts expressed in common-sized percents, which company appeared to operate more efficiently during the year? _____

Problem VII

Explain where each of the following items should appear in the financial statements of Odyssey Corporation.

1. The company maintains a stock investment portfolio as part of its business activities to enhance earnings. This year, for the first time in seven years, it sold stock for a gain of $27,000.

2. After depreciating equipment for three years based on an expected six-year life, the company decided this year that the value of the equipment would last five more years. As a result, the depreciation for the current year is $18,000 instead of $30,000.

Solutions for Chapter 13

Problem I

1. F
2. F
3. F
4. T
5. F
6. T
7. T
8. T
9. F

Problem II

1. E
2. E
3. C
4. A
5. D
6. A

Problem III

18	Business segment	19	Infrequent gain or loss
5	Common-size financial statement	8	Liquidity
3	Comparative financial statement	14	Market prospects
9	Efficiency	12	Profitability
6	Equity ratio	15	Ratio analysis
17	Extraordinary gains and losses	10	Solvency
1	Financial reporting	16	Unusual gain or loss
11	Financial statement analysis	7	Vertical analysis
2	General-purpose financial statements	4	Working capital
13	Horizontal analysis		

Problem IV

	2006	2007	2008	2009	2010
Sales	100	110	118	130	142
Cost of goods sold	100	112	122	138	150
Gross profit.....................................	100	105	108	110	122

Laker Company's sales increased each year throughout the five-year period, but its cost of goods sold increased more rapidly. This slowed the rate of increase in its gross profit.

Problem V

1. credit

2. quick assets; current liabilities

3. cost of goods sold; average inventory

4. will

5. current assets; current liabilities; ability

6. net income; average total assets

7. income taxes; fixed interest charges; fixed interest charges

8. accounts receivable; credit sales; the number of days in a year; collection efficiency (how frequently a company collects its accounts)

9. market price; earnings per share

10. net income less any preferred dividends; average common

11. higher

12. ending inventory; cost of goods sold

13. more clearly present the results of continuing operations

Problem VI

COMPANIES A AND Z
Income Statements
For Year Ended December 31, 20—

	Dollar Amounts		Common-Size Percentages	
	Company A	Company Z	Company A	Company Z
Sales..............................	$325,000	$265,000	100.0	100.0
Cost of goods sold........................	204,750	164,300	63.0	62.0
Gross profit on sales....................	120,250	100,700	37.0	38.0
Selling expenses	61,750	49,025	19.0	18.5
Administrative expenses..............	42,250	34,450	13.0	13.0
Total operating expenses.............	104,000	83,475	32.0	31.5
Net income	$ 16,250	$ 17,225	5.0	6.5

Company Z appeared to operate more efficiently during the year.

Problem VII

1. This gain is neither unusual nor infrequent. As a result, it should be reported in the income statement as part of income from continuing operations.
2. This change from an expected useful life of six to eight years is a change in an accounting estimate. The $18,000 should be reported in the income statement as part of income from continuing operations.

©The McGraw-Hill Companies, Inc., 2009

APPENDIX C
INVESTMENTS AND INTERNATIONAL OPERATIONS

Learning Objective C1:

Distinguish between debt and equity securities and between short-term and long-term investments.

Debt securities reflect a creditor relationship and include investments in notes, bonds, and certificates of deposit. *Equity securities* reflect an owner relationship and include shares of stock issued by other companies. Short-term investments in securities are current assets that meet two criteria: (1) They are expected to be converted into cash within one year or the current operating cycle of the business, whichever is longer and (2) they are readily convertible to cash, or *marketable*. All other investments in securities are long-term. Long-term investments also include assets not used in operations and those held for special purposes, such as land for expansion.

Learning Objective C2:

Identify and describe the different classes of investments in securities.

Investments in securities are classified into one of five groups: (1) trading securities, which are always short-term, (2) debt securities held-to-maturity, (3) debt and equity securities available-for-sale, (4) equity securities in which an investor has a significant influence over the investee, and (5) equity securities in which an investor has a controlling influence over the investee.

Learning Objective C3:

Describe how to report equity securities with controlling influence.

If an investor owns more than 50% of another company's voting stock and controls the investee, the investor's financial reports are prepared on a consolidated basis. These reports are prepared as if the company were organized as one entity.

Learning Objective C4 (Appendix C-A):

Explain foreign exchange rates between currencies.

A foreign exchange rate is the price of one currency stated in terms of another. An entity with transactions in a foreign currency when the exchange rate changes between the transaction dates and their settlement will experience exchange gains or losses.

Learning Objective A1:

Compute and analyze the components of return on total assets.

Return on total assets has two components: profit margin and total asset turnover. A decline in one component must be met with an increase in another if return on assets is to be maintained. Component analysis is helpful in assessing company performance compared to that of competitors and its own past.

Learning objective P1:

Account for trading securities.

Investments are initially recorded at cost, and any dividend or interest from these investments is recorded in the income statement. Investments classified as trading securities are reported at market value. Unrealized gains and losses on trading securities are reported in income. When investments are sold, the difference between the net proceeds from the sale and the cost of the securities is recognized as a gain or loss.

Learning objective P2:

Account for held-to-maturity securities.

Debt securities held-to-maturity are reported at cost when purchased. Interest revenue is recorded as it accrues. The cost of long-term held-to-maturity securities is adjusted for the amortization of any difference between cost and maturity value.

Learning objective P3:

Account for available-for-sale securities.

Debt and equity securities available-for-sale are recorded at cost when purchased. Available-for-sale securities are reported at their market values on the balance sheet with unrealized gains or losses shown in the equity section. Gains and losses realized on the sale of these investments are reported in the income statement.

Learning Objective P4:

Account for equity securities with significant influence.

The equity method is used when an investor has a significant influence over an investee. This usually exists when an investor owns 20% or more of the investee's voting stock but not more than 50%. The equity method means an investor records its share of investee earnings with a debit to the investment account and a credit to a revenue account. Dividends received reduce the investment account balance.

Learning Objective P5 (Appendix C-A):

Record transactions listed in a foreign currency.

When a company makes a credit sale to a foreign customer and sales terms call for payment in a foreign currency, the company must translate the foreign currency into dollars to record the receivable. If the exchange rate changes before payment is received, exchange gains or losses are recognized in the year they occur. The same treatment is used when a company makes a credit purchase from a foreign supplier and is required to make payment in a foreign currency.

Appendix Outline

I. **Basics of Investments**
    A. Motivation for Investments
        1. Companies transfer *excess* cash into investments to produce higher income.
        2. Some entities, such as mutual funds and pension funds, are set up to produce income from investments.
        3. Companies make investments for strategic reasons. Examples: investments in competitors, suppliers, and even customers.
    B. Short-Term versus Long-Term
        1. **Short-term investments** (temporary *investments* and *marketable* securities)—securities that must meet these two requirements:
            a. Expected to be converted into cash within one year or the current operating cycle of the business, whichever is longer.
            b. Readily convertible to cash.
        2. **Long-term investments**—investments not meeting the two requirements for short-term investments.
    C. Classification and Reporting
        1. Accounting for investments depends on three factors:
            a. Security type, either debt or equity.
            b. The company's intent to hold the security either short-term or long-term, and
            c. The company's (investor's) percent ownership in the other company's (investee's) equity securities.
        2. Using these three factors, investments are separated into five classes of securities:
            a. **Trading** – Includes debt and noninfluential equity securities that are actively traded.
            b. **Held-to-maturity** – Includes debt securities intended to be held-to-maturity.
            c. **Available-for-sale** – Includes debt and noninfluential equity securities.
            d. **Significant influence** – Includes equity securities with significant influence.
            e. **Controlling influence** – Includes equity securities with controlling influence.
    D. Basics of Accounting for Investments
        1. Accounting Basics for Debt Securities
            a. Debt securities that will be held-to maturity are recorded at cost when purchased.
            b. Interest revenue for investments in debt securities is recorded when earned.

2. Accounting Basics for Equity Securities

   a. Equity securities that are available-for-sale are recorded at cost when acquired, including commissions or brokerage fees paid.

   b. Any cash dividends received are credited to Dividend Revenue and reported in the income statement.

   c. When the securities are sold, the proceeds are compared with cost, and any gain or loss is recorded.

E. Accounting for Noninfluential Investments – companies must value and report at fair market value. Exact requirements depend on classification.

   1. Trading securities

      Trading securities are *debt and equity securities* that the company intends to actively manage and trade for profit. Frequent purchases and sales are expected and are made to earn profits on short-term price changes.

      a. Valuing and reporting trading securities

         i. The entire portfolio of trading securities is reported at its market value; this requires a "market adjustment" from the cost of the portfolio.

         ii. Any **unrealized gain (or loss)** from a change in the market value of the portfolio of trading securities is reported on the income statement.

      b. Selling trading securities

         i. When individual trading securities are sold, the difference between the net proceeds (sale price less fees) and the cost of the individual trading securities that are sold is recognized as a gain or a loss.

         ii. Any prior period market adjustment to the portfolio is *not* used to compute the gain or loss from sale of individually traded securities.

         iii. A gain is reported in the Other Revenues and Gains section of the income statement; a loss is reported in Other Expenses and Losses section.

   2. Held-to-maturity securities

      Held-to-maturity (HTM) securities are *debt securities* a company intends and is able to hold until maturity.

      a. HTM securities are reported in

         i. Current assets if their maturity dates are within one year or the operating cycle, whichever is longer.

         ii. Long-term assets when the maturity dates extend beyond one year or the operating cycle, whichever is longer.

      b. All HTM securities are recorded at cost when acquired.

        c. Interest revenue on HTM securities is recorded when earned.

        d. The portfolio of HTM securities is reported at (amortized) cost which is explained in advanced courses.

        e. There is no market adjustment to the portfolio of HTM securities.

   3. Available-for-sale securities

Available-for-sale securities (AFS) are *debt and equity securities* not classified as trading or held-to-maturity securities. AFS securities are purchased to yield interest, dividends, or increases in market value.

        a. AFS securities are reported as short-term investments if the intent is to sell the AFS securities within the longer of one year or the operating cycle; otherwise, they are classified as long-term.

        b. Valuing and reporting AFS securities

           i. The cost of the AFS securities is adjusted to reflect changes in market value (as with trading securities).

          ii. However, any unrealized gain or loss for the portfolio of AFS securities is *not* reported on the income statement; instead, it is reported in the equity section of the balance sheet (and is part of *comprehensive income*—explained below).

        c. Selling AFS securities

           i. Accounting for the sale of AFS securities is identical to that described for the sale of trading securities. (See section E.1.b above.)

          ii. The difference between the cost of the individual securities sold and the net proceeds (sales price less fees) is recognized as a gain or loss.

II.   Reporting of Influential Investments

  A. Investment in Securities with Significant Influence

A long-term investment classified as **equity securities with significant influence** implies that the investor can exert significant influence over the investee.

    1. An investor that owns 20% or more (but not more than 50%) of a company's voting stock is usually presumed to have significant influence over the investee. (In some cases, the 20% test is overruled by other, more persuasive, evidence.)

    2. The **equity method** of accounting and reporting is used for long-term investments in equity securities with significant influence.

        a. Long-term investments in equity securities with significant influence are recorded at cost in a Long-Term Investments account when acquired.

       b. When the investee reports its earnings, the investor records its share of those earnings in its investment account and credits the Earnings from Long-Term Investments account.

       c. The receipt of cash dividends is not revenue because the investor has already recorded its share of the investee's earnings; instead, the cash dividends received reduce the balance of the Long-Term Investments account.

       d. The book value of an investment under the equity method equals the cost of the investment plus (minus) the investor's equity in the *undistributed (distributed)* earnings of the investee.

       e. When the investment is sold, the gain or loss is computed by comparing the proceeds from the sale with the book value on the date of the sale.

B. Investment in Securities with Controlling Influence
A long-term investment classified as **equity securities with controlling influence** implies that the investor can exert a controlling influence over the investee.

   1. An investor who owns more than 50% of a company's voting stock has control over the investee. (In some cases, controlling influence can extend to situations of less than 50% ownership.)

   2. The *equity method with consolidation* is used to account for long-term investments in equity securities with controlling influence.

       a. The investor reports *consolidated financial statements* when owning such securities. The controlling investor is called the **parent** and the investee is called the **subsidiary**.

       b. **Consolidated financial statements** show the financial position, results of operations, and cash flows of all entities under the parent's control, including all subsidiaries; these statements are prepared as if the business were organized as one entity.

       c. The parent uses the equity method in its accounts, but the investment account is *not* reported on the consolidated financial statements.

C. Accounting Summary for Investments in Securities—See Exhibit C.8 for a summary of the accounting for investments in securities.

   1. Comprehensive Income -- **comprehensive income** refers to all changes in equity for a period except those due to investments and distributions to owners. This means that it includes:

       a. The revenues, gains, expenses, and losses reported in net income, and

       b. The gains and losses that bypass net income but affect equity.

   2. Most often this simply requires one additional column for Other Comprehensive Income in the statement of stockholders' equity.

Appendix Outline

III. **Decision Analysis—Components of Return on Total Assets**

A. A company's **return on total assets** is used to assess financial performance.

B. It can be separated into two components: profit margin and total asset turnover.

C. Return on total assets is calculated as profit margin times total asset turnover.

D. Profit margin is calculated as net income divided by net sales. It reflects the percent of net income in each dollar of net sales.

E. Total asset turnover is calculated as net sales divided by average total assets. It reflects a company's ability to produce net sales from total assets.

F. Generally, if a company is to maintain or improve its return on total assets, it must meet any decline in either profit margin or total asset turnover with an increase in the other. If not, return on assets will decline.

IV. **Investments in International Operations (Appendix C-A)**
Some entities' operations occur in so many different countries that the companies are called **multinationals**. Two major accounting challenges include accounting for sales and purchases listed in a foreign currency and preparing consolidated financial statements with international subsidiaries.

A. Exchange Rates between Currencies
The price of one currency stated in terms of another currency is called a **foreign exchange rate.**

B. Sales and Purchases Listed in a Foreign Currency

1. When a U.S. company makes a credit sale to an international customer, accounting for the sale and the account receivable is straightforward if sales terms require the international customer's payment in U.S. dollars.

2. If sale terms require (or allow) payment in a foreign currency, the U.S. company must account for the sale and the account receivable in a different manner.

   a. The sales price must be translated from the foreign currency to dollars by multiplying the sales price (stated in the foreign currency) by the exchange rate on the date of the sale; entry (for U.S. company) for sale of merchandise on credit: debit Accounts Receivable, credit Sales.

   b. If the receivable is still outstanding at the end of the end of the accounting period, the receivable must again be translated from the foreign currency to dollars by multiplying the sales price (stated in the foreign currency) by the exchange rate at the end of the accounting period. Entry assuming the amount of the receivable (when translated) is higher: debit Accounts Receivable, credit Foreign Exchange Gain.

3. When payment is received from the foreign customer, the U.S. company will immediately exchange the payment into dollars. Entry assuming the amount of the payment (when translated) is lower: debit Cash, debit Foreign Exchange Loss, credit Accounts Receivable.

4. The balance in the Foreign Exchange Gain (or Loss) account is reported on the income statement and closed to the Income Summary account at year-end.

C. Consolidated Statements with International Subsidiaries
Before preparing consolidated statements, the parent must translate financial statements of a foreign subsidiary into U.S. dollars. This topic is covered in advanced accounting courses.

2009 Jan	1	Purchased 8,000 shares (20%) of Investee Company's outstanding stock at a cost of $150,000.
May	31	Investee Company declared and paid a cash dividend of $1.50 per share.
Dec	31	Investee Company announced that its net income for the year was $100,000.
2010 Oct	1	Investee Company declared and paid a cash dividend of $1.00 per share.
Dec	31	Investee Company announced that its net income for the year was $80,000.
2011 Jan	1	Investor Corporation sold all of its shares of Investee Company for $178,000 cash.

Required:

Prepare journal entries on Investor Corporation's books using the equity method, which assumes that Investor has significant influence over Investee Company.

(If this alternative demonstration problem is not covered in class, see your instructor for the solution.)

Problem I

The following statements are either true or false. Place a (T) in the parentheses before each true statement and an (F) before each false statement.

1. ( ) Trading securities are either debt or equity securities that the company intends to actively trade for profit.

2. ( ) An investor who owns 20% or more of a corporation's voting stock is presumed to have significant influence over the investee.

3. ( ) A short-term investment in a security available-for-sale is reported on the balance sheet at cost.

4. ( ) Unrealized holding gains and losses on investments in equity securities available-for-sale are reported in the stockholders' equity section of the balance sheet.

5. ( ) An unrealized gain on a short-term investment in a trading security is reported on the income statement.

6. ( ) The equity method is used to account for investments in equity securities available-for-sale.

7. ( ) At acquisition, the purchase of equity securities is recorded at cost regardless of which method is used to account for the investment.

8. ( ) A short-term investment in a security held-to-maturity is reported on the balance sheet at its fair (market) value.

9. ( ) The only difference between accounting for debt securities held-to-maturity and debt securities available-for-sale is that interest is not accrued on debt securities held-to-maturity.

10. ( ) Investments in equity securities available-for-sale are reported on the balance sheet at their market values.

Problem II

You are given several words, phrases, or numbers to choose from in completing each of the following statements or in answering the following questions. In each case select the one that best completes the statement or answers the question and place its letter in the answer space provided.

_____1. On January 1, 20×9, Allured Company purchased 12,000 shares of More Corporation's common stock at 60-1/4 plus a $6,000 commission. On July 1, 20×9, More Corporation declared and paid dividends of $0.85 per share, and on December 31, 20×9, it reported a net income of $156,000. Assuming More Corporation has 48,000 outstanding common shares and that the market value per share at December 31, 20×9, is $65, what is the carrying value of Alfred's investment in More at December 31?
   a. $729,000.
   b. $757,800.
   c. $751,800.
   d. $723,000.
   e. $780,000.

2. On January 1, 20×9, Allured Company purchased 12,000 shares of More Corporation's common stock at 60-1/4 plus a $6,000 commission. On July 1, 20×9, More Corporation declared and paid dividends of $0.85 per share, and on December 31, 20×9, it reported a net income of $156,000. Assuming More Corporation has 96,000 outstanding common shares and that the market value per share at December 31, 20×9, is $65, what is the carrying value of Allured's investment in More at December 31?

   a. $723,000.
   b. $742,500.
   c. $738,300.
   d. $780,000.
   e. $729,000.

3. The cost and market values of Company B's short-term investments on December 31, 20×9, follow:

	Cost	Market
Securities held-to-maturity	$30,000	$28,000
Trading securities	34,000	32,500
Securities available-for-sale..................................	28,000	31,000

   What dollar amount should be reported on Company B's December 31, 20×9, balance sheet for each of the three types of short-term investments?

   a. $30,000; $34,000; $28,000.
   b. $30,000; $32,500; $31,000.
   c. $28,000; $32,500; $31,000.
   d. $28,000; $34,000; $28,000.
   e. $28,000; $32,500; $28,000.

Problem III

Many of the important ideas and concepts discussed in Appendix C are reflected in the following list of key terms. Test your understanding of these terms by matching the appropriate definitions with the terms. Record the number identifying the most appropriate definition in the blank space next to each term.

_____ Available-for-sale securities
_____ Comprehensive income
_____ Consolidated financial statements
_____ Equity method
_____ Equity securities with controlling influence
_____ Equity securities with significant influence
_____ Foreign exchange rate*

_____ Held-to-maturity securities
_____ Long-term investments
_____ Multinational*
_____ Parent
_____ Return on total assets
_____ Short-term investment
_____ Subsidiary
_____ Trading securities
_____ Unrealized gain

* Key term discussed in Appendix C-A.

1. Long-term investment when the investor is able to exert controlling influence over the investee; investors owning 50% or more of voting stock are presumed to exert controlling influence.

2. Long-term investment when the investor is able to exert significant influence over the investee; investors owning 20% or more (but less than 50%) of a voting stock are presumed to exert significant influence.

3. Long-term investments in securities held with the intent to sell them in the future.

4. Investments in debt and equity securities that are not marketable or, if marketable, are not intended to be converted into cash in the short-term; also special purpose funds and assets not used in operations.

5. Debt securities that the company has the intent and ability to hold until they mature.

6. Company that owns a controlling interest in another corporation (requires more than 50% of voting stock).

7. Accounting method used for long-term investments when the investor has "significant influence" over the investee.

8. Entity controlled by another entity (parent) when the parent owns more than 50% of the subsidiary's voting stock.

9. Financial statements that show all (combined) activities under the parent's control, including those of any subsidiaries.

10. Gain (loss) not yet realized by an actual transaction or event such as a sale.

11. Net change in equity for a period, excluding owner investments and distributions.

12. Price of one currency stated in terms of another currency.

13. Company that operates in several countries.

14. Ratio reflecting operating efficiency; defined as net income divided by average total assets for the period; also called *return on assets* or *return on investment*.

15. Debt and equity securities that management expects to convert to cash within the next 3 to 12 months (or the operating cycle if longer); also called *temporary securities* or *marketable securities*.

16. Investments in debt and equity securities that the company intends to actively trade for profit.

Problem IV

Hailey Company had no short-term investments prior to 20×9. The following transactions involving short-term investments in trading securities occurred during 20×9:

Mar. 1   Purchased 500 shares of Abco common stock at 40-3/4 plus a $200 brokerage fee.
June 20   Purchased 1,000 shares of Carr common stock at 10-1/2 plus a $100 brokerage fee.
Nov. 3   Purchased 600 shares of TCY common stock at 20-1/4 plus a $120 brokerage fee.

On December 31, 20×9, the fair market value of these trading securities held by Hailey were: Abco, 48-1/2; Carr, 9-3/4; and TCY, 22-1/2.

Prepare the journal entries to record the preceding transactions. Also prepare an adjusting entry, if necessary, to record the market adjustment of the short-term investments. Do not provide explanations. Skip a line between entries.

DATE	ACCOUNT TITLES AND EXPLANATION	P.R.	DEBIT	CREDIT

Problem V

On January 1, 2009, Large Company paid $90,000 for 36,000 of Small Company's 90,000 outstanding common shares. Small Company paid a dividend of $20,000 on November 1, 2009, and at the end of the year reported earnings of $40,000. The market value per share on December 31, 2010, was $2.10. On January 3, 2011, Large Company sold its interest in Small Company for $120,000.

1. Complete the following by filling in the blanks.

    The _____ method should be used in Large Company's books to account for the investment in Small Company since an investor that owns ____% or more, but not more than ____%, of a company's voting stock is normally presumed to have a _____ influence over the investor.

2. Prepare the journal entries for Large Company to record the facts presented above. Do not provide explanations. Skip a line between entries.

DATE	ACCOUNT TITLES AND EXPLANATION	P.R.	DEBIT	CREDIT

Problem VI

On January 1, 2009, Celestial Company paid $25,000 for 20,000 of Yardley Company's 120,000 outstanding common shares. Yardley Company paid a dividend of $.10 per share on June 1, 2009, and at the end of the year reported earnings of $500,000. The market value per share on December 31, 2009, was $1.90. Assume that Celestial did not own any investments prior to 2009. On January 1, 2010, Celestial Company sold its interest in Yardley Company for $37,900.

1. Complete the following by filling in the blanks.

   Celestial's long-term investment in Yardley would be considered as _____ because the company owns less than _____% of the outstanding voting stock of the investee.

2. Prepare the journal entries for Celestial Company to record the facts presented above. Also, prepare a journal entry, dated January 1, 2010, to remove any balances related to the market value adjustment. Do not include explanations. Skip a line between entries.

DATE	ACCOUNT TITLES AND EXPLANATION	P.R.	DEBIT	CREDIT

Solutions for Appendix C

Problem I

1. T
2. T
3. F
4. T
5. T
6. F
7. T
8. F
9. F
10. T

Problem II

1. B
2. D
3. B

Problem III

3	Available-for-sale securities		5	Held-to-maturity securities
11	Comprehensive income		4	Long-term investments
9	Consolidated financial statements		13	Multinational*
7	Equity method		6	Parent
1	Equity securities with controlling Influence		14	Return on total assets
			15	Short-term investment
2	Equity securities with significant Influence		8	Subsidiary
			16	Trading securities
12	Foreign exchange rate*		10	Unrealized gain (loss)

Key term discussed in Appendix C-A.

Problem IV

Mar. 1	Short-Term Investments—Trading	20,575	
	Cash [(500 × $40.75) + $2001..		20,575
June 20	Short-Term Investments—Trading..	10,600	
	Cash [(1,000 × $10.50) + $100]		10,600
Nov. 3	Short-Term Investments—Trading..	12,270	
	Cash [(600 × $20.25) + $120]		12,270
Dec. 31	Market Adjustment—Trading...	4,055	
	Unrealized Gain—Income		4,055

(See calculation below.)

Short-Term Investments in Trading Securities	Cost	Fair (Market) Value
Abco...	$20,575	$24,250
Carr	10,600	9,750
TCY	12,270	13,500
Total...	$43,445	$47,500

$47,500 – $43,445 = $4,055

Problem V

1. equity; 20; 50; significant

2.
2009

Jan. 1	Long-Term Investments—Small Company	90,000	
	Cash..		90,000
Nov. 1	Cash...	8,000	
	Long-Term Investments—Small Company		8,000
Dec. 31	Long-Term Investments—Small Company	16,000	
	Earnings from Long-Term Investments		16,000

2010

Jan. 3	Cash...	120,000	
	Long-Term Investments—Small Company		98,000
	Gain on Sale of Investments...		22,000

Problem VI

1. noninfluential; 20

2.
    2009

Jan. 1	Long-Term Investments—Yardley Company........................	25,000	
	Cash..		25,000
June 1	Cash..	2,000	
	Dividend Revenue		2,000
Dec. 31	Market Adjustment—Available-for-Sale (LT)........................	13,000	
	Unrealized Gain—Equity		13,000

    2010

Jan. 1	Cash..	37,900	
	Long-Term Investments—Yardley Company		25,000
	Gain on Sale of Investments...		12,900
1	Unrealized Gain—Equity...	13,000	
	Market Adjustment—Available-for-Sale (LT)..................		13,000

Financial Accounting Fundamentals